A Field Guide to the Classroom Library B

REFERENCE

A Field Guide to the Classroom Library **B**

Lucy Calkins

and

*The Teachers College
Reading and Writing
Project Community*

HEINEMANN
Portsmouth, NH

KH

Heinemann

361 Hanover Street
Portsmouth, NH 03801–3912
www.heinemann.com

Offices and agents throughout the world

Library of Congress Cataloging-in-Publication Data
Calkins, Lucy McCormick.
    A field guide to the classroom library / Lucy Calkins and the Teachers College Reading and Writing Project community.
        v. cm.
    Includes bibliographical references and index.
    Contents: [v. 2] Library B : grades K–1
     ISBN 0-325-00496-X
    1. Reading (Elementary)—Handbooks, manuals, etc.   2. Children—Books and reading—Handbooks, manuals, etc.   3. Children's literature—Study and teaching (Elementary)—Handbooks, manuals, etc.   4. Classroom libraries—Handbooks, manuals, etc.   I. Teachers College Reading and Writing Project (Columbia University).   II. Title.

LB1573 .C183 2002
372.4—dc21   2002038767

Editor: Kate Montgomery
Production: Abigail M. Heim
Interior design: Catherine Hawkes, Cat & Mouse
Cover design: Jenny Jensen Greenleaf Graphic Design & Illustration
Manufacturing: Louise Richardson

Printed in the United States of America on acid-free paper

09   VP   8 9 10

12/1/10

This field guide is dedicated to

Lynn Holcomb

The Field Guides to the Classroom Library *project is a philanthropic effort. According to the wishes of the scores of contributors, all royalties from the sale of these field guides will be given back entirely to the project in the continued effort to put powerful, beautiful, and thoughtfully chosen literature into the hands of children.*

Contents

Acknowledgments

The entire Teachers College Reading and Writing Project community has joined together in the spirit of a barn-raising to contribute to this gigantic effort to put the best of children's literature into the hands of children.

There are hundreds of people to thank. In these pages, I will only be able to give special thanks to a few of the many who made this work possible.

First, we thank Alan and Gail Levenstein who sponsored this effort with a generous personal gift and who helped us remember and hold tight to our mission. We are grateful to Annemarie Powers who worked tirelessly, launching the entire effort in all its many dimensions. Annemarie's passionate love of good literature shines throughout this project.

Kate Montgomery, now an editor at Heinemann and a long-time friend and coauthor, joined me in writing and revising literally hundreds of the field guides. Kate's deep social consciousness, knowledge of reading, and her commitment to children are evident throughout the work. How lucky we were that she became a full-time editor at Heinemann just when this project reached there, and was, therefore, able to guide the project's final stages.

Tasha Kalista coordinated the effort, bringing grace, humor, and an attention to detail to the project. She's been our home base, helping us all stay on track. Tasha has made sure loose ends were tied up, leads pursued, inquiries conducted, and she's woven a graceful tapestry out of all the thousands of books, guides, and people.

Each library is dedicated to a brilliant, passionate educator who took that particular library and the entire effort under her wing. We are thankful to Lynn Holcomb whose deep understanding of early reading informed our work; to Mary Ann Colbert who gave generously of her wisdom of reading recovery and primary texts; to Kathleen Tolan who championed the little chapter books and made us see them with new eyes; to Gaby Layden for her expertise in the area of nonfiction reading; to Isoke Nia for passionate contributions to our upper grade libraries; and to Kathy Doyle who knows books better than anyone we know.

We thank Pam Allyn for her dedication to this effort, Laurie Pessah for working behind the scenes with me, and Beth Neville for keeping the Project on course when this undertaking threatened to swamp us.

Finally, we are grateful to Mayor Guiliani for putting these libraries into every New York City school. To Judith Rizzo, Deputy Chancellor of Instruction, Adele Schroeter, Director of Office of Research, Development and Dissemination, Peter Heaney, Executive Director of the Division of Instructional Support, and William P. Casey, Chief Executive for Instructional Innovation, we also offer our heartfelt thanks for contributing their wisdom, integrity, and precious time to making this miracle happen.

Contributors

Christina Adams
Lisa Ali Chetram
Pam Allyn
Francine Almash
Janet Angelillo
Liz Arfin
Anna Arrigo
Laura Ascenzi-Moreno
Maureen Bilewich
Melissa Biondi
Pat Bleichman
Christine Bluestein
Ellen Braunstein
Dina Bruno
Theresa Burns
Lucy Calkins
Adele Cammarata
Joanne Capozzoli
Laura Cappadona
Justin Charlebois
Linda Chen
Mary Chiarella
Danielle Cione
Erica Cohen
Mary Ann Colbert
Kerri Conlon
Denise Corichi
Danielle Corrao
Sue Dalba
Linda Darro
Mildred De Stefano
Marisa DeChiara
Erica Denman
Claudia Diamond
Renee Dinnerstein
Kathy Doyle
Lizz Errico
Rosemarie Fabbricante
Gabriel Feldberg
Holly Fisher

Sofia Forgione
Judy Friedman
Elizabeth Fuchs
Jerilyn Ganz
Allison Gentile
Linda Gerstman
Jessica Goff
Iris Goldstein-
    Jackman
Ivy Green
Cathy Grimes
David Hackenburg
Amanda Hartman
Grace Heske
Caren Hinckley
Lynn Holcomb
Michelle Hornof
Anne Illardi
Maria Interlandi
Erin Jackman
Debbie Jaffe
Helen Jurios
Kim Kaiser
Tasha Kalista
Beth Kanner
Michele Kaye
Laurie Kemme
Hue Kha
Tara Krebs
Joan Kuntz Verdino
Kathleen Kurtz
Lamson Lam
Gaby Layden
Karen Liebowitz
Adele Long
Cynthia Lopez
Natalie Louis
Eileen Lynch
Theresa Maldarelli
Lucille Malka

Corinne Maracina
Jennifer Marmo
Paula Marron
Marjorie Martinelli
Esther Martinez
Debbie Matz
Teresa Maura
Leah Mermelstein
Melissa Miller
Kate Montgomery
Jessica Moss
Janice Motloenya
Marie Naples
Marcia Nass
Beth Neville
Silvana Ng
Isoke Nia
Jennie Nolan
    Buonocore
Lynn Norton Manna
Beth Nuremberg
Sharon Nurse
Liz O'Connell
Jacqueline O'Connor
Joanne Onolfi
Suzann Pallai
Shefali Parekh
Karen Perepeluk
Laurie Pessah
Jayne Piccola
Laura Polos
Annemarie Powers
Bethany Pray
Carol Puglisi
Alice Ressner
Marcy Rhatigan
Khrishmati Ridgeway
Lisa Ripperger
Barbara Rosenblum
Jennifer Ruggiero

Liz Rusch
Jennifer Ryan
Karen Salzberg
Elizabeth Sandoval
Carmen Santiago
Karen Scher
Adele Schroeter
Shanna Schwartz
India Scott
Marci Seidman
Rosie Silberman
Jessica Silver
Miles Skorpen
Joann Smith
Chandra Smith
Helene Sokol
Gail Wesson Spivey
Barbara Stavetski
Barbara Stavridis
Jean Stehle
Kathleen Stevens
Emma Suarez Baez
Michelle Sufrin
Jane Sullivan
Evelyn Summer
Eileen Tabasko
Patricia Tanzosh
Lyon Terry
Kathleen Tolan
Christine Topf
Joseph Turzo
Cheryl Tyler
Emily Veronese
Anne Marie Vira
Marilyn Walker
Gillan White
Alison Wolensky
Michelle Wolf
Eileen Wolfring

Introduction: What Is This Field Guide?

Lucy Calkins

When I was pregnant with my first-born son, the Teachers College Reading and Writing Project community organized a giant baby shower for me. Each person came with a carefully chosen book, inscribed with a message for baby Miles. Since then, we have commemorated birthdays, engagements, graduations, and good-byes by searching the world for exactly the right poem or picture book, novel or essay, and writing a letter to accompany it. Inside the letter, it says "This is why I chose this piece of literature precisely for you." In this same way, the book lists and the written guides that accompany them in this field guide have become our gift to you, the teachers of our nation's children. We have chosen, from all the books we have ever read, exactly the ones we think could start best in your classroom, and with these books, we have written notes that explain exactly why and how we think these texts will be so powerful in your children's hands.

The book lists and guides in this field guide are the Teachers College Reading and Writing Project's literacy gift to New York City and to the nation. When, two years ago, patrons Alan and Gail Levenstein came to us asking if there was one thing, above all others, which could further our work with teachers and children, we knew our answer in a heartbeat. We couldn't imagine anything more important than giving children the opportunity to trade, collect, talk over, and live by books. We want children to carry poems in their backpacks, to cry with Jess when he finds out that his friend Leslie has drowned, to explore tropical seas from the deck of a ship, to wonder at the life teeming in a drop of water. We want our children's heroes to include the wise and loving spider Charlotte, spinning her web to save the life of Wilbur, and the brave Atticus Finch.

We told the Levensteins that for teachers, as well as for children, there could be no finer gift than the gift of books for their students. We want teachers to be able to read magnificent stories aloud as the prelude to each school day, and to know the joy of putting exactly the right book in the hands of a child and adding, with a wink, "When you finish this book, there are more like it." We want teachers to create libraries with categories of books that peak their students' interests and match their children's passions, with one shelf for Light Sports Books and another shelf for Cousins of the Harry Potter books, one for Books That Make You Cry and another for You'll-Never-Believe-This Books. With this kind of a library, how much easier it becomes to teach children to read, to teach them what they need to become powerful, knowledgeable, literate people!

Even as we embarked on the effort to design magnificent classroom libraries, we knew that the best classroom library would always be the one assembled by a knowledgeable classroom teacher with his or her own students in mind. But, in so many cities, twenty new teachers may arrive in a school in a single year, having had no opportunity to learn about children's books at all. Even though some teachers have studied children's books, they may not be the ones given the opportunity to purchase books. Or, too often, there is no time to make book selections carefully—funds are discovered ten minutes before they must be spent or be taken from the budget. For these situations, we knew it would be enormously helpful to have lists and arrangements of recommended books for classroom libraries. Even without these worries, we all know the value of receiving book recommendations from friends. And so, our commitment to the project grew.

Our plan became this: We'd rally the entire Project community around a gigantic, two-year-long effort to design state-of-the-art classroom libraries and guides, exactly tailored to the classrooms we know so well. Simultaneously, we'd begin working with political, educational, and philanthropic leaders in hopes that individuals or corporations might adopt a school (or a corridor of classrooms) and create in these schools and classrooms the libraries of our dreams. Sharing our enthusiasm, colleagues at the New York City Board of Education proposed that idea to the mayor. Two years later, that dream has come true—In his January 2001 state of the city address, Mayor Giuliani promised $31.5 million of support to put a lending library in every New York City classroom, kindergarten through eighth grade.

Hearing this pronouncement, educational leaders from around the city joined with us in our philanthropic effort. People from the New York City Board of Education reviewed the lists and added suggestions and revisions. The Robin Hood Foundation, which had already been involved in a parallel effort to develop *school* libraries, contributed their knowledge. Readers from the Teachers Union and from the Office of Multicultural Education and of Early Childhood Education and of Literacy Education all joined in, coordinated by Peter Heaney, Executive Director of the Division of Instructional Support, and Adele Schroeter, Director of the Office of Research, Development and Dissemination. The book selections for the classroom libraries became even more carefully honed, and the written guides became richer still.

Over the past few months, boxes upon boxes of books have arrived across New York City, and in every classroom, children are pulling close to watch, big-eyed, as one exquisite, carefully chosen book after another is brought from the box and set on the shelf. Each teacher will receive between three and four hundred books. With most of these books, there will be a carefully crafted guide which says, "We chose this book because . . ." and "On page . . ." and "You'll notice that . . ." and "If you like this book, these are some others like it. . . . " I cannot promise that in every town and city across the nation the effort to put literature in the hands of students and guidance in the hands of their teachers will proceed so smoothly. But I'm hoping these book lists and these ready-made libraries bearing a stamp of approval will catch the eye of funders, of generous patrons, and of foresighted school leaders. And, every penny that comes to the authors from the sale of these field guides will go directly back into this project, directly back into our efforts to get more books into children's hands.

In the meantime, we needn't be idle. We'll comb through the book sales at libraries, and we'll write requests to publishers and companies. In a letter home to our children's parents, we might say, "Instead of sending in cupcakes to honor your child's birthday, I'm hoping you'll send a book. Enclosed is a list of suggestions." We can and will get books into our children's hands, by hook or by crook. And we can and will get the professional support we need for our reading instruction—our vitality and effectiveness as educators depend on it.

About the Books

When hundreds of teachers pool their knowledge of children's books as we have here, the resulting libraries are far richer than anything any one of us could have imagined on our own. We're proud as peacocks of these selections and of the accompanying literary insights and teaching ideas, and can't wait to share them both with teachers and children across the country. Here is a window into some of the crafting that has gone into the book selections:

- We suggest author studies in which the texts that students will study approximately match those they'll write and will inform their own work as authors.

- In upper-grade libraries, we include books that are relatively easy to read, but we have tried to ensure that they contain issues of concern to older children as well.

- We include books that might inform other books in the same library. For example, one library contains three books about dust storms, another contains a variety of books on spiders.

- We know that comprehension and interpretive thinking must be a part of reading from the very beginning, so we include easy to read books that can support thoughtful responses.

- We try to match character ages with student ages, approximately. For example, we have put the book in which Ramona is five in the library we anticipate will be for kindergartners, and put fourth-grade Ramona in the library we anticipate will be for fourth graders.

- We include complementary stories together when possible. For example, Ringgold's *Tar Beach* and Dorros' *Abuela* appear in the same library, anticipating that readers will recognize these as parallel stories in which the narrator has an imagined trip.

- We have never assumed that books in a series are all of the same level. For example, we have determined that some of the *Frog and Toad* books are more challenging, and this is indicated in our libraries.

- We understand that books in a series cannot always be easily read out of sequence. Because we know the *Magic Treehouse* series is best read in a particular sequence, for example, we have been careful with regard to the books we select out of that series.

- We selected our libraries to reflect multicultural values and bring forth characters of many different backgrounds and lives.

■ We try to steer clear of books that will not meet with general public approval. We do not believe in censorship, but we do believe that books purchased en masse should not bring storms of criticism upon the unsuspecting teacher.

At the same time that we are proud of the work we've done, we also know that there are countless magnificent books we have omitted and countless helpful and obvious teaching moves we have missed. We are certain that there are authors' names we have inadvertently misspelled, opinions expressed with which we don't all agree, levels assigned that perhaps should be different, and so on. We consider this work to be a letter to a friend and a work in progress, and we are rushing it to you, eager for a response. We are hoping that when you come across areas that need more attention, when you get a bright idea about a guide or booklist, that you will write back to us. We have tried to make this as easy as possible for you to do—just go to our website and contact us!

Choosing the Library for Your Class

We have created seven libraries for kindergarten through sixth grade classrooms. The libraries are each assigned a letter name (A–G) rather than a grade-level in recognition of the fact that the teacher of one class of fourth graders might find that Library D is suited to her students, and another fourth grade teacher might opt for Library E or Library F.

In order to determine which classroom library is most appropriate for a particular class in a particular school, teachers need to determine the approximate reading levels of their students in November, after the teachers have had some time to assess their students as readers. Teachers can compare the book the middle-of-the-class reader tends to be reading with the books we note for each level, and choose the library that corresponds to that average text level. More detail follows this general description. In shorthand, however, the following equivalencies apply:

Library Ⓐ is usually Kindergarten
Library Ⓑ is usually K or 1st grade
Library Ⓒ is usually 1st or 2nd grade
Library Ⓓ is usually 2nd or 3rd grade
Library Ⓔ is usually 3rd or 4th grade
Library Ⓕ is usually 4th or 5th grade
Library Ⓖ is usually 5th or 6th grade

The system of saying, "If in November, your children are reading books like these," usually doesn't work for kindergarten children. Instead, we say Library A is suitable if, in November, the average student cannot yet do a rich, story-like, emergent (or pretend) reading of a familiar storybook, nor can this child write using enough initial and final consonants that an adult can "read" the child's writing.

It is important to note that all of the books in any given library are not at the same level of difficulty. Instead, we have created a mix of levels that tend to represent the mixed levels of ability of readers in the classes we have studied. The composition of the libraries, by level, is described on pages xlvii–lvi.

Once you have chosen the library that best corresponds to the average level of your students as readers, you will need to decide which components of the library best suit your curriculum. Each library is divided into components—a core and some modules. The core is the group of books in the library we regard as essential. Each library also contains six modules, each representing a category of books. For example, in each library there is a module of nonfiction books, and in the upper-grade libraries there are modules containing five copies each of ten books we recommend for book clubs. Each module contains approximately fifty titles. The exact quantity from module to module varies slightly because we have tried to keep the cost of each module approximately equal. This means, for example, that the nonfiction module that contains more hardcover books has fewer books overall.

There are a variety of ways to assemble a library. Some teachers will want to purchase the entire library—the core plus the six modules. Sometimes, teachers on the same grade level in a school each purchase the same core but different modules, so a greater variety of books will be available across the hall for their students. In New York City, teachers automatically received the core of their library of choice, 150 books, and then could choose three of the six possible modules.

The Contents of Each Library

Researchers generally agree that a classroom should contain at least twenty books per child. Obviously, the number of books needs to be far greater than this in kindergarten and first grade classrooms, because books for beginning readers often contain fewer than 100 words and can generally only sustain a child's reading for a short while. We would have liked to recommend libraries of 750 titles but decided to select a smaller number of books, trusting that each teacher will have other books of his or her choice to supplement our recommendations.

Because we predict that every teacher will receive or buy the core of a library and only some teachers will receive any particular module, we tried to fill the core of the libraries with great books we couldn't imagine teaching, or living, without. Because we know children will borrow and swap books between classrooms, it is rare for books to be in the core of more than one library, even though some great books could easily belong there.

Usually, these classroom libraries include enough books from a particularly wonderful series to turn that series into a class rage, but the libraries frequently do not contain all the books in a series. Often, more books in the series are included in Modules One and Two, which always contain more books for independent reading, divided into the same levels as those in the core. Our expectation is that once readers have become engrossed in a series, teachers or parents can help them track down sequels in the school or public library.

Within the core of a library, we include about a dozen books of various genres that could be perfect for the teacher to read aloud to the class. These are all tried-and-true read aloud books; each title on the read-aloud list is one that countless teachers have found will create rapt listeners and generate rich conversation.

In every library we have included nonfiction books. They were not chosen to support particular social studies or science units; that would be a different and admirable goal. Instead, our team members have searched for nonfiction texts that captivate readers, and we imagine them being read within the reading workshop. The nonfiction books were chosen either because their topics are generally high-interest ones for children (animals, yo-yo tricks, faraway lands, disgusting animals), or because they represent the best of their genre.

Each library contains about fifteen books that could be splendid mentor texts for young writers. That is, they contain writing that students could emulate and learn from easily since it is somewhat like the writing they are generally able to create themselves.

In each core library, an assortment of other categories is included. These differ somewhat from one library to another. Libraries D and E, for example, contain many early chapter books, but since it is also crucial for children at this level to read the richest picture books imaginable, the core contains a score of carefully chosen picture books. Some cores also contain a set of books perfect for an author study. The categories are indicated on the book lists themselves, and under "Teaching Uses" in the guides.

The vast majority of books in each library are single copies, chosen in hopes that they will be passed eagerly from one reader to another. The challenge was not to find the number of books representing a particular level, but instead to select irresistible books. The chosen books have been field tested in dozens of New York City classrooms, and they've emerged as favorites for teachers and children alike.

The few books that have been selected in duplicate are ones we regard as particularly worthwhile to talk over with a partner. We would have loved to suggest duplicate copies be available for half the books in each library—if libraries had more duplicates, this would allow two readers to move simultaneously through a book, meeting in partnerships to talk and think about the chapters they've read. The duplicate copies would allow readers to have deeper and more text-specific book talks, while growing and researching theories as they read with each other. Duplicates also help books gain social clout in a classroom—allowing the enthusiasm of several readers to urge even more readers to pick the book up. If teachers are looking for ways to supplement these libraries, buying some duplicate copies would be a perfect way to start.

Many of the libraries contain a very small number of multiple (four or five) copies of books intended for use in guided reading and strategy lessons. Once children are reading chapter books, we find teachers are wise to help children into a new series by pulling together a group of four readers, introducing the text, and guiding their early reading. Teachers may also want to offer extra support to children as they read the second book in a series, and so we suggest having a duplicate of this next book as well, so that each child can read it with a partner, meeting to retell and discuss it.

The Levels Within the Libraries

We've leveled many, but purposely not all, of the books in every classroom library. The fact that we have leveled these books doesn't mean that teachers should necessarily convey all of these levels to children. We expect teachers will often make these levels visible on less than half of their books (through the use of colored tabs), giving readers the responsibility of choosing appropriate books for themselves by judging unmarked books against the template of leveled books. "This book looks a lot like the green dot books that have been just-right for me, so I'll give it a try and see if I have a smooth read," a reader might say. It is important that kids learn to navigate different levels of difficulty within a classroom library on their own or with only minimal support from a teacher.

We do not imagine a classroom lending library that is divided into levels as discrete as the levels established by Reading Recovery© or by Gay Su Pinnell and Irene Fountas' book, *Guided Reading: Good First Teaching for All Children* (Heinemann, 1996). These levels were designed for either one-to-one tutorials or intensive, small group guided reading sessions, and in both of these situations a vigilant teacher is present to constantly shepherd children along toward more challenging books. If a classroom lending library is divided into micro-levels and each child's entire independent reading life is slotted into a micro-level, some children might languish at a particular level, and many youngsters might not receive the opportunities to read across a healthy range of somewhat-easier and somewhat-harder books. Most worrisome of all, because we imagine children working often with reading partners who "like to read the same kinds of books as you do," classroom libraries that contain ten micro-levels (instead of say, five more general levels) could inadvertently convey the message that many *children* as well as many *books* were off-limits as partners to particular readers.

There are benefits to micro-levels, however, and therefore within a difficulty level (or a color-dot), some teachers might ascribe a plus sign to certain books, signifying that this book is one of the harder ones at this level. Teachers can then tell a child who is new to a level to steer clear of the books with plus signs, or to be sure that he or she receives a book introduction before tackling a book with this marker.

When assigning books to levels, we have tried to research the difficulty levels that others have given to each text and we have included these levels in our guides. Fairly frequently, however, our close study of a particular text has led us to differ somewhat from the assessments others have made. Of course leveling books is and always will be a subjective and flawed process; and therefore teachers everywhere *should* deviate from assigned levels, ours and others, when confident of their rationale, or when particularly knowledgeable about a reader. You can turn to the tables at the back of this section, on pages xxvii–lx, to learn more about our leveling system.

Building the Libraries

When we started this project two years ago, we initiated some intensive study groups, each designed to investigate a different terrain in children's literature. Soon, a group led by Lynn Holcomb, one of the first Reading Recovery teachers in Connecticut, was working to select books for a K–1 library. Members of this group also learned from Barbara Peterson, author of *Literary Pathways: Selecting Books to Support New Readers* (Heinemann, 2001), who conducted groundbreaking research at Ohio State University, examining how readers actually experience levels of text complexity. The group also learned from Gay Su Pinnell, well-known scholar of literacy education and coauthor with Irene Fountas of many books including *Guided Reading*. Of course, the group learned especially from intensive work with children in classrooms. The group searched for books that:

- Represent a diverse range of shapes, sizes, authors, and language patterns as possible. The committee went to lengths to be sure that when taken as a whole, primary-level libraries looked more like libraries full of real books than like kits full of "teaching materials."

- Use unstilted language. A book that reads, "Come, Spot. Come, Spot, come," generally would not be selected.

- Contain many high frequency words. If one book contained just one word on a page ("Scissors/paste/paper/etc.") and another book contained the reoccurring refrain of "I see the scissors./ I see the paste." we selected the second option.

- Carry meaning and were written to communicate content with a reader. If the book would probably generate a conversation or spark an insight, it was more apt to be included than one that generally left a reader feeling flat and finished with the book.

- Represent the diversity of people in our world and convey valuable messages about the human spirit.

A second group, under the leadership of Kathleen Tolan, an experienced teacher and staff developer, spent thousands of hours studying early chapter books and the children who read them. This group pored over series, asking questions: Is each book in the series equally difficult? Which series act as good precursors for other series? Do the books in the series make up one continuous story, or can each book stand alone? What are the special demands placed on readers of this series?

Yet another group, led by Gaby Layden, staff developer at the Project, studied nonfiction books to determine which might be included in a balanced, independent reading library. The group studied levels of difficulty in nonfiction books, and found authors and texts that deserved special attention. Carefully, they chose books for teachers to demonstrate and for children to practice working through the special challenges of nonfiction reading.

Meanwhile, renowned teacher-educator Isoke Nia, teacher extraordinaire Kathy Doyle, and their team of educators dove into the search for the very best chapter books available for upper-grade readers. Isoke especially helped us select touchstone texts for writing workshops—books to help us teach children to craft their writing with style, care, and power.

Teacher, staff developer, and researcher Annemarie Powers worked full-time to ensure that our effort was informed by the related work of other groups across the city and nation. We pored over bibliographies and met with librarians and literature professors. We searched for particular kinds of books: books featuring Latino children, anthologies of short stories, Level A and B books which looked and sounded like literature. We researched the classrooms in our region that are especially famous for their classroom libraries, and took note of the most treasured books we found there. All of this information fed our work.

Reading Instruction and the Classroom Library: An Introduction to Workshop Structures

These classroom libraries have been developed with the expectation that they will be the centerpiece of reading instruction. When I ask teachers what they are really after in the teaching of reading, many answer, as I do, "I want children to be lifelong readers. I cannot imagine anything more important than helping children grow up able to read and loving to read. I want students to initiate reading in their own lives, for their own purposes."

There is, of course, no one best way to teach reading so that children become lifelong readers. One of the most straightforward ways to do this is to embrace the age-old, widely shared belief that children benefit from daily opportunities to read books they choose for their own purposes and pleasures (Krashen 1993, Atwell 1987, Cambourne 1993, Smith 1985, Meek 1988).

More and more, however, we've come to realize that students benefit not only from opportunities to read, read, read, but also from instruction that responds to what students do when they are given opportunities to read. I have described the reading workshop in my latest publication, *The Art of Teaching Reading* (Calkins 2001). The reading workshop is an instructional format in which children are given long chunks of time in which to read appropriate texts, and also given explicit and direct instruction. Teachers who come from a writing workshop background may find it helpful to structure the reading workshop in ways that parallel the writing workshop so that children learn simultaneously to work productively inside each of the two congruent structures. Whatever a teacher decides, it is important that the structures of a reading workshop are clear and predictable so that children know how to carry on with some independence, and so that teachers are able to assess and coach individuals as well as partnerships and small groups.

Many teachers begin a reading workshop by pulling students together for a minilesson lasting about eight minutes (unless the read aloud is, for that day, incorporated into the minilesson, which then adds at least twenty minutes). Children then bring their reading bins, holding the books they are currently reading, to their assigned "reading nooks." As children read independently, a teacher moves among them, conferring individually with a child or bringing a small group of readers together for a ten- to fifteen-minute guided reading or strategy lesson. After children have read independently for about half an hour, teachers ask them to meet with their partners to talk about their books and their reading. After the partners meet, teachers often call all the readers in a class together for a brief "share session" (Calkins 2001). The following table shows some general guidelines for the length of both independent reading and the partnership talks based on the approximate level of the texts students are reading in the class.

How Long Might a Class Have Independent Reading and Partnership Talk?		
Class Reading Level	*Independent Reading Duration*	*Partnership Talk Duration*
Library A	10 minutes	20 minutes
Library B	15 minutes	20 minutes
Library C	20 minutes	20 minutes
Library D	30 minutes	10 minutes
Library E	40 minutes	10 minutes
Library F	40 minutes	10 minutes
Library G	40 minutes	10 minutes

Periodically, the structure of the minilesson, independent reading, partnership, and then share time is replaced by a structure built around book clubs or "junior" book clubs, our own, reading-intensive version of reading centers.

Minilessons

During a minilesson, the class gathers on the carpet to learn a strategy all readers can use not only during the independent reading workshop but also throughout their reading lives. The content of a minilesson comes, in part, from a teacher deciding that for a period of time, usually a month, he needs to focus his teaching on a particular aspect of reading. For example, many teachers begin the year by devoting a month to reading with stamina and understanding (Calkins 2001). During this unit, teachers might give several minilessons designed to help children choose books they can understand, and they might give others designed to help readers sustain their reading over time. Another minilesson might be designed to help readers make more time for reading in their lives or to help them keep a stack of books-in-waiting to minimize the interval between finishing one book and starting another.

The minilesson, then, often directs the work readers do during independent reading. If the minilessons show students how to make sure their ideas are grounded in the details of the text, teachers may establish an interval between independent reading time and partnership conversations when children can prepare for a talk about their text by marking relevant sections that support their ideas.

Sometimes minilessons are self-standing, separate from the interactive read aloud. Other minilessons include and provide a frame for the day's read aloud. For example, the teacher may read aloud a book and direct that day's talk in a way that demonstrates the importance of thinking about a character's motivations. Then children may be asked to think in similar ways about their independent reading books. Perhaps, when they meet with a partner at the end of reading, the teacher will say, "Please talk about the motivations that drive your central characters and show evidence in the text to support your theories."

Conferences

While children read, a teacher confers. Usually this means that the teacher starts by sitting close to a child as he or she continues reading, watching for external behaviors that can help assess the child. After a moment or two, the teacher usually says, "Can I interrupt?" and conducts a few-minute-long conversation while continuing the assessment. A teacher will often ask, "Can you read to me a bit?" and this, too, informs any hunches about a child and his or her strengths and needs as a reader. Finally, teachers intervene to lift the level of what the child is doing. The following table offers some examples of this.

General Examples of the Conferring That Can Help Readers Grow	
If, in reading, the child is . . .	*Teachers might teach by . . .*
able to demonstrate a basic understanding of the text	nudging the child to grow deeper insights, perhaps by asking: ■ Do any pages (parts) go together in a surprising way? ■ Why do you think the author wrote this book? What is he (she) trying to say? ■ If you were to divide the book into different sections, what would they be? ■ How are you changing as a reader? How are you reading this book differently than you've read others? ■ What's the work you are doing as you read this?
talking mostly about the smallest, most recent details read	generalizing what kind of book it is, giving the child a larger sense of the genre. If it is a story, we can ask questions that will work for any story: ■ How is the main character changing? ■ How much time has gone by? ■ What is the setting for the story? If the text is a non-narrative, we could ask: ■ What are the main chunks (or sections) in the text? ■ How would you divide this up? ■ How do the parts of this text go together? ■ What do you think the author is trying to teach you?
clearly enthralled by the story	asking questions to help the reader tap into the best of this experience to use again later. ■ What do you think it is about this story that draws you in? ■ You seem really engaged, so I'm wondering what can you learn about this reading experience that might inform you as you read other books. ■ When I love a book, as you love this one, I sometimes find myself reading faster and faster, as if I'm trying to gulp it down. But a reading teacher once told me this quote. "Some people think a good book is one you can't put down, but me, I think a good book is one you must put down—to muse over, to question, to think about." Could you set some bookmarks throughout this book and use them to pause in those places to really think and even to write about this book? Make one of those places right now, would you?

Partnerships

When many of us imagine reading, we envision a solitary person curled up with a book. The truth is that reading is always social, always embedded in talk with others. If I think about the texts I am reading now in my life and ask myself, "Is there something *social* about my reading of those texts?" I quickly realize that I read texts because people have recommended them. I read anticipating conversations I will soon have with others, and I read noticing things in this one text that I have discussed with others. My reading, as is true for many readers, is multilayered and sharper because of the talk that surrounds it.

There are a lot of reasons to organize reading time so that children have opportunities to talk with a reading partner. Partner conversations can highlight the social elements of reading, making children enjoy reading more. Talking about books also helps children have more internal conversations (thoughts) as they read. Putting thoughts about texts out into the world by speaking them allows other readers to engage in conversation, in interpretations and ideas, and can push children to ground their ideas in the text, to revise their ideas, to lengthen and deepen their ideas.

For young children, talking with a partner usually doubles the actual unit of time a child spends working with books. In many primary classrooms, the whole class reads and then the teacher asks every child to meet with a partner who can read a similar level of book. Each child brings his bin of books, thus doubling the number of appropriate books available to any one child. The child who has already read a book talks about it with the other child, giving one partner a valuable and authentic reason to retell a book and another child an introduction to the book. Then the two readers discuss how they will read together. After the children read aloud together, the one book held between them as they sit hip to hip, there is always time for the partners to discuss the text. Sometimes, teachers offer students guidance in this conversation.

More proficient readers need a different sort of partnership because once a child can read short chapter books, there are few advantages to the child reading aloud often. Then too, by this time children can sustain reading longer. Typically in third grade, for example, individuals read independently for thirty minutes and then meet with partners for ten minutes to talk over the book. Again, the teacher often guides that conversation, sometimes by modeling—by entertaining with the whole-class read-aloud text—the sort of conversations she expects readers will have in their partnerships.

Book Clubs

Teaching children to read well has a great deal to do with teaching children to talk well about books, because the conversations children have in the air between one another become the conversations they have in their own minds as they read. Children who have talked in small groups about the role of the suitcase in Christopher Paul Curtis's book, *Bud, Not Buddy* will be far more apt to pause as they read another book, asking, "Might *this* object play a significant role in this book, like the suitcase did in *Bud, Not Buddy*?"

When we move children from partnership conversations toward small-group book clubs, we need to provide some scaffolding for them to lean on at first. This is because partnerships are generally easier for children to manage than small group conversations. It is also generally easier for students to read for thirty-minute reading sessions with ten-minute book talks than it is to read for a few days in a row and then sustain extended book talks, as they are expected to do in book clubs.

Children need some support as they begin clubs. One way to do this is to begin with small book club conversations about the read aloud book—the one book we know everyone will be prepared to talk about. Another way to get started with book clubs is for the teacher to suggest that children work in small groups to read multiple copies of, say, a mystery book. The teacher will plan to read a mystery book aloud to the class during the weeks they work in their clubs. Meanwhile, each group of approximately four readers will be reading one mystery that is at an appropriate level for them. The whole class works on and talks about the read-aloud mystery, and this work then guides the small group work. On one day, for example, after reading aloud the whole-class mystery, the teacher could immerse the class in talk about what it's like to read "suspiciously," suspecting everything and everyone. For a few days, the class can try that sort of reading as they listen to the read aloud. Meanwhile, when children disperse to their small groups to read their own mysteries, they can read these books "suspiciously."

Eventually the book clubs can become more independent. One small group of children might be reading several books by an author and talking about what they can learn from the vantage point of having read so many. Another group might read books that deal with a particular theme or subject. Either way, in the classrooms I know best, each book club lasts at least a few weeks. Teachers observe, and coach and teach into these talks, equipping kids with ways to write, talk, and think about texts. However, teachers neither dominate the clubs nor steer readers toward a particular preordained interpretation of a text. Instead, teachers steer readers toward ways of learning and thinking that can help them again and again, in reading after reading, throughout their lives.

Library Ⓑ Contents Description

Library B consists of

I.	Independent Reading & Partner Reading (Levels 1–5)			
		Level 1	81 Titles	81 Texts
		Level 2	83 Titles	83 Texts
		Level 3	88 Titles	88 Texts
		Level 4	76 Titles	76 Texts
		Level 5	61 Titles	61 Texts
	Emergent Literacy/Shared Reading		18 Titles	75 Texts
	Nonfiction/Concept Books		10 Titles	10 Texts
	Poetry		6 Titles	6 Texts
II.	Guided Reading		20 Titles	80 Texts
III.	Reading Centers/Literature Circles		20 Titles	20 Texts
IV.	Author Study		10 Titles	10 Texts
V.	Read Alouds		31 Titles	31 Texts
VI.	Books to Support the Writing Process		8 Titles	8 Texts
Total Number of Texts in Library B			**512 Titles**	**629 Texts**

(Because of substitutions made in the ordering process, this number may not be precise.)

CORE

Group Description	Level	#	Author	Title	ISBN	Publisher	Quantity	Heinemann Write-Up
Independent Reading		1		Mas Pinata		Celebration Press	1	
		2	Brown, Marc	Arthur Writes a Story	590394835	Scholastic Inc.	1	Y
		3	Walsh, Jill Patton	Green Book, The	374428026	Farrar Strauss & Giroux	1	
	1	1	Annie-Jo	In the Woods	1572555386	Mondo Publishing	1	Y
		2	Armstrong, Shane	I Like Shapes	439116600	Scholastic Inc.	1	
		3	Bancroft, Gloria	What Do I See?	780288734	Wright Group	1	
		4	Berger, Samantha	In the Air	439081246	Scholastic Inc.	1	
		5	Bissett, Isabel	Mixing Colors	763560588	Rigby	1	
		6	Cowley, Joy	Gotcha Box, The	780272617	Wright Group	1	Y
		7	Cowley, Joy	I Love My Family	780249070	Wright Group	1	Y
		8	Cowley, Joy	Mrs. Wishy-Washy's Tub	780272609	Wright Group	1	Y
		9	Depree, Helen	I Can Paint	1556246374	Wright Group	1	
		10	Depree, Helen	Toys	780232739	Wright Group	1	
		11	Depree, Simon	Making Pictures	780234618	Wright Group	1	
		12	Frost, Miriam	Clown Face	78029050X	Wright Group	1	
		13	McMillan, Bruce	Growing Colors	688131123	William Morrow & Co	1	Y
		14	Mitchell, Claudette	Basketball	780281020	Wright Group	1	
	2	1	Burton, Margie	Old and New	1583442189	Early Connections	1	
		2	Cowley, Joy	Where Is Skunk?	780273001	Wright Group	1	
		3	Douglas, Doreen	Rosie, the Nosy Goat	78026326X	Wright Group	1	
		4	Giles, Jenny	Little Snowman, The	763515043	Rigby	1	Y
		5	Gosset, R. & M. Ballinger	How Many Fish?	5902996	Scholastic	1	
		6	Martin, Bill	Brown Bear, Brown Bear, What Do You See?	805047905	Henry Holt & Co	1	Y

Group Description	Level	#	Author	Title	ISBN	Publisher	Quantity	Heinemann Write-Up
		7	Moreton, Daniel	Day in Japan, A	439045711	Scholastic Inc.	1	
		8	Randell, Beverly	Ben's Teddy Bear	435067486	Rigby	1	Y
		9	Randell, Beverly	Home for Little Teddy, A	763515108	Rigby	1	Y
		10	Randell, Beverly	Tiger, Tiger	435049003	Rigby	1	Y
		11	Tuchman, Gail	Swing, Swing, Swing	590275569	Scholastic Inc.	1	Y
		12	Wildsmith, Brian	All Fall Down	198490062	Oxford University Press	1	
		13	Williams, Rebel	Call 911	780290712	Wright Group	1	Y
	3	1	Ballinger, Margaret	Making a Memory	590237926	Scholastic Inc.	1	Y
		2	Bishop, Nic	Green Snake, The	322001463	Wright Group	1	
		3	Blenus, Debra	I Smell Smoke!	780263308	Wright Group	1	
		4	Burton & Cogan	Soccer	1557348944	Teacher Created Materials	1	
		5	Christensen, Nancy	Good Night, Little Kitten	51605354X	Children's Press	1	Y
		6	Cowley, Joy	Splishy-Sploshy	780283309	Wright Group	1	Y
		7	Cowley, Joy	Sunflower Seeds	78027282X	Wright Group	1	
		8	Cutting, Brian & Jillian	Our Skeleton	780202570	Wright Group	1	Y
		9	Cutting, Jillian	School Bus, The	780264088	Wright Group	1	
		10	Eggleton, Jill	House for a Mouse, A	763559091	Rigby	1	
		11	Eggleton, Jill	Scarecrow's Hair	763559083	Rigby	1	
		12	Gomi, Taro	My Friends	590486152	Scholastic Inc.	1	
		13	Goss, Janet	It Didn't Frighten Me	157255097X	Mondo Publishing	1	
		14	Hessell, Jenny	Good Night, Little Brother	7010184X	Rigby	1	Y
		15	Hughes, Monica	What's It Made Of?	763560839	Rigby	1	
		16	Iversen, Sandra	Boxes	78026570X	Wright Group	1	
		17	Lynch, Patricia Ann	Fix It, Fox		Silver Burdett Ginn	1	
		18	Martin, Lee Ann	Animals Hide and Seek	78028898X	Wright Group	1	
		19	Martin, Lee Ann	My Body Works	322001536	Wright Group	1	

Group Description	Level	#	Author	Title	ISBN	Publisher	Quantity	Heinemann Write-Up
		20	Melser, June	Big Toe, The	780274695	Wright Group	1	
		21	O'Connor, Jane	Teeny Tiny Woman, The	394883209	Random House	1	Y
		22	Prince, Sarah	Twins	760819106	Wright Group	1	
		23	Randell, Beverly	Baby Bear Goes Fishing	435066978		1	Y
		24	Randell, Beverly	Friend for Little White Rabbit, A	435067079	Rigby	1	Y
		25	Randell, Beverly	Hermit Crab	435066994	Rigby	1	Y
		26	Seuss, Dr.	Foot Book, The	394809378	Random House	1	Y
		27	Shaw, Charles G.	It Looked Like Spilt Milk	64431592	Harper Trophy	1	Y
		28	Snow, Pegeen	Eat Your Peas, Louise!	516420674	Children's Press/Rookie Readers	1	
		29	Windsor, Jo	Carrying Babies	763559023	Rigby	1	
		30	Windsor, Jo	Feathered Friends	763558966	Rigby	1	
	4	1	Andrew, Moira	Best Present, The	763566357	Rigby	1	
		2	Armstrong, Jennifer	Sunshine, Moonshine	679864423	Random House	1	Y
		3	Barton, Byron	Dinosaurs, Dinosaurs	6443298X	Harper Collins	1	
		4	Barton, Byron	I Want to be an Astronaut	64432807	Harper Collins	1	
		5	Bonsall, Crosby	Mine's the Best	64442136	Harper Collins	1	Y
		6	Burton, Margie	My Five Senses	1892393646	Early Connections	1	
		7	Capucilli, Alyssa	Biscuit	64442128	Harper Collins	1	
		8	Cartwright, Pauline	Night Noises	780263383	Wright Group	1	
		9	Gardner, Marjory	Five Little Monkeys	1572550554	Mondo Publishing	1	
		10	Hoff, Syd	Who Will Be My Friends?	64440729	Harper Trophy	1	
		11	Hutchins, Pat	Rosie's Walk	20437501	Simon & Schuster	1	Y
		12	Kroniger, Stephen	If I Crossed the Road	68981190X	Simon & Schuster	1	
		13	Maccarone, Grace	I Shop with My Daddy	590501968	Scholastic Inc.	1	Y

Group Description	Level	#	Author	Title	ISBN	Publisher	Quantity	Heinemann Write-Up
		14	McKissack, Patricia	Messy Bessey	516270036	Children's Press/Rookie Readers	1	Y
		15	Randell, Beverly	Ben's Dad	435066935	Rigby	1	Y
		16	Randell, Beverly	Honey for Baby Bear	435067192	Rigby	1	Y
		17	Randell, Beverly	Lion and the Mouse, The	435067435	Rigby	1	Y
		18	Semple, Cheryl	Pancakes for Supper	732702011	Wright Group	1	Y
		19	Vaughan, Marcia	Hands, Hands, Hands	1572550155	Mondo Publishing	1	
		20	Ziefert, Harriet	Nicky Upstairs and Downstairs	140368523	Penguin Publishing	1	Y
	5	1	Archambault, John & Bill Martin	Here Are My Hands	805011684	Henry Holt & Co	1	
		2	Bunting, Eve	Flower Garden	152023720	Harcourt Brace	1	Y
		3	Carle, Eric	Very Busy Spider, The	399229191	Penguin Putnam	1	Y
		4	Crews, Donald	Sail Away	688110533	Greenwillow Books	1	Y
		5	Ehlert, Lois	Red Leaf, Yellow Leaf	152661972	Harcourt Brace	1	Y
		6	Giles, Jenny	Hide and Seek	780212169	Wright Group	1	
		7	Johnson, Crockett	Picture for Harold's Room, A	64440850	Harper Trophy	1	
		8	Kalan, Robert	Jump, Frog, Jump	68813954X	Scholastic Inc.	1	
		9	Krauss, Ruth	Happy Day, The	64431916	Harper Trophy	1	
		10	Kuskin, Karla	City Dog	395900166	Clarion Books	1	Y
		11	Martin, Bill	Chicka Chicka Boom Boom	68983568X	Simon & Schuster	1	
		12	Nodset, Joan	Who Took the Farmers Hat	590029509	Scholastic Inc.	1	Y
		13	Randell, Beverly	Ben's Tooth	435067613	Rigby	1	Y
		14	Sendak, Maurice	Seven Little Monsters	64431398	Harper Collins	1	
		15	Wood, Audrey	Napping House, The	152567089	Harcourt Brace	1	Y
		16	Ziefert, Harriet	Clean House For Mole and Mouse, A	140508104	Penguin Putnam	1	Y

Group Description	Level	#	Author	Title	ISBN	Publisher	Quantity	Heinemann Write-Up
	6	1	Adler, David	Young Cam Jansen Series/and the Baseball Mystery	141311061	Penguin Putnam	1	
		2	Aesop's Fables	City Mouse and Country Mouse	590411551	Scholastic Inc.	1	
		3	Barbour, Karen	Little Nino's Pizzeria	152463216	Harcourt Brace	1	
		4	Hoff, Syd	Danny and the Dinosaur Go to Camp	64442446	Harper Trophy	1	Y
		5	Howe, James	Day the Teacher Went Bananas, The	140547444	Penguin Publishing	1	
		6	Hutchins, Pat	Doorbell Rang, The	590411098	Scholastic Inc.	1	Y
		7	Lobel, Arnold	Mouse Soup	64440419	Harper Trophy	1	Y
		8	McDonald, Megan	Beezy Series/Beezy	531071626	Orchard Books	1	Y
	7	1	Bemelmans, Ludwig	Madeline Series/Madeline in America	590043064	Scholastic Inc.	1	Y
		2	Fowler, Allan	It Could Still Be a Mammal	516449036	Children's Press	1	Y
		3	Fowler, Allan	It Could Still Be a Rock	516460102	Children's Press	1	
		4	Havill, Juanita	Jamaica's Find	590425048	Scholastic Inc.	1	Y
		5	Ross, Pat	M&M Series/Bad News Babies	140318518	Penguin Publishing	1	Y
		6	Sharmat, Marjorie Weinman	Big Fat Enormous Lie, A	590967991	Scholastic Inc.	1	
		7	Van Leeuwen, Jean	Tales of Oliver Pig	140365494	Penguin Puffin	1	
Big Books–1 Big Book + 6 Small Copies		1	Williams, Sue	I Went Walking	152380116	Harcourt Brace	1 BB + 6 small copies	Y
Concept Books		1	Bang, Molly	Ten, Nine, Eight	688104800	William Morrow & Co	1	
		2	Berenstain, Stan	Bears on Wheels	39480967X	Random House	1	
		3	Fowler, Allan	It Could Still Be a Fish	516449028	Children's Press	1	Y
		4	Isadora, Rachel	City Seen from A to Z	688120326	William Morrow & Co	1	
		5	Morris, Ann	Bread, Bread, Bread	688122752	William Morrow & Co	1	Y
Emergent Literacy		1	Sendak, Maurice	Where the Wild Things Are	64431789	Harper Trophy	4	Y
		2	Ziefert, Harriet	Gingerbread Boy, The	140378189	Penguin Puffin	4	Y

Group Description	Level	#	Author	Title	ISBN	Publisher	Quantity	Heinemann Write-Up
		3	Ziefert, Harriet	Little Red Hen, The	140378170	Penguin Puffin	4	Y
Teaching Writing		1	Baylor, Byrd	Other Way to Listen, The	689810539	Simon & Schuster	1	Y
		2	Fox, Mem	Wilfrid Gordon McDonald Partridge	91629126X	Kane/Miller Book Publishers	1	Y
		3	Kroll, Steven	Patches Lost and Found	1890817538	Winslow Press	1	
		4	Showers, Paul	Listening Walk, The	64433226	Harper Collins	1	Y
Poetry/Song Collections		1	Florian, Douglas	Beast Feast	152017372	Harcourt Brace	1	
		2	Hoberman, Mary Ann	Fathers, Mothers, Sisters, Brothers	140548491	Penguin Publishing	1	
		3	Steptoe, Javaka	In Daddy's Arms I Am Tall	1584300167	Lee & Low Books	1	
		4	Stevenson, James	Sweet Corn	688173047	William Morrow & Co	1	
		5	Worth, Valerie	All the Small Poems & Fourteen More	374403457	Farrar Strauss & Giroux	1	
Read-Aloud Texts		1	Cleary, Beverly	Ramona the Brave	380709597	William Morrow & Co	1	Y
		2	Crews, Donald	Freight Train	688149006	William Morrow & Co	1	
		3	de Paola, Tomie	Bill and Pete	698114000	Penguin Putnam	1	
		4	Delaney, Antoinette	Gunnywolf, The	64433048	Harper Trophy	1	
		5	Fox, Mem	Harriet, You'll Drive Me Wild!	152019774	Harcourt Brace	1	Y
		6	Gannett, Ruth S.	My Father's Dragon	394890485	Random House	1	Y
		7	Henkes, Kevin	Jessica	688158471	Mulberry Books	1	Y
		8	Hesse, Karen	Come On, Rain!	590331256	Scholastic Inc.	1	Y
		9	Hoffman, Mary	Amazing Grace	803710402	Dial Books	1	
		10	Isadora, Rachel	Ben's Trumpet	688801943	Harper Collins	1	
		11	Johnston, Tony	Amber on the Mountain	14056408X	Penguin Puffin	1	
		12	Kraus, Robert	Leo the Late Bloomer	06443348X	Harper Trophy	1	Y
		13	Lionni, Leo	Matthew's Dream	67987318X	Random House	1	
		14	Mitchell, Margaree King	Uncle Jed's Barbershop	590223135	Scholastic Inc.	1	Y

Group Description	Level	#	Author	Title	ISBN	Publisher	Quantity	Heinemann Write-Up
		15	Rollins, Susan	New Shoes, Red Shoes	531302687	Scholastic Inc.	1	Y
		16	Seeger, Pete	Abiyoyo	590427202	Scholastic Inc.	1	Y
		17	Soto, Gary	Chato's Kitchen	590897489	Scholastic Inc.	1	Y
		18	Steig, William	Amos & Boris	274403600	Farrar Strauss & Giroux	1	
		19	Steig, William	Sylvester & the Magic Pebble	671662694	Simon & Schuster	1	Y
		20	Van Allsburg, Chris	Polar Express	395389496	Houghton Mifflin	1	Y
		21	Waber, Bernard	Ira Sleeps Over	395205034	Houghton Mifflin	1	
		22	Williams, Vera	Chair for My Mother, A	590331558	William Morrow & Co	1	Y
		23	Yolen, Jane	Owl Moon	590420445	Scholastic Inc.	1	Y

MODULE 1: More Independent and Partnership Reading: Filling in the Lower Portion of the Library

Group Description	Level	#	Author	Title	ISBN	Publisher	Quantity	Heinemann Write-Up
	1	1	Cowley, Joy	Brenda's Birthday	780272544	Wright Group	1	
		2	Crosbie, Michael J.	Architecture: Shapes	471143669	Wiley, John & Sons	1	
		3	Frost, Miriam	Desert Day	780288688	Wright Group	1	
		4	Klein, Adria	I Am	439064546	Scholastic Inc.	1	
		5	Malka, Lucy	Fun With Hats	1572550430	Mondo Publishing	1	Y
		6	Meadows, Graham	Big and Little	780232712	Wright Group	1	
		7	Mitton, Tony	Snowman	763541850	Rigby	1	
		8	Peters, Catherine	Hats	395882974	Houghton Mifflin	1	
		9	Ramsey, Joe	My Room	780288645	Wright Group	1	
		10	Randell, Beverly	At the Zoo	763541478	Rigby	1	Y
		11	Randell, Beverly	Dad	763541389	Rigby	1	
		12	Randell, Beverly	Dressing-up	763541427	Rigby	1	
		13	Randell, Beverly	Mom	763541370	Rigby	1	
		14	Randell, Beverly	Way I Go To School, The	763541540	Rigby	1	
		15	Savage, Elizabeth	Rainy Day Counting	780288750	Wright Group	1	

Group Description	Level	#	Author	Title	ISBN	Publisher	Quantity	Heinemann Write-Up
		16	Smith, Sue	Honk!	1572550376	Mondo Publishing	1	
		17	Teft-Cousin, Patricia	My Mama	780281535	Wright Group	1	
		18	Vernali, Stephanie	Eat It, Print It	763560642	Rigby	1	
		19	White, Coral	Shells	763560669	Rigby	1	
		20	Williams, Rozanne	Buttons Buttons	916119319	Creative Teaching Press	1	
		21	Williams, Rozanne	I Can Write	916119564	Creative Teaching Press	1	
		22	Wing-Jan, Lesley	Friends	763560626	Rigby	1	
		23	Young, Christine	Zoo, The	780210581	Wright Group	1	
	2	1		Crayola Counting Book		Creative Teaching Press	1	
		2		I Need to Clean My Room		Creative Teaching Press	1	
		3		Magic Money Box		Creative Teaching Press	1	
		4		Safety Counts		Creative Teaching Press	1	
		5		Under the Sky		Creative Teaching Press	1	
		6		What Do You See?		Creative Teaching Press	1	
		7		Where Do Monsters Live?		Creative Teaching Press	1	
		8	Canizares, Susan	Sun	590107313	Scholastic Inc.	1	
		9	Canizares, Susan	Who Lives in the Arctic?	590761501	Scholastic Inc.	1	
		10	Cartwright, Pauline	Tails	1556246331	Wright Group	1	
		11	Chanko, Pamela	Writing Places	439046092	Scholastic Inc.	1	Y
		12	Chanko, Pamela & Daniel Moreton	Weather	590107305	Scholastic Inc.	1	
		13	Cutting, Jillian	Eating Out	780239113	Wright Group	1	
		14	Frost, Miriam	Boats	780289021	Wright Group	1	
		15	Hawes, Alison	Snake Goes Away	763566101	Rigby	1	
		16	Lockyer, John	Astronaut, The	780237145	Wright Group	1	
		17	Nelson, May	My Baby	1572576995	Wright Group	1	

Group Description	Level	#	Author	Title	ISBN	Publisher	Quantity	Heinemann Write-Up
		18	Nelson, May	My Bike	1572577045	Wright Group	1	
		19	Randell, Beverly	Baby Owls, The	76351506X	Rigby	1	Y
		20	Randell, Beverly	Photo Book, The	435067265	Rigby	1	Y
		21	Riley, Kana	Green, Green	669445193	Houghton Mifflin	1	
		22	Saksie, Judy	Seed Song, The	916119386	Creative Teaching Press	1	
		23	Smith, Annette	Fishing	763541737	Rigby	1	Y
		24	Young, Sharon L.	Randy's Room	761983066	Sage Publications	1	

MODULE 2: More Independent and Partnership Reading: Filling in the Middle of the Library

Group Description	Level	#	Author	Title	ISBN	Publisher	Quantity	Heinemann Write-Up
	3	1	Heller, Ruth	Up, Up and Away	698116631	Paper Star	1	
		2		Voyage of Mae Jemison		Scholastic Inc.	1	
		3	Avery, Dorothy	What Is It?	1572576944	Wright Group	1	
		4	Birnbaum, Bette	Jane Goodall and the Wild Chimpanzees	811467090	Raintree Steck Vaughn	1	
		5	Canizares, Susan	Coral Reef	59076182X	Scholastic Inc.	1	
		6	Canizares, Susan	Italy	43904572X	Scholastic Inc.	1	
		7	Canizares, Susan	Meet Jim Henson	439045754	Scholastic Inc.	1	
		8	Canizares, Susan	Pele the King of Soccer	439045770	Scholastic Inc.	1	
		9	Cowley, Joy	Bears' Picnic, The	780272900	Wright Group	1	
		10	Cowley, Joy	Meanies	1559112468	Wright Group	1	Y
		11	Graves, Kimberlee	I Can't Sleep	916119440	Creative Teaching Press	1	
		12	Graves, Kimberlee	Mom Can Fix Anything	916119467	Creative Teaching Press	1	
		13	Kenny, Ann	Night Walk	1572740213	Richard C. Owen Publishers	1	
		14	Randell, Beverly	Ben's Treasure Hunt	435067508	Rigby	1	Y
		15	Riley, Kana	Peaches the Pig	669445274	Houghton Mifflin	1	
		16	Sloan, Peter	Washing the Dog	760803609	Sundance	1	

Group Description	Level	#	Author	Title	ISBN	Publisher	Quantity	Heinemann Write-Up
		17	Williams, Rebel	Tracks	780290909	Wright Group	1	Y
		18	Williams, Rozanne Lanczak	Who Lives Here?	916119378	Creative Teaching Press	1	
	4	1	Bailey, Debbie	My Mom	1550371630	Firefly Books/Annick	1	
		2	Beck, Jennifer	BMX Billy	79011424	Rigby	1	
		3	Birchall, Brian	How Animals Hide	780245806	Wright Group	1	
		4	Canizares, Susan	Storms	590107291	Scholastic Inc.	1	
		5	Cowley, Joy	Papa's Spaghetti	790101491	Rigby	1	Y
		6	Eggleton, Jill	Fat Ducks	763559229	Rigby	1	
		7	Frost, Helen	Bird Families	73680224X	Pebble Books	1	
		8	Frost, Helen	Bird Nests	736802258	Pebble Books	1	
		9	Giles, Jenny	Soccer at the Park	763515167	Rigby	1	
		10	Goodrow, Anne	Ten Yellow Buses	322001897	Wright Group	1	
		11	Greydanus, Rose	Mike's New Bike	893752827	Troll Communications	1	
		12	Hardin, Suzanne	No Dogs Allowed	1572741147	Richard C. Owen Publishers	1	Y
		13	Hughes, Monica	Bobbie and the Play	763566330	Rigby	1	
		14	Hughes, Monica	Try This!	763560928	Rigby	1	
		15	Lewison, Wendy	Buzz Said the Bee	590907417	Scholastic Inc.	1	
		16	Maccarone, Grace	Monster Math School Time	590308599	Scholastic Inc.	1	
		17	Marzollo, Jean	City Sounds	590275631	Scholastic Inc.	1	
		18	Mayer, Mercer	Critters of the Night Series/Midnight Snack	679887067	Random House	1	
		19	McPhail, David	Bug, A Bear, and A Boy, A	590149040	Scholastic Inc.	1	
		20	Moffat, Judith	Who Stole the Cookies?	590065971	Scholastic Inc.	1	
		21	Powell, Jillian	Mrs. Mog's Cats	763566373	Rigby	1	
		22	Randell, Beverly	House Hunting	435067559	Rigby	1	
		23	Randell, Beverly	Lion and the Rabbit	4350675X	Rigby	1	

Group Description	Level	#	Author	Title	ISBN	Publisher	Quantity	Heinemann Write-Up
		24	Randell, Beverly	Sally's Red Bucket	435067052	Rigby	1	Y
		25	Randell, Beverly	Tabby in the Tree	435067273	Rigby	1	
		26	Rendall, Jenny	When Goldilocks Went to the House of the Bears	1572550538	Mondo Publishing	1	
		27	Smith, Annette	Mitch to the Rescue	763519626	Rigby	1	
		28	Wilhelm, Hans	I Lost My Tooth	590642308	Scholastic	1	
		29	Windsor, Jo	Helping Out	763358907	Rigby	1	
		30	Windsor, Jo	Watch Out for Trash Cans	763559156	Rigby	1	

MODULE 3: More Independent and Partnership Reading: Filling in the Upper Portion of the Library

Group Description	Level	#	Author	Title	ISBN	Publisher	Quantity	Heinemann Write-Up
	5	1	Caldwell, V.M.	Solar-Powered Sam	1572742828	Richard C. Owen Publishers	1	
		2	Comber, Barbara	I Can Do It	1572551003	Mondo Publishing	1	
		3	Cowley, Joy	Red-Eyed Tree Frog	590871765	Scholastic Inc.	1	Y
		4	Degen, Bruce	Jamberry	694006513	Harper Collins	1	
		5	Falwell, Cathryn	Feast for 10	395620376	Houghton Mifflin	1	
		6	Fear, Sharon	Ginger	66945436	Houghton Mifflin	1	
		7	Henkes, Kevin	Bailey Goes Camping	688152880	William Morrow & Co	1	Y
		8	Hoff, Syd	Lighthouse Children, The	64441784	Harper Trophy	1	Y
		9	Hoff, Syd	Mrs. Brice's Mice	64441458	Harper Collins	1	Y
		10	Jackson, Marjorie	Shintaro's Umbrellas	1572740256	Richard C. Owen Publishers	1	
		11	Mazzone, Kelly	House for Hickory, A	1572550279	Mondo Publishing	1	
		12	Noonan, Diana	My Friend Jess	780212266	Wright Group	1	
		13	Pilkey, Dav	Dragon's Series/Dragon's Fat Cat	531070689	Orchard Books	1	
		14	Pilkey, Dav	Dragon's Series/Dragon's Merry Christmas	531070557	Orchard Books	1	
		15	Porter, Gracie	Going on a Field Trip	780291891	Wright Group	1	
		16	Reiser, Lynn	Any Kind of Dog	688133722	Mulberry Books	1	

Group Description	Level	#	Author	Title	ISBN	Publisher	Quantity	Heinemann Write-Up
		17	Trussell-Cullen, Alan	Whistle Tooth, The	769900380	Wright Group	1	
		18	Ziefert, Harriet	Turnip, The	140380825	Penguin Puffin	1	
	6	1	Adler, David	Young Cam Jansen Series/the Missing Cookie	140380507	Viking Penguin	1	Y
		2	Aruego, Jose	Rockabye Crocodile: A Folktale from the Philippines	688123333	William Morrow & Co	1	Y
		3	Bornstein, Ruth	Little Gorilla	899194214	Clarion Books	1	
		4	Brown, Margaret Wise	Little Fireman, The	64433897	Harper Collins	1	
		5	Bulla, Clyde Robert	Daniel's Duck	64440311	Harper Trophy	1	Y
		6	Cole, Joanna	Bony Legs	590405160	Scholastic Inc.	1	
		7	Fowler, Allan	Friendly Dolphins	516262564	Children's Press	1	
		8	Galdone, Paul	Henny Penny	899192254	Clarion Books	1	
		9	Kessler, Leonard	Here Comes the Strikeout	64440117	Harper Trophy	1	
		10	Krueger, Carol	Rainbows	763561029	Rigby	1	
		11	Lobel, Arnold	Uncle Elephant	64441040	Harper Collins	1	
		12	Mareollo, Claudio	Kenny and the Little Kickers	59045417X	Scholastic Inc.	1	
		13	Minarik, Else Holmelund	Little Bear Series/Little Bear's Friend	64440516	Harper Trophy	1	Y
		14	Riley, Kana	Building Strong Bridges	322018455	Wright Group	1	
		15	Robins, Joan	Addie's Bad Day	64441830	Harper Trophy	1	Y
		16	Rylant, Cynthia	Henry and Mudge Series/In Puddle Trouble	689810032	Simon & Schuster	1	Y
		17	Schwartz, Alvin	In a Dark, Dark Room	64440907	Harper Collins	1	Y
		18	Skofield, James	Detective Dinosaur Series/Detective Dinosaur Lost & Found	64442578	Harper Trophy	1	
		19	Washington, Linda	Jamall's City Garden	763561215	Rigby	1	
	7	1	Baker, Jeannie	Where the Forest Meets the Sea	688063632	Greenwillow Books	1	

Group Description	Level	#	Author	Title	ISBN	Publisher	Quantity	Heinemann Write-Up
		2	Berenstain, Stan & Jan	Berenstain Bear Scouts Series/the Whitewater Mystery	590565222	Scholastic Inc.	1	
		3	Berger, Melvin	Oil Spill!	64451216	Harper Collins	1	
		4	de Paola, Tomie	Quicksand Book, The	823402916	Holiday House	1	
		5	Fowler, Allan	Giant Pandas: Gifts from China	516460315	Childrens Press/Rookie Read-About Science	1	
		6	Fowler, Allan	These Birds Can't Fly		Childrens Press/Rookie Read-About Science	1	
		7	Freeman, Don	Corduroy	140501738	Penguin Puffin	1	Y
		8	Hoban, Lillian	Arthur's Funny Money	64440486	Harper Collins	1	
		9	Hoban, Russell	Frances Books Series/A Baby Sister for Frances	64430065	Harper Collins	1	
		10	Lionni, Leo	Inch by Inch	688132839	William Morrow & Co	1	
		11	Lionni, Leo	Swimmy	590430491	Scholastic Inc.	1	Y
		12	Lundell, Margo	Girl Named Helen Keller, A	590479636	Scholastic Inc.	1	
		13	Marzollo, Jean	Basketball Buddies	590384015	Scholastic Inc.	1	
		14	Mills, Claudia	Gus and Grandpa at Basketball			1	
		15	Munsch, Robert	Paper Bag Princess, The	920236162	Firefly Books	1	
		16	Ross, Pat	M&M Series/The Haunted House Game	140387307	Penguin Puffin	1	
		17	Sharmat, Marjorie Weinman	Nate the Great and the Boring Beach Bag	440401682	Bantam Doubleday Dell	1	
		18	Slobodkina, Esphyr	Caps for Sale	590410806	Scholastic Inc.	1	Y
		19	Van Leeuwen, Jean	Tales of Amanda Pig	14036840X	Penguin Putnam	1	
		20	Young, Ed	Seven Blind Mice	590469711	Scholastic Inc.	1	

MODULE 4: Genre and Author Studies

Group Description	Level	#	Author	Title	ISBN	Publisher	Quantity	Heinemann Write-Up
Alphabet Books		1	Bender, Robert	A to Z Beastly Jamboree	140562133	Penguin Putnam	1	
		2	Carlson, Nancy	ABC I Like Me	140564853	Penguin	1	

Group Description	Level	#	Author	Title	ISBN	Publisher	Quantity	Heinemann Write-Up
		3	Ellwand, David	Emma's Elephant and Other Favorite Animal Friends	525457925	Dutton	1	
		4	Lionni, Leo	Alphabet Tree, The	679808353	Alfred A Knopf	1	Y
		5	Palotta, Jerry	Icky Bug Alphabet Book, The	881064564	Charlesbridge Publishing	1	
Author Studies		1	Freeman, Don	Beady Bear	140501975	Penguin Putnam	1	
		2	Freeman, Don	Dandelion	140502181	Penguin Putnam	1	
		3	Freeman, Don	Mop Top	140503269	Penguin Putnam	1	
		4	Freeman, Don	Pocket For Corduroy, A	140503528	Penguin Putnam	1	
		5	Freeman, Don	Rainbow of My Own	140503285	Penguin Putnam	1	
		6	Keats, Ezra Jack	Kitten for a Day	689717377	Simon & Schuster	1	
		7	Keats, Ezra Jack	Letter to Amy, A	14056442X	Penguin Putnam	1	Y
		8	Keats, Ezra Jack	Peter's Chair	140564411	Penguin Putnam	1	Y
		9	Keats, Ezra Jack	Snowy Day, The	140501827	Penguin Puffin	1	Y
		10	Keats, Ezra Jack	Whistle for Willie	140502025	Penguin Publishing	1	
		11	Wells, Rosemary	Bunny Cakes	140566678	Penguin Publishing	1	Y
		12	Wells, Rosemary	Bunny Money	803721463	Penguin Putnam	1	
		13	Wells, Rosemary	Max and Ruby in Pandora's Box	140564152	Penguin Publishing	1	
		14	Wells, Rosemary	Max's Birthday	803722680	Dial Books	1	
		15	Wells, Rosemary	Max's Dragon Shirt	140567275	Penguin Publishing	1	
Family Stories (Memoir)		1	de Paola, Tomie	Nana Upstairs, Nana Downstairs	698118367	Penguin Puffin	1	Y
		2	Fox, Mem	Wilfrid Gordon McDonald Partridge	91629126X	Kane/Miller Book Publishers	1	Y
		3	Houston, Gloria	My Great Aunt Arizona	64433749	Harper Collins	1	
		4	Pomerantz, Charlotte	Chalk Doll, The	64433331	Harper Collins	1	
		5	Stevenson, James	I Meant to Tell You	688141773	William Morrow & Co	1	
How-To Books		1	Gibbons, Gail	My Baseball Book	688171370	William Morrow & Co	1	

Group Description	Level	#	Author	Title	ISBN	Publisher	Quantity	Heinemann Write-Up
		2	Henessey, B.G	Road Builders	140542760	Penguin	1	
		3	Lucuero, Jaime	How To Make Salsa	1572551194	Mondo Publishing	1	
		4	Wellington, Monica	Mr. Cookie Baker	140562346	Viking Penguin	1	
		5	Williams, Vera	It's A Gingerbread House!	688149804	William Morrow & Co	1	
		6	Witt, Alexa	It's Great to Skate	689825900	Simon & Schuster	1	
List Books		1	Brown, Margaret Wise	Important Book, The	64432270	Harper Collins	1	Y
		2	Desimini, Lisa	My House	805055169	Henry Holt & Co	1	
		3	Fox, Mem	Time for Bed	152010661	Harcourt Brace	1	
		4	Porter-Gaylord, Laurel	I Love My Daddy Because…	525446249	Penguin Putnam	1	
		5	Wild, Margaret	Our Granny	395670233	Houghton Mifflin	1	
Nonfiction		1	Butterfield, Moira	Quick, Quiet, and Feathered	81727233X	Steck-Vaughn	1	
		2	Dussling, Jennifer	Slinky Scaly Snakes	789434393	DK Publishing	1	Y
		3	Gibbons, Gail	Moon Book, The	823413640	Holiday House	1	
		4	Rockwell, Anne	At the Beach	689714947	Simon & Schuster	1	
Poetry		1		Small Child's Book of Cozy Poems, A	590383647	Scholastic Inc.	1	
		2	Adoff, Arnold	Touch the Poem	590479709	Scholastic Inc.	1	
		3	Hopkins, Lee Bennett	April Bubbles Chocolate: An ABC of Poetry	671759116	Simon & Schuster	1	
		4	Shange, Ntozake	I Live in Music	941807096	Welcome Enterprises	1	
		5	Worth, Valerie	All the Small Poems & Fourteen More	374403457	Farrar Strauss & Giroux	1	
Wordless Books		1	Carle, Eric	I See a Song	590252135	Scholastic Inc.	1	
		2	Mayer, Mercer	Frog Goes to Dinner	140546332	Penguin	1	Y
		3	Mayer, Mercer	Frog on His Own	140546340	Penguin	1	
		4	Spier, Peter	Peter Spier's Rain	440413478	Bantam Doubleday Dell	1	

Group Description	Level	#	Author	Title	ISBN	Publisher	Quantity	Heinemann Write-Up
MODULE 5: Talking Across Books								
Character—Biscuit		1	Capucilli, Alyssa	Bathtime for Biscuit	64442640	Harper Collins	1	
		2	Capucilli, Alyssa	Biscuit	64442128	Harper Collins	1	
		3	Capucilli, Alyssa	Biscuit Finds a Friend	64442438	Harper Collins	1	
		4	Capucilli, Alyssa	Happy Birthday Biscuit	60283556	Harper Collins	1	Y
Character—Clifford		1	Bridwell, Norman	Clifford the Big Red Dog	059044297X	Scholastic Inc.	1	
		2	Bridwell, Norman	Clifford's Birthday Party	590442791	Scholastic Inc.	1	
		3	Bridwell, Norman	Clifford's Kitten	590442805	Scholastic Inc.	1	
		4	Bridwell, Norman	Clifford's Manners	590442856	Scholastic Inc.	1	
Character— Curious George		1	Rey, Hans Augusto	Curious George	39515023X	Houghton Mifflin	1	
		2	Rey, Hans Augusto	Curious George Goes to the Hospital	395070627	Houghton Mifflin	1	
		3	Rey, Hans Augusto	Curious George Makes Pancakes	395919088	Houghton Mifflin	1	
		4	Rey, Hans Augusto	Curious George Rides a Bike	395174449	Houghton Mifflin	1	
Character—Harold		1	Johnson, Crocket	Harold and the Purple Crayon	64430227	Harper Collins	1	
		2	Johnson, Crocket	Harold's Fairy Tale	64433471	Harper Collins	1	
		3	Johnson, Crocket	Harold's Trip to the Sky	64430251	Harper Collins	1	
		4	Johnson, Crocket	Picture for Harold's Room, A	64440850	Harper Trophy	1	
Character—Spot		1	Hill, Eric	Spot Series/Spot Bakes a Cake	140555293	Penguin Publishing	1	
		2	Hill, Eric	Spot Series/Spot Goes to School	140552820	Penguin Publishing	1	
		3	Hill, Eric	Spot Series/Spot Goes to the Circus	140552979	Penguin Publishing	1	
		4	Hill, Eric	Spot Series/Where's Spot	399234950	Penguin Publishing	1	
Nonfiction—All Seasons		1	Fowler, Susi L.	When Summer Ends	140544720	Penguin Puffin	1	
		2	Helldorfer, Mary	Gather Up Gather In	140548475	Viking Penguin	1	
		3	Nayer, Judy	Fall	1567849059	Newbridge Educational Publishing	1	

Group Description	Level	#	Author	Title	ISBN	Publisher	Quantity	Heinemann Write-Up
		4	Nayer, Judy	In Spring	1567849091	Newbridge Educational Publishing	1	
		5	Pearson, Susan	My Favorite Time of the Year	60246812	Harper Collins	1	
Nonfiction—Animal Home		1	Bancroft, Henrietta	Animals In Winter	64451658	Harper Collins	1	
		2	Bolton, Faye	Animal Shelters	1572551925	Mondo Publishing	1	
		3	Zoehfeld, Kathleen	What Lives in a Shell?	64451240	Harper Collins	1	
Nonfiction—Bugs		1	Brimner, Larry Dane	How Many Ants?	516262513	Children's Press	1	
		2	Dobkin, Bonnie	Great Bug Hunt, The	516420178	Children's Press	1	
		3	Reid, Mary	Bugs, Bugs, Bugs	590397923	Scholastic Inc.	1	
Nonfiction—Days of the Week		1	Caines, Jeannette	I Need a Lunch Box	64433412	Harper Collins	1	
		2	Carle, Eric	Today Is Monday	698115635	Putnam Publishing	1	
		3	Ward, Cindy	Cookie's Week	698114353	Penguin Publishing	1	Y
Nonfiction—Dinosaurs		1	Aliki	Dinosaur Bones	64450775	Harper Collins	1	
		2	Barton, Byron	Dinosaurs, Dinosaurs	6443298X	Harper Collins	1	
		3	Most, Bernard	How Big Were the Dinosaurs?	152008527	Harcourt	1	
		4	Most, Bernard	If the Dinosaurs Came Back	152380213	Harcourt Brace	1	
		5	Parish, Peggy	Dinosaur Time	64440370	Harper Collins	1	
Nonfiction—Growing Things		1		One Square Inch			1	
		2	Ehlert, Lois	Growing Vegetable Soup	152325808	Harcourt Brace	1	Y
		3	Krauss, Ruth	Carrot Seed, The	64432106	Harper Trophy	1	Y
Nonfiction—Seeds/Flowers		1	Bunting, Eve	Sunflower House	152019529	Harcourt	1	
		2	Halpern, Monica	How Many Seeds?	817282750	Steck-Vaughn	1	
		3	Jordan, Helene	How a Seed Grows	64451070	Harper Collins	1	

Group Description	Level	#	Author	Title	ISBN	Publisher	Quantity	Heinemann Write-Up
Versions of The Three Bears		4	Trumbauer, Lisa	Grow, Seed, Grow			1	
		1	Brett, Jan	Goldilocks and the Three Bears	698113586	Putnam Publishing	1	
		2	Galdone, Paul	Three Bears, The	395288118	Clarion Books	1	Y
		3	Marshall, James	Goldilocks and the Three Bears	140563660	Penguin	1	
Versions of The Three Little Pigs		1	Galdone, Paul	Three Little Pigs, The	395288134	Clarion Books	1	Y
		2	Pfeifer, Larissa	Three Little Pigs, The		Wright Group	1	
		3	Van Lille, Katrin	Three Little Pigs, The	669445266	Great Source	1	
		4	Ziefert, Harriet	Three Little Pigs, The	140376240	Penguin Puffin	1	

MODULE 6: Shared Reading and Read Aloud

Group Description	Level	#	Author	Title	ISBN	Publisher	Quantity	Heinemann Write-Up
Big Book-1 Big Book – 4 Small Copies		1	Barton, Byron	Three Bears, The	694009989	Harper Collins	1	
		2	Martin, Bill	Sounds of An Owly Night				
		3	Marzollo, Jean	I'm a Seed	590265865	Scholastic Inc.	1	
		4	Snow, Pegeen	Eat Your Peas, Louise!	516420674	Children's Press/Rookie Readers	1	
		5	Titherington, Jeanne	Pumpkin Pumpkin	688099300	William Morrow & Co	1	
Chapter Books		1	Atwater, Richard	Mr. Popper's Penguins	590477331	Little Brown & Co	1	Y
		2	Cameron, Ann	Stories That Julian Tells, The	394828925	Alfred A Knopf	1	Y
		3	Dahl, Roald	Charlie & the Chocolate Factory	141301155	Penguin Putnam	1	
		4	Gannett, Ruth	Elmer and the Dragon	394890493	Alfred A. Knopf	1	
		5	King-Smith, Dick	Babe: The Gallant Pig	679883614	Random House	1	
Cumulative Texts		1	Cole, Henry	Jack's Garden	68815283X	William Morrow & Co	1	
		2	Fox, Mem	Shoes from Grandpa	53107031X	Orchard Books	1	Y
Emergent Literacy		1	Eastman, Patricia	Are You My Mother?	394800184	Random House	4	Y

Group Description	Level	#	Author	Title	ISBN	Publisher	Quantity	Heinemann Write-Up
Repetitive Texts		2	Galdone, Paul	Gingerbread Boy, The	899191630	Clarion Books	4	
		3	Piper, Watty	Little Engine That Could, The	448405202	Putnam Publishing	4	
		1	Barchas, Sarah E.	I Was Walking Down the Road	590718835	Scholastic Inc.	1	
		2	Cabrera, Jane	Cat's Colors	014056487X	Penguin Putnam	1	
		3	Carter, David	In a Dark, Dark Wood	671741349	Simon & Schuster	1	
		4	Fleming, Denise	Where Once There Was Wood	805064826	Henry Holt & Co	1	
		5	Frasier, Debra	On the Day You Were Born	152579958	Harcourt Brace	1	
		6	Shelby, Anne	Someday House, The	53108860X	Orchard Books	1	
		7	Tafuri, Nancy	Spots Feathers and Curly Tails	688075363	William Morrow & Co	1	
		8	Zolotow, Charlotte	Sky Was Blue, The	60278773	Harper Collins	1	
Rhyming Texts		1	Baker, Keith	Who Is the Beast?	152001220	Harcourt	1	
		2	Brown, Margaret Wise	Little Donkey Close Your Eyes	64435075	Harper Collins	1	
		3	Bunting, Eve	Flower Garden	152023720	Harcourt Brace	1	Y
		4	Cushman, Doug	ABC Mystery, The	64434591	Harper Collins	1	
		5	Stewart, Sarah	Library, The	374443947	Farrar Strauss & Giroux	1	Y
		6	Zolotow, Charlotte	Some Things Go Together	64431339	Harper Collins	1	
Songs		1	Adams, Pam	Old MacDonald Had a Farm	859530531	Child's Play-International	1	
		2	Adams, Pam	There Was an Old Lady Who Swallowed a Fly	859530183	Child's Play-International	1	
		3	Eagle, Kin	It's Raining, It's Pouring		Charlesbridge Publishing	1	
		4	Garcia, Jerry	Teddy Bear's Picnic, The	6027302X	Harper Collins	1	
		5	Hoberman, Mary Ann	Eensy Weensy Spider, The	316363308	Little Brown & Co	1	
		6	Kaye, Buddy	A You're Adorable, B You're Beautiful	1564025667		1	
		7	Wescott, Nadine	Peanut Butter and Jelly	140548521	Viking Penguin	1	
		8	Wescott, Nadine Bernard	Lady With the Alligator Purse, The	316930741	Little Brown & Co	1	

Benchmark Books for Each Text Level

TC Level	Benchmarks: Books that Represent Each Level
1	*A Birthday Cake* (Cowley) *I Can Write* (Williams) *The Cat on the Mat* (Wildsmith)
2	*Rain* (Kaplan) *Fox on the Box* (Gregorich)
3	*It Looked Like Spilt Milk* (Shaw) *I Like Books* (Browne) *Mrs. Wishy-Washy* (Cowley)
4	*Rosie's Walk* (Hutchins) *The Carrot Seed* (Krauss) *Cookie's Week* (Ward)
5	*George Shrinks* (Joyce) *Goodnight Moon* (Brown) *Hattie and the Fox* (Fox)
6	*Danny and the Dinosaur* (Hoff) *Henry and Mudge* (Rylant)
7	*Nate the Great* (Sharmat) *Meet M&M* (Ross)
8	*Horrible Harry* (Kline) *Pinky and Rex* (Howe) Arthur Series (Marc Brown)
9	*Amber Brown* (Danziger) *Ramona Quimby, Age 8* (Cleary)
10	*James and the Giant Peach* (Dahl) *Fudge-A-Mania* (Blume)
11	*Shiloh* (Naylor) *The Great Gilly Hopkins* (Paterson)
12	*Bridge to Terabithia* (Paterson) *Baby* (MacLachlan)
13	*Missing May* (Rylant) *Where the Red Fern Grows* (Rawls)
14	*A Day No Pigs Would Die* (Peck) *Scorpions* (Myers)
15	*The Golden Compass* (Pullman) *The Dark Is Rising* (Cooper) *A Wizard of Earthsea* (Le Guin)

Descriptions of Text Levels One Through Seven

TEXT LEVEL ONE

This level roughly corresponds to the following levels in other systems:

Reading Recovery© (RR) Levels 1–2
Developmental Reading Assessment (DRA) Levels A–2

Text Characteristics for TC Level One

- The font is large, clear, and is usually printed in black on a white background.

- There is exaggerated spacing between words and letters. (In some books, publishers have enlarged the print but have not adjusted the spacing which can create difficulties for readers.)

- There is usually a single word, phrase, or simple sentence on a page, and the text is patterned and predictable. For example, in the book *I Can Read*, once a child knows the title (which is ideally read to a Level One reader) it is not hard for the child to read "I can read the newspaper," "I can read the cereal box." These readers are regarded as "preconventional" because they rely on the illustrations (that support the meaning) and the sounds of language (or syntax) and not on graphophonics or word/letter cues to read a sentence such as, "I can read the newspaper."

- Usually each page contains two or three sight words. A Level One book *may* contain one illustrated word on a page (such as "Mom," "Dad," "sister," "cat") but it's just as easy for a child to read "I see my mom. I see my Dad. I see my sister. I see my cat." because the sight words give the child a way into the text.

- The words are highly supported by illustrations. No one would expect a Level One reader to solve the word "newspaper." We would, however, expect a child at this level to look at the picture and at the text and to read the word "newspaper."

- Words are consistently placed in the same area of each page, preferably top left or bottom left.

Characteristics of the Reader

Readers in this group will demonstrate most of these behaviors.

- Remember the pattern in a predictable text
- Use picture cues

- Use left to right directionality to read one or two lines of print

- Work on matching spoken words with printed words and self-correcting when these don't "come out even"

- Rely on the spaces between words to signify the end of one word and the beginning of another. These readers read the spaces as well as the words, as the words are at first black blobs on white paper

- Locate one or two known words on a page

Benchmarks

The following titles are representative of the kinds of books found in this grouping.

A Birthday Cake, Joy Cowley
Cat on the Mat, Brian Wildsmith
The Farm, Literacy 2000/Stage 1
Growing Colors, Bruce McMillan
I Can Write, Rozanne Williams
Time for Dinner, PM Starters

Assessment

The following titles can be used to determine if a reader is ready to move on to the next grouping of books. This type of assessment is most effective if the text is unfamiliar to the reader. If these titles will be used as assessment texts, they should *not* be part of the classroom library.

My Home, Story Box
The Tree Stump, Little Celebrations
DRA Assessments A–2

We move children from Level One to Level Two books when they are consistently able to match one spoken word with one word written on the page. This means that they can point under words in a Level One book as they read and know when they haven't matched a spoken word to a written word by noticing that, at the end of the line, they still have words left on the page or they've run out of words. When children read multisyllabic words and compound words and point to multiple, instead of one, word on the page, we consider this a successful one-to-one match.

TEXT LEVEL TWO

This level roughly corresponds to the following levels in other systems:

Reading Recovery© (RR) Levels 3–4
Developmental Reading Assessment (DRA) Levels 3–4

Text Characteristics of TC Level Two

- There are usually two lines of print on at least some of the pages in these books, and sometimes there are three. This means readers will become accustomed to making the return sweep to the beginning of a new line.

- The texts are still patterned and predictable, but now the patterns tend to switch at intervals. Almost always, the pattern changes at the end of the book. The repeating unit may be as long as two sentences in length.

- The font continues to be large and clear. The letters might not, however, be black against white although this is generally the case.

- Children still rely on the picture but the pictures tend to give readers more to deal with; children need to search more in the picture to find help in reading the words.

- High frequency words are still helpful and important. The sentences in Level One books tend to begin with 2 to 3 high frequency words, for example, "I like to run. I like to jump." At this level, the pages are more apt to begin with a single high frequency word and then include words that require picture support and attention to first letters, for example, "A mouse has a long tail. A bear has a short tail."

- Sentences are more varied, resulting in texts that include a full range of punctuation.

Characteristics of the Reader

Readers in this group will demonstrate most of these behaviors.

- Get the mouth ready for the initial sound of a word

- Use left to right directionality as well as a return sweep to another line of print

- Locate one or two known words on a page

- Monitor for meaning: check to make sure it makes sense

Benchmarks

The following titles are representative of the kinds of books found in this grouping.

All Fall Down, Brian Wildsmith
I Went Walking, Sue Williams
Rain, Robert Kalan
Shoo, Sunshine

Assessment

The following titles can be used to determine if a reader is ready to move on to the next grouping. This type of assessment is most effective if the text is unfamiliar to a reader. If these titles will be used as assessment texts, they should *not* be part of the classroom library.

The Bus Ride, Little Celebrations, DRA 3
Fox on the Box, School Zone, DRA 4

We generally move children from Level Two to Level Three texts when they know how to use the pictures and the syntax to generate possibilities for the next word, when they attend to the first letters of unknown words. These readers will also read and rely on high frequency words such as *I, the, a, to, me, mom, the child's name, like, love, go,* and *and*.

TEXT LEVEL THREE

This level roughly corresponds to the following levels in other systems:

Reading Recovery© (RR) Levels 5–8
Developmental Reading Assessment (DRA) Levels 6–8

Text Characteristics of TC Level Three

It is important to note that this grouping includes a wide range of levels. This was done deliberately because at this level, readers should be able to select "just right" books for themselves and be able to monitor their own reading.

- Sentences are longer and readers will need to put their words together in order to take in more of the sentence at a time. When they are stuck, it's often helpful to nudge them to reread and try again.

- The pictures are not as supportive as they've been. It's still helpful for children to do picture walks prior to reading an unfamiliar text, but now the goal is less about surmising what words the page contains and more about seeing an overview of the narrative.

- Readers must rely on graphophonics across the whole word. If readers hit a wall at this level, it's often because they're accustomed to predicting words based on a dominant pattern and using the initial letters (only) to confirm their predictions. It takes readers a while to begin checking the print closely enough to adjust their expectations.

- Children will need to use sight words to help with unknown words, using parts of these familiar words as analogies, helping them unlock the unfamiliar words.

- The font size and spacing are less important now.

- Words in the text begin to include contractions. We can help children read these by urging them to look all the way across a word.

Characteristics of the Reader

Readers in this group will demonstrate most of these behaviors.

- Reread and self-correct

- Read with some fluency

- Cross check one cue against another

- Monitor for meaning: check to make sure what has been read makes sense and sounds right

- Recognize common chunks of words

Benchmarks

The following titles are representative of the kinds of books found in this grouping.

Bears in the Night Stan and Jan, Berenstain
The Chick and the Duckling, Ginsburg
It Looked Like Spilt Milk, Charles G. Shaw
Mrs. Wishy-Washy, Joy Cowley

Assessment

The following titles can be used to determine if a reader is ready to move on to the next grouping. This type of assessment is most effective if the text is unfamiliar to a reader. If these titles will be used as assessment texts, they should *not* be part of the classroom library.

Bread, Story Box, DRA 6
Get Lost Becka, School Zone, DRA 8

We move a child to Level Four books if that child can pick up an unfamiliar book like *Bread* or *It Looked Like Spilt Milk* and read it with a little difficulty, but with a lot of independence and with strategies. This reader should know to reread when she is stuck, to use the initial sounds in a word, to chunk word families within a word, and so on.

TEXT LEVEL FOUR

This level roughly corresponds to the following levels in other systems:

Reading Recovery© (RR) Levels 9–12
Developmental Reading Assessment (DRA) Levels 10–12

Text Characteristics of TC Level Four

- In general, the child who is reading Level Four books is able to do more of the same reading work he could do with texts at the previous level. This child reads texts that contain more words, lines, pages, and more challenging vocabulary.

- These texts contain even less picture support than earlier levels.

- Fluency and phrasing are very important for the Level Four reader. If children don't begin to read quickly enough, they won't be able to carry the syntax of the sentence along well enough to comprehend what they are reading.

■ These books use brief bits of literary language. That is, in these books the mother may turn to her child and say, "We shall be rich."

■ These books are more apt to have a plot (with characters, setting, problem, solution) and they tend to be less patterned than they were at the previous level.

Characteristics of the Reader

Readers in this group will demonstrate most of these behaviors.

■ Reread and self-correct

■ Read with fluency

■ Integrate cues from meaning, structure, and visual sources

■ Monitor for meaning: check to make sure what has been read makes sense, sounds right, and looks right

■ Make some analogies from known words to figure out unknown words

■ Read increasingly difficult chunks within words

Benchmarks

The following titles are representative of the kinds of books found in this grouping.

The Carrot Seed, Ruth Krauss
Cookie's Week, Cindy Ward
Rosie's Walk, Pat Hutchins
Titch, Pat Hutchins

Assessment

The following titles can be used to determine if a reader is ready to move on to the next grouping. This type of assessment is most effective if the text is unfamiliar to a reader. If these titles will be used as assessment texts, they should *not* be part of the classroom library.

Are You There Bear?, Ron Maris, DRA 10
The House in the Tree, Rigby PM Story Books
Nicky Upstairs and Downstairs, Harriet Ziefert
William's Skateboard, Sunshine, DRA 12

We move a child to Level Five books if that reader can independently use a variety of strategies to work through difficult words or parts of a text. The reader must be reading fluently enough to reread quickly, when necessary, so as to keep the flow of the story going. If a reader is reading very slowly, taking too much time to work through the hard parts, then this reader may not be ready to move on to the longer, more challenging texts in Level Five.

TEXT LEVEL FIVE

This level roughly corresponds to the following levels in other systems:

Reading Recovery© (RR) Levels 13–15
Developmental Reading Assessment (DRA) Level 14

Text Characteristics

■ Sentences in Level Five books tend to be longer, more varied, and more complex than they were in previous levels.

■ Many of the stories are retold folktales or fantasy-like stories that use literary or story language, such as: "Once upon a time, there once lived, a long, long time ago. . . . "

■ Many books may be in a cumulative form in which text is added to each page, requiring the reader to read more and more text as the story unfolds, adding a new line with every page turn.

■ The illustrations tend to be a representation of just a slice of what is happening in the text. For example, the text may tell of a long journey that a character has taken over time, but the picture may represent just the character reaching his destination.

■ There will be more unfamiliar and sometimes complex vocabulary.

Characteristics of the Reader

Readers in this group will demonstrate most of these behaviors.

■ Reread and self-correct regularly

■ Read with fluency

■ Integrate a balance of cues

■ Monitor for meaning: check to make sure what has been read makes sense, sounds right, and looks right

■ Demonstrate fluent phrasing of longer passages

■ Use a repertoire of graphophonic strategies to problem solve through text

Benchmarks

The following titles are representative of the kinds of books found in this grouping.

George Shrinks, William Joyce
Goodnight Moon, Margaret Wise Brown
Hattie and the Fox, Mem Fox
Little Red Hen, Parkes

Assessment

The following titles can be used to determine if a reader is ready to move on to the next grouping. This type of assessment is most effective if the text is unfamiliar to a reader. If these titles will be used as assessment texts, they should *not* be part of the classroom library.

> *The Old Man's Mitten*, Bookshop, Mondo
> *Who Took the Farmer's Hat?*, Joan Nodset, DRA 14

We move children from Level Five to Level Six texts when they are consistently able to use a multitude of strategies to work through challenges quickly and efficiently. These challenges may be brought on by unfamiliar settings, unfamiliar language structures, unfamiliar words, and increased text length. The amount of text on a page and the length of a book should not be a hindrance to the reader who is moving on to Level Six. The reader who is ready to move on is also adept at consistently choosing appropriate books that will make her a stronger reader.

TEXT LEVEL SIX

This level roughly corresponds to the following levels in other systems:

> Reading Recovery© (RR) Levels 16–18
> Developmental Reading Assessment (DRA) Level 16

Text Characteristics of TC Level Six

- The focus of the book is evident at its start

- Descriptive language is used more frequently than before

- Dialogue often tells a large part of the story

- Texts may include traditional retellings of fairy tales and folktales

- Stories are frequently humorous

- Considerable amount of text is found on each page. A book in this grouping may be a picture book, or a simple chapter book. These books offer extended stretches of text.

- Texts are often simple chapter books, and often have episodic chapters in which each chapter stands as a story on its own

- Texts often center around just two or three main characters who tend to be markedly different from each other (a boy and a girl, a child and a parent)

- There is limited support from the pictures

- Texts includes challenging vocabulary

Characteristics of the Reader

Readers in this group will demonstrate most of these behaviors.

- Reread and self-correct regularly

- Read with fluency

- Integrate a balance of cues

- Demonstrate fluent phrasing of longer passages

- Use a repertoire of graphophonic strategies to problem solve through text

Benchmarks

The following titles are representative of the kinds of books found in this grouping.

Danny and the Dinosaur, Syd Hoff
The Doorbell Rang, Pat Hutchins
Henry and Mudge, Cynthia Rylant
The Very Hungry Caterpillar, Eric Carle

Assessment

The following titles can be used to determine if a reader is ready to move on to the next grouping. This type of assessment is most effective if the text is unfamiliar to a reader. If these titles will be used as assessment texts, they should *not* be part of the classroom library.

Bear Shadow, Frank Asch, DRA 16
Jimmy Lee Did It, Pat Cummings, DRA 18

TEXT LEVEL SEVEN

This level roughly corresponds to the following levels in other systems:

Reading Recovery© (RR) Levels 19–20
Developmental Reading Assessment (DRA) Level 20

Text Characteristics of TC Level Seven

- Dialogue is used frequently to move the story along

- Texts often have 2 to 3 characters. (They tend to have distinctive personalities and usually don't change across a book or series.)

- Texts may include extended description. (The language may set a mood, and may be quite poetic or colorful.)

- Some books have episodic chapters. (In other books, each chapter contributes to the understanding of the entire book and the reader must carry the story line along.)

- There is limited picture support

- Plots are usually linear without large time-gaps

- Texts tend to have larger print and double spacing between lines of print

Characteristics of the Reader

Readers in this group will demonstrate most of these behaviors.

- Reread and self-correct regularly

- Read with fluency, intonation, and phrasing

- Demonstrate the existence of a self-extending (self-improving) system for reading

- Use an increasingly more challenging repertoire of graphophonic strategies to problem solve through text

- Solve unknown words with relative ease

Benchmarks

The following titles are representative of the kinds of books found in this grouping.

A Baby Sister for Frances, Russell Hoban
Meet M&M, Pat Ross
Nate the Great, Marjorie Sharmat
Poppleton, Cynthia Rylant

Asessment

The following titles can be used to determine if a reader is ready to move on to the next grouping. This type of assessment is most effective if the text is unfamiliar to a reader. If these titles will be used as assessment texts, they should *not* be part of the classroom library.

Peter's Pockets, Eve Rice, DRA 20
Uncle Elephant, Arnold Lobel

More Information to Help You Choose the Library That is Best for Your Readers

Library A

Library A is appropriate if your children enter kindergarten in October as very emergent readers with limited experiences hearing books read aloud. Use the following chart to help determine if Library A is about right for your class.

Approximate Distribution of Reading Levels of a Class Matched to Library A		
Benchmark Book	Reading Level	Percentage of the Class Reading at about This Level
The Cat on the Mat, by Wildsmith	TC Level 1	45%
Fox on the Box, by Gregorich	TC Level 2	30%
Mrs. Wishy-Washy, by Cowley	TC Level 3	25%

Library B

Library B is appropriate for a class of children if, in October, they are reading books like *I Went Walking*. Use the following chart to help determine if Library B is about right for your class. (Note to New York City teachers: Many of your students would score a 3 on the ECLAS correlated with titles such as, *Things I Like to Do* and *My Shadow*.)

Approximate Distribution of Reading Levels of a Class Matched to Library B		
Benchmark Book	Reading Level	Percentage of the Class Reading at about This Level
The Cat on the Mat, by Wildsmith	TC Level 1	10%
Fox on the Box, by Gregorich	TC Level 2	10%
Mrs. Wishy-Washy, by Cowley	TC Level 3	30%
The Carrot Seed, by Krauss	TC Level 4	25%
Goodnight Moon, by Brown	TC Level 5	15%
Henry and Mudge, by Rylant	TC Level 6	5%
Nate the Great, by Sharmat	TC Level 7	5%

Library C

Library C is appropriate for a class of children if, in October, many of your students are approaching reading books like *Mrs. Wishy-Washy* and *Bears in the Night*. (Note to New York City teachers: Many of your students would be approaching a 4 on the ECLAS that would be correlated with *Baby Bear's Present* and *No Where and Nothing*.)

Approximate Distribution of Reading Levels of a Class Matched to Library C		
Benchmark Book	Reading Level	Percentage of the Class Reading at about This Level
Fox on the Box, by Gregorich	TC Level 2	8%
Mrs. Wishy-Washy, by Cowley	TC Level 3	8%
The Carrot Seed, by Krauss	TC Level 4	20%
Goodnight Moon, by Brown	TC Level 5	20%
Henry and Mudge, by Carle	TC Level 6	20%
Nate the Great, by Sharmat	TC Level 7	15%
Pinky and Rex, by Howe	TC Level 8	5%
Ramona Quimby, by Cleary	TC Level 9	2%
James and the Giant Peach, by Dahl	TC Level 10	2%

Library D

Use the following chart to help determine if Library D is right for your class.

Approximate Distribution of Reading Levels of a Class Matched to Library D		
Benchmark Book	Reading Level	Percentage of the Class Reading at about This Level
Good Night Moon, by Brown	Level 5	8%
Henry and Mudge, by Rylant	Level 6	20%
Nate the Great, by Sharmat	Level 7	25%
Pinky and Rex, by Howe	Level 8	30%
Ramona Quimby, by Cleary	Level 9	10%
James and the Giant Peach, by Dahl	Level 10	2%

Library E

Library E is appropriate for a class of children if, in October, a readers list tends to look approximately like the following chart.

Approximate Distribution of Reading Levels of a Class Matched to Library E		
Benchmark Book	*Reading Level*	*Percentage of the Class Reading at about This Level*
Nate the Great, by Sharmat	Level 7	10%
Pinky and Rex, by Howe	Level 8	25%
Ramona Quimby, by Cleary	Level 9	30%
James and the Giant Peach, by Dahl	Level 10	22%
Shiloh, by Naylor	Level 11	5%
Baby, by MacLachlan	Level 12	5%
Missing May, by Rylant	Level 13	2%
Scorpions, by Myers	Level 14	1%

Library F

Library F is appropriate for a class of children if, in October, a readers list tends to look approximately like the following chart.

Approximate Distribution of Reading Levels of a Class Matched to Library F		
Benchmark Book	*Reading Level*	*Percentage of the Class Reading at about This Level*
Pinky and Rex, by Howe	Level 8	2%
Ramona Quimby, by Cleary	Level 9	20%
James and the Giant Peach, by Dahl	Level 10	25%
Shiloh, by Naylor	Level 11	30%
Baby, by MacLachlan	Level 12	20%
Missing May, by Rylant	Level 13	2%
Scorpions, by Myers	Level 14	1%

Library G

Library G is appropriate for a class of children if, in October, a readers list tends to look approximately like the following chart.

Approximate Distribution of Reading Levels of a Class Matched to Library G		
Benchmark Book	*Reading Level*	*Percentage of the Class Reading at about This Level*
James and the Giant Peach, by Dahl	Level 10	10%
Shiloh, by Naylor	Level 11	10%
Baby, by MacLachlan	Level 12	30%
Missing May, by Rylant	Level 13	30%
Scorpions, by Myer	Level 14	20%

About the Guides

Soon we'd begun not only accumulating titles and honing arrangements for dream libraries, but also writing teaching advice to go with the chosen books. Our advice to the contributors was, "Write a letter from you to others who'll use this book with children. Tell folks what you notice in the book, and advise them on teaching opportunities you see. Think about advice you would give a teacher just coming to know the book." The insights, experience, and folk wisdom poured in and onto the pages of the guides.

A written guide accompanies many of the books in the libraries. These guides are not meant to be prescriptions for how a teacher or child should use a book. Instead they are intended to be resources, and we hope thoughtful teachers will tap into particular sections of a guide when it seems fit to do so. For example, a teaching guide might suggest six possible minilessons a teacher could do with a book. Of course, a teacher would never try to do all six of these! Instead we expect one of these minilessons will seem helpful to the teacher, and another minilesson to another teacher. The teaching guides illustrate the following few principles that are important to us.

Teaching One Text Intensely in Order to Learn About Many Texts

When you take a walk in the woods, it can happen that all the trees look the same, that they are just a monotony of foliage and trunks. It is only when you stop to learn about a particular tree, about its special leaf structure and the odd thickness of its bark, about the creatures that inhabit it and the seeds it lets fall, that you begin to see that particular kind of tree among the thickets. It is when you enter a forest knowing something about kinds of trees that you begin to truly see the multiplicity of trees in a forest and the particular attributes and mysteries of each one. Learning about the particulars of one tree leads you to thinking about all of the trees, each in its individuality, each with its unique deep structure, each with its own offerings.

The same is true of texts. The study of one can reveal not just the hidden intricacies of that story, but also the ways in which truths and puzzles can be structured in other writings as well. When one book holds a message in the way a chapter ends, it gives the reader the idea that any book may hold a message in the structure of its chapter's conclusions. When one book is revealed to make a sense that is unintended by the author, we look for unintended sense in other books we read. Within these guides, then, we hope that readers like you will find truths about the particular books they are written about, but more, we hope that you find pathways into all the books you read. By showing some lengthy thinking and meditations on one book, we hope to offer you paths toward thinking about each and every book that crosses your desk and crosses your mind.

Suggesting Classroom Library Arrangements

Many the attributes of a book, detailed in a guide, can become a category in a classroom library. If a group of students in a class seems particularly energized by the Harry Potter books, for example, the guide can be used to help determine which books could be in a bin in the library marked, "If You Like *Harry Potter*—Try These." The similarity between the *Harry Potter* books and the other books in this group may be not only in difficulty gradient, but also in content, story structure, popularity, or genre. That is, a class of children that like *Harry Potter* might benefit from a bin of books on fantasy, or from a collection of best-selling children's books, or from a bin of "Long-Books-You-Can't-Put-Down," or from stories set in imagined places. As you browse through the guides that accompany the books you have chosen, the connections will pop out at you.

Sometimes, the guides will help you determine a new or more interesting placement for a book. Perhaps you have regarded a book as historical fiction, but now you realize it could alternatively be shelved in a collection of books that offer children examples of "Great Leads to Imitate in Your Own Writing." Or, perhaps the guides will suggest entirely new categories that will appeal to your class in ways you and your students haven't yet imagined. Perhaps the guides will help you imagine a "Books That Make You Want to Change the World" category. Or maybe you'll decide to create a shelf in your library titled, "Books with Odd Techniques That Make You Wonder What the Author Is Trying To Do."

Aiding in Conferring

Teachers' knowledge of what to ask and what to teach a reader who says, "this book is boring" comes not only from their knowledge of particular students but also from their knowledge of the text they are talking about. Does "boring" mean that the book is too easy for the reader? Perhaps it means instead that the beginning few chapters of the book are hard to read—confusing because of a series of flashbacks. A guide might explain that the book under discussion has mostly internal, emotional action, and, if the reader is accustomed to avalanche-and-rattlesnake action in books, she may need some time to warm up to this unfamiliar kind of "quiet" action. The guide can point out the kinds of reactions, or troubles, other readers have had with particular books. With the guides at our fingertips, we can more easily determine which questions to ask students, or which pages to turn to, in order to get to the heart of the conference.

Providing a Resource for Curriculum Planning

One Friday, say, we leave the classroom knowing that our students' writing shows that they are thirsting for deeper, more complicated characters to study and imitate. As we plan lessons, we can page through the guides that correspond with some of the books in our library, finding, or remembering, books that students can study that depict fascinating characters.

On the other hand, perhaps we need a book to read aloud to the class, or perhaps we need to recommend a book to a particular struggling reader.

Maybe a reader has finished a book he loves and has turned to you to help him plan his reading for the next weeks. When designing an author study or an inquiry into punctuation and its effects on meaning, it also helps to have the guides with you to point out books that may be helpful in those areas. In each of these cases, and many more, the guides can be a planning aid for you.

Reminding Us, or Teaching Us, About Particular Book Basics

No teacher can read, let alone recall in detail, every book that every child will pick up in the classroom. Of course, we read many of them and learn about many more from our colleagues, but there are far too many books in the world for us to be knowledgeable about them all. Sometimes, the guides will be a reminder of what you have read many years ago. Sometimes, they will provide a framework for you to question or direct your students more effectively than you could if you knew nothing at all about the book. "Probably, you will have to take some time to understand the setting before you can really get a handle on this book, why don't you turn to the picture atlas?" you might say after consulting the guide, or "Sharlene is reading another book that is similar to this one in so many ways! Why don't you go pair up with her to talk." You might learn to ask, "What do you think of Freddy?" in order to learn if the student is catching on to the tone of the narrator, or you might learn you could hint, "Did you get to chapter three yet? Because I bet you won't be bored any more when you get there. . . ." The guides provide a bit of what time constraints deny us: thoughtful insights about the content or unusual features of a given book.

Showcasing Literary Intricacies in Order to Suggest a Reader's Thinking

Sometimes, when we read a book, our idea of the author's message is in our minds before we even finish the story. Because we are experienced readers, much of our inferring and interpreting, our understanding of symbols and contexts, can come to us effortlessly. In the guides, we have tried to slow down some of that thinking so that we can all see it more easily. We have tried to lay out some of the steps young readers may have to go through in order to come to a cohesive idea of what the story is about, or a clear understanding of why a character behaved the way she did. As experienced readers, we may not even realize that our readers are confused by the unorthodox use of italics to show us who is speaking, for example. We may not remember the days when we were confused by changing narrators, the days when it took us a few chapters to figure out a character wasn't to be believed. In these guides, we have tried to go back to those days when we were more naïve readers, and have tried to fill in those thoughts and processes we are now able to skip over so easily.

By bringing forth the noteworthy features of the text, features experienced readers may not even notice, we are reminded of the thinking that our students need to go through in order to make sense of their reading. It gives us an idea of where to offer pointers, of where readers may have gone off in an unhelpful direction, or of where their thinking may need to go instead of where it has gone. By highlighting literary intricacies, we may remember that every bit about the construction of texts is a navigation point for students, and every bit is something we may be able to help students in learning.

Providing a Community of Readers and Teachers

The guides are also intended to help teachers learn from the community of other teachers and readers who have used particular texts already. They make available some of the stories and experiences other teachers have had, in order that we might stand on their shoulders and take our teaching even higher than they could reach. These guides are intended to give you some thinking to go with the books in your classroom library, thinking you can mix with your own ideas.

In the end, we don't all have a community of other teachers with whom we can talk about children's literature. The guides are meant not to stand in for that community, but instead to provide a taste, an appetizer, of the world of supportive professional communities. We hope that by reading these guides and feeling the companionship, guidance and insight they offer, teachers will be nudged to recreate that experience for the other books that have no guides, and that they will ask their colleagues, librarians, and the parents of their students to talk with them about children's literature and young readers. Then, when teachers are creating these guides for themselves, on paper or in their minds' eyes, we will know this project has done the work for which it was created.

Bibliography

Atwell, Nancie. 1987. *In the Middle: Writing, Reading, and Learning with Adolescents*. Portsmouth, NH: Boynton/Cook.

Calkins, Lucy. 2001. *The Art of Teaching Reading*. New York: Addison-Wesley Educational Publishers, Inc.

Cambourne, Brian. 1993. *The Whole Story: Natural Learning and the Acquisition of Literacy in the Classroom*. Auckland, NZ: Ashton Scholastic.

Krashen, Stephen. 1993. *The Power of Reading: Insights from the Research*. Englewood, CO: Libraries Unlimited.

Meek, Margaret. 1988. *How Texts Teach What Readers Learn*. Thimble Press.

Smith, Frank. 1985. *Reading Without Nonsense*. 2nd ed. New York: TC Press.

A Chair For My Mother
Vera B. Williams

Book Summary

In this vividly illustrated story, a young girl describes her family's quest for an armchair. After they lose everything in a fire and get a new apartment, she, her mother and her grandmother save their coins in a big glass jar, working toward the moment when they will have enough for the chair. In the end, the family's perseverance earns them the "wonderful, beautiful, fat, soft armchair" they have wanted so much.

Basic Book Information

All but two pages in this 29-page book share the same layout: full-page illustrations are on the left of each pair of facing pages, and two or three paragraphs of text are on the right. Beneath the text is a small, simple illustration as well. *A Chair For My Mother* was named a Caldecott Honor Book. Its other accolades include The Boston Globe/Horn Book Award for Illustration and an American Library Association Notable Book selection. Vera B. Williams lives in Brooklyn.

Noteworthy Features

In many ways, the story of *A Chair For My Mother* is quite accessible. The girl, her mother, her grandmother and their cat are the only characters mentioned more than once, and thus the only characters readers need to remember from page to page. The girl herself narrates. Her voice is colloquial and clear. There is, however, a subtle shift in time, present to past to present: the fifth page of text flashes back to the fire one year earlier. A large capital letter accentuates the start of each new time, with a very large "M" at the start of the book, another large "M" at the start of the flashback and an equally large "T" at the start of the final, present-tense segment.

Much of the story is conveyed through the illustrations. For example, the narrator never explicitly states that work exhausts her mother but the image of her mother, shoes off, eyes closed, body slumped awkwardly around the kitchen table suggests why a comfortable armchair in which to relax might be so important. The small illustrations beneath the text also provide information. The narrator says that "it took a while" to find her cat after the fire; the tail poking from a garbage can under the text implies where the cat hid. The borders around facing pages convey yet more.

Teaching Ideas

A Chair For My Mother is a wonderful read aloud, but children should be able to hold this book and scrutinize its rich illustrations at their own pace. This book provides excellent opportunities for readers to practice using

Illustrator
Vera B. Williams

Publisher
Morrow, 1982

ISBN
0590331558

TC Level
8

pictures to expand their comprehension. On a first or second time through the book, readers might note details in Williams' large paintings opposite the text, inferring as much as they can. What do the thirteen coins at the bottom of the enormous jar on the second page tell about how far this family is from buying a new chair? What do the family's expressions say about how they are feeling when they have finally purchased a stuffed chair and loaded it onto their truck? During later readings, readers might also note smaller details, such as the borders. For example, they can see how the borders around the three pages in which the narrator and her mother return to find their home on fire go from a sunny blue sky with cottony clouds to angular orange flames shooting upward to drooping, blackened tulips. They might notice a more hopeful mood when those singed tulips give way on the next page to a border of rejuvenated, upright flowers.

When readers get together in partnerships to talk over what they notice about the book, teachers may want to nudge them to use every bit of information possible, from the pictures and from the text, to develop theories about the characters. Students may note that one member of the family, the mother, appears to support three. This may explain why the family cannot simply buy everything they need to furnish their new apartment, and why their neighbors treat them so generously. They can also infer the characters' attitudes and emotions. For instance, what does it say about the grandmother's sense of self that, when thanking the neighbors for the gifts, she says, "It's lucky we're young"? In what ways *is* she young?

Book Connections

Vera B. Williams has illustrated many of the books she has authored, including *Cherries And Cherry* Pits; *Something Special For Me*; and *Music, Music For Everyone*, which also involves collecting coins in a jar. Tomie dePaola's *The Art Lesson* and Patricia Polacco's *Chicken Sunday* are two other picture books at this level that have been illustrated by the author. *Aunt Flossie's Hats (and Crab Cakes Later)*, written by Elizabeth Fitzgerald Howard, is yet another realistic picture book at this level. Many of its facing pages are laid out similarly to those in *A Chair For My Mother*, with whole-page paintings on one side, text opposite them, and small illustrations beneath the text.

Genre
Picture Book

Teaching Uses
Partnerships; Read Aloud; Independent Reading

A Field Guide to the Classroom Library, Lucy Calkins and the Teachers College Reading and Writing Project, Heinemann, ©2002 Teachers College, Columbia University; http://www.heinemann.com/fieldguides

A Clean House for Mole and Mouse

Harriet Ziefert

Book Summary

Mole helps Mouse clean their dirty house. "Then everything looked just fine." But to Mole's surprise, Mouse does not allow him to cook, take a bath, or nap in the clean house. Mouse does, however, suggest that he eat, nap, and shower outside so that everything inside stays "just fine."

Basic Book Information

There are 200 words over 32 pages. There is some repetition of chunks of language. The use of quotation marks indicates dialogue. In addition, italics and exclamation marks are used to indicate expression and emphasis.

Noteworthy Features

This is an engaging story about Mouse's determination to keep the house clean. In addition, it tells another story about Mole's dedication to the task. Mole takes some short cuts to cleaning that the reader will find entertaining and perhaps familiar. Although the illustrations provide some support, readers cannot use them to obtain the precise message. This story is longer and more than a simple sequence of events. The reader is given a few additional twists to the simple storyline of cleaning the house.

Teaching Ideas

Readers need to recognize that the illustrations are only moderately supportive of the text, and they need to solve more complex words through a range of word analysis skills. There are teaching opportunities to encounter, notice, and solve words with regular spelling patterns.

The illustrations in this particular book enhance and extend the meaning rather than provide all or most of the information. The teacher can take advantage of the extensions that the illustrations provide to aid in the comprehension and enjoyment of the text. Mole's cleaning methods provide an excellent opportunity to compare the characteristics of Mole and Mouse.

The use of quotation marks lends itself to the instruction of how to read dialogue. In addition, the reader can use the italics and exclamation points to read with expression.

Readers will want to take the time to ask, "What is the author's message here? What is she trying to tell us? How does this book tell us to change our life?"

Genre
Picture Book

Illustrator
David Prebenna

Publisher
Scholastic, 1988

ISBN
0140508104

TC Level
5

Teaching Uses
Independent Reading; Language Conventions; Interpretation; Partnerships

A Field Guide to the Classroom Library, Lucy Calkins and the Teachers College Reading and Writing Project, Heinemann, ©2002 Teachers College, Columbia University; http://www.heinemann.com/fieldguides

A friend for little white rabbit

Beverley Randell

Book Summary

Little white rabbit wants a friend to play with. She goes to the little white lamb and the little white duck, and asks them if they will play with her. They both respond, "No I will not." Finally, the little white rabbit sees a little brown rabbit who plays with her.

Basic Book Information

This book, which is part of Rigby's PM Storybooks, was written by Beverley Randell. More than 25 million of Beverley Randell's books have been sold. She wrote the series when she was a classroom teacher, and has written a 125-page document carefully detailing all the component elements in her series. These elements include:

A heavy reliance on the use of sight words, and a tendency to write full sentences rather than shorter captions.

A traditional storyline with characters, a problem, and a resolution: Sometimes the PM books appear to belist-like, but a closer look always shows the presence of a strong storyline.

A steadfast commitment to sense: These books never include nonsense words, magic, or reference to the supernatural. A strong priority is set on children expecting logical, concrete meaningfulness so they learn to monitor for sense, and learn to self-correct when it's absent.

Noteworthy Features

The book includes many high frequency words (*little, play, said, go, no, me, is, come*) and the repetition of these will give readers a way into the new content on each page. Some sentences have as many as seventeen words, but most sentences are short. Readers who read this book will be pointing under the words, and the font, white space, and frequent occurrence of familiar words will all help to pin a reader's focus onto the print. Illustrations provide high to moderate support.

Teaching Ideas

In a guided reading lesson, or in a one-to-one conference with a child who may need some support on a first read of this book, a teacher may give an introduction. One teacher did so by saying, "Little white rabbit is looking for a friend. What are some things that friends do together?" Soon the teacher said, "Let's see if she finds a friend." The children predicted that the brown rabbit on the cover would become her friend. The teacher will probably need to talk about the word *who* on page 10. Interestingly enough, in these little books it will often be the words that begin with *w* that are the hardest,

Illustrator
Drew Aitken

Publisher
Rigby, 1994

ISBN
0435067079

TC Level
3

and this is especially true because the context can't help with *what, when, where* or *who.* "The little rabbit looks so upset in this picture," a teacher said. "The rabbit says, 'Who will play with me?'" Then the teacher said, "Let me show you the word *who.* Notice you can't sound this word out; it is a word that we just learn by sight." Often we'll ask children to point to *who* and say it, or to tell us what they notice about the word.

This book is appropriate for readers learning to match one spoken word to one written one. If a teacher wants to help readers self-correct when the matching doesn't work, the teacher can cue the reader to find a known sight word, which will then serve as an anchor for a one-to-one match. References can be made to the word wall in the classroom if the sight word is on it.

Opportunities to crosscheck will be presented in this book. That is, there are places in the text where readers will need to use information from the picture and the print in order to read the story. For example, there is a picture of a lamb on page two and a duck on page six. A teacher should be able to observe children using the picture as a source of information and then checking against the letters. The teacher can then praise the children for doing this.

The teacher can also ask students to find an unknown word by using the initial letter. For example, "Can you find the word *hello* on page 14? What letter would you expect *hello* to start with?"

Teachers will also find the opportunity to teach other early reading behaviors such as prompting the children to reread, looking at the picture, and getting their mouths ready for the first sound. Also, it is helpful to ask children, "Does that make sense?"

This small book has large and important ideas at its core. Children, even young children, can discuss the reasons why the first few white animals of different species would not play with each other and then why the animal of the same species but different color would play. How is this like how people get along? What is this author saying about people? As the children interpret the author's message, they can also critique it and the world, asking "Is this book fair? Is this situation fair?"

Genre
Emergent Literacy Book

Teaching Uses
Independent Reading; Small Group Strategy Instruction; Whole Group Instruction

A Home for Little Teddy

Beverley Randell

Book Summary

In this story, Little Teddy decides he cannot sleep on the shelf with the other stuffed animals. He wanders around asking various creatures if he can sleep with them. The bulk of the text is a repeating pattern where Teddy asks animals if he can live with them. The names of the animals are the only things that change on each page. The animals all say no. Finally, the dolls in the dollhouse say "yes" and Little Teddy happily moves in with them.

Basic Book Information

The PM Storybooks, developed in New Zealand and published by Rigby, place a priority on including the traditional story elements. Even texts that at first appear to be lists are, in fact, stories with characters, a problem, and a resolution. The only exceptions are their very earliest books. The PM Readers are known for including a large number of high frequency words, and for controlling vocabulary so that in books of a comparable level of difficulty, the same high frequency words reoccur. The PM Readers use complete sentences: I see a bird./ I see a frog./ to reinforce repetition of high frequency words and simple sentence syntax.

The fact that PM Readers include many high frequency words means that sometimes the resulting sentences seem stilted and unnatural.

Noteworthy Features

About half of this book is dialogue between Little Teddy and the creatures he meets. All dialogue is marked with quotation marks and is referenced with a "speaker tag."

The word "not" in the story is in bold type, to help children catch this crucial word. This helps readers notice the word in particular, and perhaps read it with emphasis, so that they understand that the animals are refusing to offer shelter to the teddy. Without this, some readers would undoubtedly skim over the word and become confused.

The pictures in the story match the text, but will not help readers figure out many particular words, as they are general depictions of scene. They also do not show expressions that would reveal characters' emotions, so they don't offer many clues about the story between the lines either.

Teaching Ideas

Certainly, this book is good for the general teaching uses particular to this level including left to right directionality, one-to-one correspondence, and

---

Illustrator
Chantal Stewart

Publisher
Rigby PM Story Book
Collection, 1997

ISBN
0763515108

TC Level
2

monitoring to a known and unknown word. Specifically, this book provides practice in reading dialogue, and reading with expression. There aren't any unusual or challenging vocabulary words in the text.

This book is appropriate for readers learning to match one spoken word to one written one. The teacher can cue the reader to find a known sight word, which will serve as an anchor for a one-to-one match. The child who is reading books on this level will probably recognize a few sight words and can use those words to "anchor" or pin-down his pointing. Teachers may refer students to their classroom word wall to check for sight words.

Children who are able to work successfully with a book on this level will benefit not only from the teacher's encouragement to do a one-to-one match, but to "cross-check" as well. Successful reading happens when a reader cross-checks or integrates cues from a variety of sources including sight words, the picture, and the initial letter sound.

In most literature, it is useful for readers to ask themselves why the characters act the way they do in the story. This is particularly true in this book, and this sort of discussion will probably help children gain a deeper understanding of what is going on in the text.

As soon as readers focus on what is really happening, they will undoubtedly have questions for themselves and each other. Why is Little Teddy so adamant about not sleeping with the other stuffed animals? Children sometimes decide from the picture clues that it is too crowded there, or that the cars and trucks on the shelf above make too much noise. Others think Little Teddy just doesn't like the other animals, or that he has been walking along with his suitcase for a long time and this is just another place he won't stop. In any case, when partners are asked to stop and talk after each page, issues generally come up in their book talk right away.

There are also questions about why the other animals turn the teddy away. They say they do it because he is not like them. This can be a great opportunity for children to discuss what they think of reasoning like that. Is that a good reason to turn away someone who needs shelter? And why do the dolls finally let Little Teddy live with them? What is different about them? Is a dollhouse any more suited to a bear than a mouse house? This kind of critical thinking about the book will help children develop their interpretation and critique skills.

Sometimes teachers coach children to read the story looking for the "understory," the emotions under the words-using personal experience to educate their guesses. What is Little Teddy feeling when he is refused shelter? What are the rabbit and the mouse feeling? What are the dolls feeling as they look at the teddy before they tell him he can stay? Why do they feel differently than the other creatures the teddy asked?

Genre
Emergent Literacy Book

A Field Guide to the Classroom Library, Lucy Calkins and the Teachers College Reading and Writing Project, Heinemann, ©2002 Teachers College, Columbia University; http://www.heinemann.com/fieldguides

Teaching Uses

Independent Reading; Language Conventions; Interpretation; Critique; Partnerships; Small Group Strategy Instruction; Whole Group Instruction

A Field Guide to the Classroom Library, Lucy Calkins and the Teachers College Reading and Writing Project, Heinemann, ©2002 Teachers College, Columbia University; http://www.heinemann.com/fieldguides

A Letter to Amy

Ezra Jack Keats

Book Summary

Young Peter writes a letter to Amy to invite her to his birthday party-a letter instead of a call to make it special. When he goes out to mail it, the wind carries it just out of his reach. As he chases it, he bumps into Amy herself and knocks her over. In his haste to mail the letter before she sees it and ruins the surprise, he doesn't talk to Amy at all. She runs away crying. His birthday arrives and the party has started. Finally, Amy arrives with her talking parrot, Pepe. The boys make comments about a girl coming to the party. The cake comes out and everybody gives Peter suggestions for what to wish for. Peter makes his own private wish and blows out the candles.

Basic Book Information

This beautiful picture book has Ezra Jack Keats' award-winning illustrations in his trademark paper-collage style.

Noteworthy Features

The book contains richly textured collage illustrations with details of family and city life. Peter's letter to Amy flies across the graffiti-covered landscape of his neighborhood "skipping across a hopscotch game," before he finally catches it.

The text may be difficult to comprehend, especially for younger students who'll need to be encouraged to make inferences to decipher Peter's feelings and the reasons for his actions in the story. Students will need to look closely at and analyze the pictures in order to understand what characters are referring to and thinking.

Teaching Ideas

Rarely does a book come along that seems so perfectly created to help launch children into rich discussion. Issues are brought up and left for the reader to discuss throughout the story. Students may be encouraged to read or hear the whole story through once, before the teacher rereads it, stopping often to talk and figure things out. The following are some of the issues that children may raise: Why does Peter write Amy a letter instead of calling her as he had with his other friends? Peter says it is to make this invitation special. Does the reader believe him, or could it be for another reason? Why does Peter want to make Amy's invitation special? Why is a letter special? Many readers decide that Peter feels the need to treat Amy differently because she will be the only girl at the party. Then, of course, readers wonder about Peter's behavior when he bumps into Amy outside in the rain. Why is he ignoring her? Why didn't he just hand her the letter? Why

Illustrator

Ezra Jack Keats

Publisher

Puffin Penguin, 1968

ISBN

014056442X

TC Level

6

A Field Guide to the Classroom Library, Lucy Calkins and the Teachers College Reading and Writing Project, Heinemann, ©2002 Teachers College, Columbia University; http://www.heinemann.com/fieldguides

does she cry?

Students will also benefit from class discussions about what Peter wishes for as he blows out his birthday candles at the end of the story. Why does the book seem to end so abruptly? A large number of readers usually think that Peter wishes for something related to Amy. They decide that the story ends there because the book is really about how Peter is dealing with his feelings for Amy. This discussion makes readers really think about what the book is about.

Teachers who are using the text in their author studies may want to compare events and themes of other Keats' books, especially those that feature the character of Peter.

The story begins as Peter announces that he's writing a letter to Amy to invite her to his birthday party. This kind of start can be a great example of a hook for children who are working on the beginnings of their own pieces of writing.

Book Connections

Ezra Jack Keats has written and illustrated many books for children. He has won the Caldecott Medal for *The Snowy Day*. Some of his books include *Whistle For Willie*; *Hi,Cat!*; *Apt. 3*; *Goggles!*; and *Peter's Chair*.

Genre
Picture Book

Teaching Uses
Author Study; Interpretation; Teaching Writing; Partnerships

Abiyoyo
Pete Seeger

Book Summary

In this storysong, a boy and his father annoy the townsfolk. The boy constantly plays his ukulele and the boy's father uses his magic wand to perform practical jokes and make things disappear. Tired of their tricks, the angry townspeople make the boy and his father live on the edge of town.

One day a terrible giant named Abiyoyo approaches. The giant eats the cows and sheep, and the townspeople flee in terror. The boy and his father have a plan. If they can get Abiyoyo to lie down, then the father can make him disappear. They run to the giant, and just as he is about to eat them, the boy begins to play a song, singing the giant's name over and over, "Abiyoyo."

The giant loves it and dances until he is so tired that he collapses on the ground. The boy's father quickly uses his magic wand and "zoop," makes Abiyoyo disappear. The people rejoice and carry the two back into town, singing all the way.

Basic Book Information

This beautiful picture book was written by the famous folksinger, Pete Seeger. The book contains a musical refrain, and it is hard to resist bursting into song when reading it. The story is simple and memorable enough that children who want to hear it read aloud several times (and perhaps listen to Pete Seeger's audiotaped readings) will soon be able to "read" the book or tell the story from memory.

Noteworthy Features

Kids don't need to be able to read music or know this Pete Seeger song to enjoy *Abiyoyo*. This written account is an exact transcription of the Seeger tapes available to children.

Pete Seeger's preface is meant for adult readers. Many children will not understand all of it, even if it is read aloud to them. Nevertheless, after reading the book, it may be worthwhile to direct children toward certain sections of Seeger's note, and read those aloud, particularly sections about the power and creativity of storytelling and of art. Students might enjoy learning how Seeger created the story (adapted from a South African folktale), told it as a bedtime story to his children, later singing and performing it on stage.

Teaching Ideas

If students have been thinking about the components and structure of stories, they will find this story offers a great deal to talk about. The tale fits

Illustrator
Michael Hays

Publisher
Scholastic, 1986

ISBN
0590427202

A Field Guide to the Classroom Library, Lucy Calkins and the Teachers College Reading and Writing Project, Heinemann, ©2002 Teachers College, Columbia University; http://www.heinemann.com/fieldguides

into the classical definition of a story, with characters and setting, and an igniting action that starts a sequence of events, which can be described as the problem and solution.

Many teachers appreciate the illustrations of the village and its people of various complexions and cultures in this story. Pointing this out can lead to productive conversations about culture, nationality, and religion. Some teachers though, might not make the composition of this village a topic of conversation, but instead just let it seep into the reader's consciousness.

It is fairly easy to find the recording of this book by Pete Seeger, and children can learn a lot from reading along and performing the story. If children hear the recording before reading the story, it may be worthwhile for students to attempt their own illustrations first (especially of the giant Abiyoyo), and then share and compare their work. This may also be an opportunity to discuss the illustrator's role in supporting the text to make meaning.

The story itself is full of possible interpretations and messages. Seeger's own suggestions for interpretations in his note, add even more possibilities. Children often begin by pointing out that the giant seems to be made of metal. Why would this be so? Why would the illustrator of the book make the giant machine-like? Why would the song that is the giant's undoing be his own name repeated over and over again? Some readers see in *Abiyoyo* that the outcasts of society are the ones who end up saving it. It is also worth noting that the village was saved by two generations-a father and a son-combining their skills on behalf of the village. Then, too, it is music, not might, that saves the day. Readers will find many opportunities for rich discussion.

Book Connections

Readers may see parallels between this story and countless others. The outcast and underdog often rise to the status of hero or heroine in the literary world. Additionally, as in *Little Red Riding Hood*, *Goliath*, and many other stories, the victor is not the mighty wolf or giant, but the wise and resourceful child.

Genre
Picture Book; Fairy and Folk Tale

Teaching Uses
Read Aloud; Independent Reading; Interpretation; Critique; Whole Group Instruction

Addie's Bad Day

Joan Robins

Book Summary

Addie's Bad Day is about two best friends, Addie and Max. It's Max's birthday and Addie tells him that she cannot come to his party, so she wants to give him his birthday present and card early. After Max reads her card, he still doesn't understand why Addie can't come. Addie tells him it is because she cannot take off her hat. When Max begs her to tell him why, she finally tells him about her bad day. She's had a horrible haircut and is convinced "everyone will laugh" because she looks like an "ugly-wugly." In sympathy, Max calls himself a "pugly-mugly." Addie gives Max a jungle suit as a gift. When he convinces her to wear her matching suit to the party so no one will be able to tell them apart, or see her haircut, Addie agrees and the party is on! The last page of the story is a drawing of Addie and Max in matching jungle suits. It's a thank you card to Addie that reads "to Ugly-Wugly/My Best Birthday/from Pugly-Mugly."

Basic Book Information

Addie's Bad Day is *An I Can Read Book*. This humorous book is 32 pages long. Each page averages three to five sentences, each of which has a bright illustration that supports the main action of the text.

Addie's Bad Day is one of three books about the two main characters, Addie and Max. The others are *Addie Runs Away* and *Addie Meets Max*.

Noteworthy Features

Addie's Bad Day is a great book for readers who are beginning to be able to sustain independent reading with some fluency. The sentences are simple and straightforward, yet somewhat longer and more descriptive than those in earlier books. The story is long enough so that early readers will not race through it, yet short enough to be read in one independent reading session.

The most challenging section of the book will probably be the lead, where the story does not follow the classic story structure, and so it may throw the reader off. The story begins with Addie peeking around trees, pulling her cap low, peering in through the windows and in general, acting altogether suspicious. For almost a third of the book, even readers who comprehend the text may be mystified.

Teaching Ideas

Readers who understand this text may be mystified by the first eight to ten pages of this book and certainly by Addie's cryptic poem on page 10. This

Illustrator
Sue Truesdell

Publisher
Harper and Row, 1993

ISBN
0064441830

TC Level
6

A Field Guide to the Classroom Library, Lucy Calkins and the Teachers College Reading and Writing Project, Heinemann, ©2002 Teachers College, Columbia University; http://www.heinemann.com/fieldguides

will probably be a new experience for children. Usually, if children are confused by a text this means the book is above their reach. In this book, the reader's initial confusion may be a sign that they *are* experiencing the text as it was designed to be experienced. A teacher may want to see if readers are confused, and point out that some books *are meant to be* confusing, at least for the first few pages, to keep us reading.

Once children get past the puzzling pages, then the story becomes straightforward. In a conference, we might nudge children to reread for smoothness and information, to think more deeply about the text, and to make inferences and draw conclusions. With a second reading of the book, many children may still find the poem on page 10 to be puzzling. What could Addie's poem mean? In discussing the text, reading partners may work through the puzzle of the poem and see the parallel between the bare tree in autumn and how Addie feels about her haircut: bare. "Poor tree/Poor me," Addie writes in her poem. Teachers may guide the readers to draw the conclusion that it's because Addie is embarrassed by her haircut that she wears a hat and doesn't want to be seen.

This book can be used to teach a strategy lesson on reading dialogue. A teacher might select a page of text that includes dialogue, and either share it with a small group of readers on an overhead projector, or give copies of the book to each member of a small group. Readers may look for, and discuss how the quotation marks, exclamation points, words in italics or all caps can be read aloud to emphasize meaning. Readers may practice reading the dialogue in the characters' voices. Then the teacher might say, "As you all return to your independent reading today, I will be coming around and admiring the work you do as a reader. And I'll pay special attention to whether you are giving voice to your characters."

Addie's Bad Day can be used in conjunction with the other two books about the same characters: *Addie Runs Away* and *Addie Meets Max*. In a conference with one reader or in a small group, the teacher may want to highlight the way readers read within a series. Although the characters and the plot are not particularly well developed, there is enough in these books for the readers to discuss similarities and differences among the three titles. Readers may notice how the characters are the same in each book, how the author seems to write about friendship, and how Ginger the dog is always included. Readers can speculate about what a new "Addie and Max" book might be about, brainstorm ideas, or even write a letter to the author offering their suggestions.

Book Connections

Other titles similar in vocabulary, length and content to the *Addie* books are the *Henry and Mudge* series by Cynthia Rylant, and the *Little Bear* books by Else Holmelund Minarik.

Genre
Picture Book

A Field Guide to the Classroom Library, Lucy Calkins and the Teachers College Reading and Writing Project, Heinemann, ©2002 Teachers College, Columbia University; http://www.heinemann.com/fieldguides

Teaching Uses
Independent Reading; Character Study; Small Group Strategy Instruction;
Language Conventions; Interpretation

Airport

Byron Barton

Book Summary

Airport is a book that describes the various happenings of different airplanes at an airport. The reader learns about an airplane that dusts the crops and one that writes a message in the sky. They also learn about a helicopter, a cargo plane and finally follow a jet plane from the beginning of a journey to the end, and then start again at the beginning of the process.

Basic Book Information

More than many other books in this library, this book looks like a picture book. It contains 31 unnumbered pages, with 14 sentences stretched across these pages. The first sentence stretches across four pages, and then successive sentences are stretched across two pages, with illustrations on all pages.

Noteworthy Features

The text placement is fairly consistent on the bottom of each page. After the first page, we read a list of different airplanes and their jobs, spread across the rest of the pages of the book. . However, there is an inconsistent use of words to introduce each sentence shifting between *this, here, there,* and *these.* Some of the concepts will be unfamiliar to many children. "Dusting the crops" and "writing a message" are examples of what may be tricky parts for many.

At first some children may be confused to find that each sentence crosses over to the next page, but once they become familiar with this structure, they're often able to adapt to it.

Teaching Ideas

Airport is a simple nonfiction book that can be used to introduce a conversation about various types of planes and their purposes. Many teachers will let children study and read the book as best they can with independence because the non-narrative and non-patterned nature of the book makes it good to read in a "dip-in" sort of a way.

After the child has done some work with the text, the teacher may want to introduce the book. One way to do this would be to say, "*Airport* is a book about different types of airplanes and their different jobs." If the reader needed more support, the teacher might incorporate the terms used in the book in her discussions using *here, there,* and *this.* A teacher may introduce the tricky pages first. "Let's see what happens when a jet plane starts to journey into the sky," she could say.

Children have loved studying this book as part of an author study of

Illustrator
Byron Barton

Publisher
HarperTrophy, 1982

ISBN
0064431452

TC Level
5

Byron Barton. Some children found that this book was similar to many of Barton's other books, such as *Dinosaurs, Dinosaurs*. Students were able to make connections to his list-like writing and bold illustrations, across books. Children who've read other Byron Barton books had more experience negotiating the sentences across two pages.

One teacher used this book as part of a reading center on airplanes. Readers discussed similar books, and with help, thought about how different airplanes have different purposes. This book could be a great addition to a center on airplanes where children can compare various planes and discuss their purposes.

Students might substitute the word *people* for *passengers*, probably because they don't look across the entire word. On a reread of the entire sentence, they are usually able to self-correct.

Genre
Picture Book; Nonfiction

Teaching Uses
Content Area Study; Author Study; Independent Reading

A Field Guide to the Classroom Library, Lucy Calkins and the Teachers College Reading and Writing Project, Heinemann, ©2002 Teachers College, Columbia University; http://www.heinemann.com/fieldguides

At the Zoo

Beverley Randell; Jenny Giles

Book Summary

The first picture shows a girl pointing to a monkey, smiling at the reader (or at an unseen companion). "Come and see the monkey," the text says and then continues, eventually dropping out the photos of the girl and showing only the animals. The text continues, substituting names of different animals at the ends of the sentences.

Basic Book Information

This book contains 43 words over 8 pages of print. The repetitive pattern consists of two sentences. The pattern changes on the last page to reflect the animals "seeing" the girl.

Noteworthy Features

The book uses real photos of animals in a zoo, which many readers will find engaging. The photos are clear and concrete without distracting details. The text simply lists the animals the girl sees. There is no title page in this book. The story begins on the first page.

Teaching Ideas

A possible book introduction could be, "The girl in this story went to the zoo. She saw many animals and they saw her. Read to find out what animals she saw." A picture walk will help the teacher to set up the repetitive pattern of, "I went to the zoo. I saw a _____." The teacher should also use this opportunity to insure that the reader is familiar with the zoo animals pictured, especially the pelican and the koala.

The use of a natural oral language pattern and the depiction of familiar animals makes the text suitable for teaching the strategy of searching meaning and syntax to make predictions about the text.

One-to-one matching and checking the initial letter/sound relationship to the pictures of the koala, pelican, and alligator are especially necessary. If the reader calls one of these animals by the incorrect name, such as *bear* for *koala*, the teacher has an excellent opportunity to model the strategies of monitoring and crosschecking with the visual.

The teacher could use this list book to identify other animals in a zoo, as part of an interactive writing activity, or in writing workshop as students use it as a model or mentor list book text.

Publisher
Rigby, 1996

ISBN
0763541478

Genre
Emergent Literacy Book

Teaching Uses
Independent Reading; Teaching Writing; Whole Group Instruction; Language Conventions

A Field Guide to the Classroom Library, Lucy Calkins and the Teachers College Reading and Writing Project, Heinemann, ©2002 Teachers College, Columbia University; http://www.heinemann.com/fieldguides

Baby Bear Goes Fishing

Beverley Randell

Book Summary

Mother Bear thinks that Baby Bear is too little to go fishing with Father Bear. Baby Bear goes fishing anyway. Father Bear gives up, because the fish are not coming. Baby Bear goes on fishing and is very successful. Baby Bear proves that he is not too little to go fishing.

Basic Book Information

This book contains 108 words over 16 pages. The size and spacing of the print are appropriate for the emergent reader. The border around each picture provides a clear distinction between the illustrations and the print. The illustrations are supportive and have few added details. The language patterns, though varied, are close to the natural oral language of the reader. The author uses exclamation points, quotation marks, and bold-faced print. Many high frequency words are repeated. The book is a simple sequence of events that can be told through the pictures. The main characters are Mother, Father and Baby Bear.

Noteworthy Features

This storyline may be very familiar to readers. Baby Bear is being told he is too little to go fishing. Many readers can relate to the "too little" Baby Bear. This familiarity, along with the use of natural oral language, aids the reader in using meaning and syntax to predict the text. These predictions must be monitored and confirmed through the use of visual cues.

Teaching Ideas

A possible book introduction may be: "Mother Bear thought that Baby Bear was too little to go fishing. Read to find out what happened when Baby Bear went fishing and did not give up even though Father Bear did." The supportive pictures will lend themselves to a book walk. During the book walk the teacher can familiarize the reader with some of the language. Also, the bear's method of fishing should be discussed and possibly compared with a human's traditional method of fishing.

This text provides opportunities to model and/or practice crosschecking visual (graphophonic) cues with information in the picture. Readers can also be coached to confirm or revise any predictions they made, based on their experiences and expectations, before reading. The use of many words with regular spelling patterns provides opportunities for readers to use all they've learned as they encounter, notice and solve these words while reading.

Illustrator
Isabel Lowe

Publisher
Rigby, 1994

ISBN
0435066978

TC Level
3

Genre
Emergent Literacy Book

Teaching Uses
Independent Reading; Language Conventions; Interpretation; Whole Group
Instruction

Bailey Goes Camping

Kevin Henkes

Book Summary

Bruce and Betty are going camping, leaving their younger brother Bailey at home. "Don't feel bad, Bailey," Bruce says. "It's not *that* great. All we do is eat hot dogs and live in a tent and go swimming and fishing...." Betty adds, "And don't forget roasting marshmallows." The older children leave and Bailey is dejected and inconsolable. He doesn't want to play baseball or bake cookies; he wants to go camping. "Don't feel badly," Papa says, "It's not *that* great." "Oh yes, it is," Bailey responds and then quotes his big brother, "You get to eat hot dogs and live in a tent...."

Mama saves the day by suggesting Bailey can do *all* those things at home, and the book shows inventive ways in which he does just that. He fishes in the bathtub, toasts marshmallows over the burner on the stove, and is content. By the story's end, Bailey falls asleep under the stars in his own bed.

Basic Book Information

Booklist describes this Mulberry picture book as "a cozy, comfortable book that will leave youngsters smiling." This is a 22-page book with one to seven lines of type per page. Though the type is small for young readers, the text usually appears beneath the pictures.

Noteworthy Features

Booklist describes this Mulberry picture book as "a cozy, comfortable book that will leave youngsters smiling." The full-color illustrations are framed in small squares on the page, emphasizing Bailey's "smallness," and the intimacy of the story. The illustrations also support the action and mood of each scene, supporting the text.

Teaching Ideas

Teachers may want to read and reread this story to give children an internalized sense of how stories go. Following a read aloud, teachers may point out how they use their voices and the words in italics, to emphasize the meaning of the story.

The sense of harmony one gets from this book comes from its perfect circular shape. It folds back onto itself, suggesting that with a bit of ingenuity we can make everything right with the world.

The grace and charm of this book comes in part from all that is not said, or from what is implied. The older children leave, and the text says only, "Bailey watched Bruce and Betty leave." He says, "It's not fair." Meanwhile, the reader sees Bailey walking alone and dejected through the field of dandelions. Teachers may ask students "How do you think Bailey is feeling?

A Field Guide to the Classroom Library, Lucy Calkins and the Teachers College Reading and Writing Project, Heinemann, ©2002 Teachers College, Columbia University; http://www.heinemann.com/fieldguides

Illustrator
Kevin Henkes

Publisher
Greenwillow Books, 1985

ISBN
0688152880

TC Level
5

How would you feel if this happened to you?"

The story offers many opportunities for discussions about making inferences and drawing conclusions. For example, the text doesn't say that the father desperately wanted to console his youngest child. It simply shows him in the field, baseball bat over his shoulder saying, "Come on.... Let's play baseball."

When used in guided or independent reading, children will reread this in an emergent fashion, approximating as best they can, but the picture-support isn't explicit enough to make this a perfect book for emergent readers. Some children though, will grow to be able to read the words themselves with support from the patterned, predictable text. But all children can savor and delight in the story.

When used in writing workshop, teachers may help readers turn back to notice particular things Henkes has done, such as writing in the perfect circular shape, using repetition, and "showing not telling." Teachers may point out the story shows a problem and a solution, and offer students an opportunity to draw or write about a problem they've had and solved in their own lives.

Book Connections

Children who enjoyed reading about Bailey will enjoy other books by Kevin Henkes, who has won numerous awards for his picture books which include: *Chrysanthemum, Julius the Baby of the World, Sheila Rae, the Brave, A Weekend with Wendell, Owen,* and *Lilly's Purple Plastic Purse.*

Genre
Picture Book

Teaching Uses
Independent Reading; Interpretation; Read Aloud; Teaching Writing; Small Group Strategy Instruction; Language Conventions

Beezy
Megan McDonald

Book Summary

The book is a collection of three stories about a girl named Beezy, her grandmother, and her best friend Merlin. The first story is about an evening when the winds pick up, the electricity goes out, and Beezy's family and friends chase away their worries of a hurricane by telling hurricane stories by candlelight. Mr. Gumm begins by talking about when he was a young boy. The second story focuses more on Beezy, who seems to be a seven- or eight-year-old girl. Beezy befriends a dog that follows her. Gran posts a sign, "Found-small cute dog" and Beezy prays no one will claim Funnybone, as she has named the dog. The final story tells of a rather exotic new girl, Sarafina Zippy, who is from the circus that is passing through town. Sarafina knows how to ride a unicycle, to do a double flip, and to make a dog bone disappear.

Basic Book Information

The book is 48 pages long and includes a table of contents and three stories each of varied length. The majority of the text is in dialogue form. The color pictures illustrate the main action of each scene to support comprehension.

Noteworthy Features

This book is surprising in a number of ways. First, although it is titled *Beezy*, the name of the pert seven- or eight-year-old whose picture dominates the cover, in fact Beezy plays a supporting role in two of the three stories. The stories all include Merlin, a boy who is Beezy's age. Most include Gran, the hip-looking grandmother with whom Beezy lives, and Mr. Gumm, a shopkeeper and family friend.

The book often uses sentence fragments: "The light blinked. Off. On. Off. On." Also, "She gave him an old bone. A funny-looking bone. He followed her. To school. To Mr. Gumm's store... Home."

The book includes a number of colorful expressions, which could mystify readers. These include for example, Mr. Gumm's description of his long relationship with Gran. "I knew your Gran back in the days when stones were soft." He remembers Hurricane Jane, "She blew up the coast;" the sky was "sunset red as a beet" and winds were "faster than a car can drive."

Children who don't know much about hurricanes may not comprehend how the eye of a storm dropped a washing machine right in the front yard.

Teaching Ideas

In a conference, a teacher might ask a reader whether the book is *mainly* about Beezy, as the title suggests. If the child isn't sure, this may be an

Illustrator
Nancy Poydar

Publisher
Scholastic, 2000

ISBN
0531071626

TC Level
6

interesting topic of discussion. "What *do* we learn of Beezy?" the teacher might ask, allowing the reader to reread to cull information such as the fact that Beezy lives with her Gran in Soda Springs, on the coast of Florida, that she plays softball and has a tree fort, and that she has known Merlin since she was two.

A teacher might also suggest that sometimes we get to know characters not by what is explicitly written in the text, but by *what* the character *says* and *how she says it*. A look at Beezy's comments will yield little, but Mr. Gumm, on the other hand, has dramatic and unusual ways of talking that are worth noting.

One of the interesting points for discussion around the book is this: how do the three stories overlap? At first glance, they overlap only in that many of the characters are the same. In all three stories, these children (and the grownups who surround them) invent creative ideas for how to have a good time. They don't watch television, play video games, or even do a lot of sports. They do tell stories, sing songs, chase dandelion seeds, play in the tree fort, roll down the grassy hill, play checkers, jump rope, and look for pirate's treasure. The dog, which is found and adopted in the second story, reappears at the end of the third story.

In writing workshop, children may notice the story-within-a-story feature of Chapter One. The winds blow, the lights go out, and the family gathers to tell stories. To reinforce a text-to-self connection, a teacher may offer a writing (or conversation) prompt for her students by asking "Has your family ever gathered to tell stories? What stories were told?"

Genre
Picture Book

Teaching Uses
Independent Reading; Interpretation; Teaching Writing

A Field Guide to the Classroom Library, Lucy Calkins and the Teachers College Reading and Writing Project, Heinemann, ©2002 Teachers College, Columbia University; http://www.heinemann.com/fieldguides

Ben's dad

Beverley Randell

Book Summary

Mom tells Ben that Dad is coming home today. Ben goes to school and tells the teacher and the boys and girls that his dad is coming home. During school, Ben paints a picture of his dad taking care of the engines on a ship. Ben's dad comes to school and takes him home.

Basic Book Information

The PM Series was developed by Beverley Randell who continues-at age 70-to be an important contributor to the series. She began to write the books after ten years as a New Zealand classroom teacher. The PM Readers always rely upon a traditional story structure, which includes a central character that has a problem, a climax or pivotal moment where readers wonder if the problem will be solved, and then a resolution, when the problem is solved.

Noteworthy Features

This book has many high frequency words including: *went, coming, today, said, my, look, on, the,* and *here.* The repetition of these words will give readers a way into the new content on each page. This book will support early reading behaviors such as directionality, one-to-one correspondence, and monitoring both known and unknown words.

Teaching Ideas

Some teachers may decide to do a book introduction to help a reader (or a small group of readers) to fluently process this text. A teacher might begin her introduction by saying, "Here is a picture of Ben and his dad on the cover. Look at the uniform that Ben's dad is wearing. What job do you think he has?"

This book is appropriate for readers learning to match one spoken word to one written one. The teacher can cue the reader to find a known sight word, which will serve as an anchor for a one-to-one match. The child who is reading books of this level will probably recognize a few sight words and can use those words to "anchor" or pin-down his or her pointing.

Teachers may refer students to their classroom word walls to check for sight words. Children who are able to work successfully with a book at this level will benefit not only from the teacher's encouragement to do a one-to-one match, but to crosscheck as well. Successful reading happens when a reader crosschecks or integrates cues from a variety of sources. For example, there is a picture of Ben with a jar of paint on page seven. A teacher can observe whether the reader uses the picture as a source of

A Field Guide to the Classroom Library, Lucy Calkins and the Teachers College Reading and Writing Project, Heinemann, ©2002 Teachers College, Columbia University; http://www.heinemann.com/fieldguides

Illustrator
Genevieve Rees

Publisher
Rigby, 1996

ISBN
0435066935

TC Level
4

information and then checks it against the letters *p-a-i-n-t,* and if so, then praise the child for doing this.

A reader who uses sight words, the picture and the initial letters in known words, may still encounter difficulty on page 11 when Ben says, "Look at the engines." If a child reads this alone, she may end up substituting a word-*machines?* -and then continue reading. If a child encounters this word when a teacher is near, we may want to let them do a bit of work first and then say, "Could it be *engines?*"

Another option for teachers may be a mini-lesson in phonics. For example, the word *ship* and the word *shouted* are used in the text. The teacher may call attention to the *sh* blend and help students generate other words using /*sh*/.

Once a child has read this book, it'll be important for the child to talk about the story. If the child has read other books about Ben, she will probably notice the accumulating details about this character. In many books, Ben's teddy bear plays a role. Will the bear be less important to him once his father returns? In other stories, we've seen paintings on Ben's bedroom wall. Now we see the painting Ben makes of his father.

Book Connections

Ben's dad is part of a series written by Beverley Randell. Other books in the series include: *A birthday cake for Ben, Ben's treasure hunt, Ben's Teddy Bear, Ben's tooth* and *Ben's red car.*

Genre
Emergent Literacy Book

Teaching Uses
Independent Reading; Interpretation; Whole Group Instruction; Small Group Strategy Instruction

A Field Guide to the Classroom Library, Lucy Calkins and the Teachers College Reading and Writing Project, Heinemann, ©2002 Teachers College, Columbia University; http://www.heinemann.com/fieldguides

Ben's Teddy Bear

Beverley Randell

Book Summary

Ben's mom tucks him into bed and tells him to go to sleep but Ben is quickly up looking for his teddy bear. Mom joins him in the search for his bear. She finds it under the clothes on a chair in his room. Ben thanks her, and Mom tucks both Ben and the teddy bear into bed. Ben and his teddy bear are asleep on the last page.

Basic Book Information

The PM Readers is a series published by Rigby. The PM Readers tend to come in kits where every book looks exactly like every other book. The PM Readers are an important resource for teachers because first, there is an exorbitant amount of them available at the early reading levels and second, the publishers recognize the supports that early readers need and try to offer these. Instead of saying, "I see the cow/ the pig/ the horse," a PM Reader is likely to say, "I see the cow./ I see the pig./ I see the horse." Some researchers feel the PM Readers are especially good at providing a lot of easy text, full of high frequency words.

Another advantage of the PM Readers is that a great many, of even the earliest books, are stories. Other early books tend to be label-books, organized in a repetitive list structure, and it's nice to be able to also give beginning readers the opportunity to read stories that have a central character that has a problem that is resolved by the end of the story. The PM Readers contain many books about Ben and his family that are written at a variety of levels.

Noteworthy Features

The book includes many high frequency words such as *look, is, up, go, to, for,* and *here.* The repetition of these will give readers a way into the new content on each page. This book will support early reading behaviors such as directionality and one-to-one correspondence. The text is highly supported by colorful illustrations. The print is large and well spaced, and includes a variety of punctuation. Sentences are short, but there are up to four lines of text on some pages.

Teaching Ideas

It might be helpful for a teacher to look over a book and think, "If this book is roughly appropriate for a child, what features of the book will support the child's reading? What will be easy for the child?" The teacher may also want to think, "What challenges will the book probably pose for a child?"

A child who is reading a book with multiple lines of print such as this

Illustrator

Genevieve Rees

Publisher

Rigby, 1994

ISBN

0435067486

TC Level

2

one, will have already shown that he can point to written words as he says oral words in texts which have only one line of print. It will still be important for the child to point crisply under the words, and the teacher will probably want to watch the way the child's focus wraps around from the end of one line to the start of the next. That is, pointing will be difficult for this child only because the sentences are longer and pages hold more text. This reader should have a collection of words he knows well, and chances are these words will probably include *mom, look, go, is, to* and *here*. The child who knows any of these words easily, by sight, can use this knowledge to make sure that spoken and written words are in sync as they move along, pointing and speaking.

If a teacher sees a child having some difficulty with one-to-one-pointing, it will help to remind that child of one or two known words. "So whenever you see this '*M-o-m*,' you'll say this-'Mom.' What do you notice about this word?"

A reader of this text will have been using both pictures *and* print to solve unknown words. In most of the texts this child has been reading, unknown words are supported either by the syntax of the sentence or by the illustration. In this book, page 7 may pose difficulties. The text shows a boy standing in the doorway of his bedroom. It says, "Mom, Mom! Where is Teddy Bear?" Neither Mom nor the teddy bear are visible in the picture. The reader who has been thinking about the story and is putting together one page with the next, predicting the way this story will probably go, may be able to guess that the boy is searching for his bear, but this information will come from the cover, the title page (and from a picture-walk if the child has done this) and not from the sources of information available on page 7. What an opportunity this page gives us, then, to see whether children are following the story, holding early information in their minds as they read on. Or are they solving words in a page-by-page and word-by-word way?

If the reader *can't* do much on his own with page 7, a teacher might suggest that sometimes it can help to go back and reread the text, turning one's brain on to *high* and *really* thinking. If we join the child in noticing the cover photo and take note of the bear together, the reader may surmise that on page 7, the boy is asking for his bear. If the child needs more support, a quick look-through of the book will help. We can reinforce the importance for readers at this level to carefully *read* the cover and title and use that information to read the text more successfully.

Children who are reading this level of text are developing the skills and experiences necessary to look all the way across words, noticing chunks. A teacher may, then, want to do a bit of work around the *-ing* ending in looking. Pointing to the word *go*, the teacher could ask, "So what if Beverley Randell had wanted to say *going*? How would she have written that?"

A teacher may want to encourage children to retell the story. When the books are as sparsely written as this one is, we hope that children will retell by adding the inferred text to the actual text. A teacher may need to demonstrate a retelling so that children understand what we mean by a retelling. The page says, "Mom, Mom! Where is Teddy Bear?" and *shows* Ben standing in the door. In a retelling or think aloud the reader might add, "Ben got out of bed and went to the hall and called his Mom, saying 'Where is my Teddy Bear?'"

A teacher may want to remind children that when we reread books each time, we notice more and think more. The child who is prompted to reread, expecting a deeper level of comprehension, will probably be gratified. In a reread, an observant child will notice that the bear's paw was always peeking out from under the pile full of clothes (on page 6).

If the children have read *Ben's red car*, or *A birthday cake for Ben* or *Ben's treasure hunt*, the teacher and students can have a discussion about Ben and his family across books.

Teachers may also take the opportunity to point out the author's use of bold print for emphasis, as well as how punctuation is used, and that these factors affect how the text is read.

Book Connections

Ben's Teddy Bear is part of a series written by Beverley Randell. Other books in the series include *Ben's red car* , *A birthday cake for Ben, Ben's treasure hunt, Ben's dad* and *Ben's tooth.*

Genre
Emergent Literacy Book

Teaching Uses
Independent Reading; Language Conventions; Small Group Strategy Instruction; Whole Group Instruction

A Field Guide to the Classroom Library, Lucy Calkins and the Teachers College Reading and Writing Project, Heinemann, ©2002 Teachers College, Columbia University; http://www.heinemann.com/fieldguides

Ben's tooth

Beverley Randell

Book Summary

Ben is eating an apple at school and his tooth comes out. His teacher, Mrs. Green, gives him a little box for his tooth. Ben goes home after school and shows his mom. Mom tells him the tooth fairy might come tonight. Ben doubts this and calls his mom "silly" because fairies are in fairy tales, but he still puts his tooth by the bed. As he goes to sleep he asks, "Will a fairy come or won't she?" In the morning, Ben finds his tooth gone and some money in the little box and he runs to show his mom.

Basic Book Information

The PM Storybooks, developed in New Zealand and published by Rigby, place a priority on including the traditional story elements. Even texts that at first appear to be lists are, in fact, stories with characters, a problem and a resolution. The only exceptions are their very earliest books. The PM Readers are known for including a large number of high frequency words, and for controlling vocabulary so that in books of a comparable level of difficulty, the same high frequency words reoccur. The PM Readers use complete sentences (e.g., "*I see a bird./ I see a frog.*") to reinforce repetition of high frequency words.

The fact that PM Readers include many high frequency words means that sometimes the resulting sentences may seem stilted and unnatural.

Noteworthy Features

The author uses varied sentence patterns. Some sentences have as many as fifteen words. Most pages have six or seven lines of text. Due to this amount of text, the book will provide plenty of opportunities for strategies such as self-correcting, self-monitoring and searching for visual information. The print is large and well spaced.

Many children will be familiar with various events in Ben's life, which will support their comprehension of the story.

Teaching Ideas

If a child has read other PM Readers about Ben before coming to this one, the child probably won't need a book introduction. The same characters are here and the same syntax as in the other *Ben* books. If, however, the teacher decided for some reason to give a child the support of a book introduction, she could say, "This book is called Ben's tooth. Let's look at the picture on the cover. What do you think happened when Ben ate the apple?" The teacher may encourage the students to make predictions and discuss if they have ever lost a tooth making a text-to-self connection. In this discussion,

Illustrator
Genevieve Rees

Publisher
Rigby, 1996

ISBN
0435067613

TC Level
5

A Field Guide to the Classroom Library, Lucy Calkins and the Teachers College Reading and Writing Project, Heinemann, ©2002 Teachers College, Columbia University; http://www.heinemann.com/fieldguides

the teacher will probably want to mention the concept of the tooth fairy.

This book is appropriate to support early reading behaviors such as directionality and one-to-one matching. The text will provide opportunities for readers to read longer text and make predictions. For example, on page 11, if a teacher is near as the child reads, the teacher might intervene to ask the child to predict what Mom will do with Ben's tooth or similarly, on page13, to predict if the tooth fairy will come.

Once the child has finished reading this book, the teacher may want to revisit a few pages with the child in order to teach for word-solving strategies. The teacher and child might turn to the word *bedroom* on page 11, and the word *bedtime* on page 13, and use these two words as a springboard for talking about compound words.

If the children have read *Ben's red car, A birthday cake for Ben, Ben's treasure hunt, Ben's Teddy Bear, or Ben's dad,* they may discuss Ben and his family, comparing the books.

Book Connections

Ben's tooth is part of a series written by Beverley Randell. Other books in the series include *Ben's red car, A birthday cake for Ben, Ben's treasure hunt, Ben's Teddy Bear*, and *Ben's dad.*

Genre
Emergent Literacy Book

Teaching Uses
Independent Reading; Interpretation; Small Group Strategy Instruction; Whole Group Instruction; Character Study

Ben's treasure hunt

Beverley Randell

Book Summary

The story begins as Mom tells Ben that she has a clue for him. The clue says, "Look on the swing." Ben goes to the swing on the next page and finds a clue, which leads him to the TV, and this continues until the final clue leads him to Mom's pocket where he finds a toy plane. The last page ends with Ben telling Mom that he loves her.

Basic Book Information

The PM Series was developed by Beverley Randell who continues-at age 70-to write books for this series. She began to write the books after ten years as a New Zealand classroom teacher. The PM Readers always rely upon a traditional story structure, which includes a central character that has a problem, a climax or pivotal moment where readers wonder if the problem will be solved and the resolution, when the problem is in fact solved.

Noteworthy Features

The book includes many high frequency words: *come, here, is, look, went, he, to, on, in,* and *said*. The repetition of these will give readers a way into the new content on each page. The phrase "Ben went to look" is repeated several times throughout the book. This book will support early reading behaviors such as directionality, one-to-one correspondence and self-monitoring for comprehension. Sentences are short, and most pages have three lines of text.

Teaching Ideas

In this book, as in so many books, the hardest bit of the text will probably be the title. The word *treasure* is a long one and the illustration showing a clue will only help children who've followed trails of clues on treasure hunts or heard of others who've done this. Although we often expect children to test whether a book will be okay for them by reading a tiny bit of it, we'll also want to let kids know that titles can be hard sometimes, and they can try reading past a perplexing title, coming back later to work with it.

A teacher who observes a child as she reads the book or who gathers a small group of children together, may want to support the readers by saying, "When I start a new book, I pay very close attention to the information I get at first because sometimes I can figure out how the book will probably go. The title page has a drawing of a clue, which says, 'Clue 4 Look on Teddy Bear.'" If children really think about this, the clue becomes a clue for them as readers as well as a clue for Ben. The numeral four (4) suggests a trail of clues has been laid, each sending Ben to a new destination in a cumulative structure.

Illustrator
Genevieve Rees

Publisher
Rigby, 1994

ISBN
0435067508

TC Level
3

 A Field Guide to the Classroom Library, Lucy Calkins and the Teachers College Reading and Writing Project, Heinemann, ©2002 Teachers College, Columbia University; http://www.heinemann.com/fieldguides

If a child reads this book independently, she may mark pages to talk about, or mark the pages that connect to each other or to other books. On the opening page, Mom is studying books for school and reviewing her lecture notes. The TV has a newspaper above it and a TV guide near. The bedside table features a row of books, and the story itself is all about how written clues create a treasure hunt. The children may note the books Mom is reading throughout the story. If they've already read *Ben's tooth*, they will have seen Mom with anthropology texts. Now it is clear that she is a student.

Book Connections

Ben's treasure hunt is part of a series written by Beverley Randell. Other books in the series include *Ben's red car*, *A birthday cake for Ben*, *Ben's Teddy Bear*, *Ben's dad*, and *Ben's tooth*.

Genre
Emergent Literacy Book

Teaching Uses
Small Group Strategy Instruction; Independent Reading; Teaching Writing; Whole Group Instruction

A Field Guide to the Classroom Library, Lucy Calkins and the Teachers College Reading and Writing Project, Heinemann, ©2002 Teachers College, Columbia University; http://www.heinemann.com/fieldguides

Bunny Cakes
Rosemary Wells

Book Summary

This book tells the story of Rosemary Wells' famous bunny characters, Max and Ruby, making a birthday cake for their grandmother. Ruby, Max's older sister, has decided that the pair should make their grandmother an angel surprise cake instead of the earthworm cake that Max is preparing. Unfortunately, each time Max tries to help he spills some of the ingredients on the floor. Each time he spills, Ruby gets further exasperated and sends Max to the store with a list of replacement ingredients. Max would really like to buy some Red Hot Marshmallow Squirters for the cake, as well, but every time he tries to add this item to the list, the grocer is unable to read his writing. Finally, after his third trip to the store, Max figures out how to write in a way that the grocer will understand: he draws a picture! He gets his Marshmallow Squirters and Grandma is given two cakes: angel food with butter cream roses and sugar hearts AND an earthworm cake with Red Hot Marshmallow Squirters!

Basic Book Information

Bunny Cakes is Rosemary Wells' fourteenth book about the much-loved Max, and one of several that also feature his bossy big sister, Ruby. Wells illustrated the book as well, using colorful, almost cartoon-like pictures that are contained in a box centered on the top of the page. This is a 22-page text.

Noteworthy Features

As is true in many books where the author is also the illustrator, some of the important information in the book is given only in the pictures. For example, the text never tells you that Max spilled the milk. You get this information from the picture, as the text reads simply, "But it was too late."

Most pages have about three to four lines of text. In addition, there is some dialogue in the book, though the characters do not talk back and forth to each other. This book has a very high picture-word correlation, with the pictures telling the story very clearly. Teachers will want readers to notice the repeated use of a colon, and a picture of a grocery list that serves as an important part of the text.

Teaching Ideas

In the A library, *Bunny Cakes* is intended primarily to be used as an emergent literacy read aloud. This instruction is based on the research of Elizabeth Sulzby, whose work with kindergarten children informed her of the importance of recreating parent-child interactions around books in the

Series
Max books

Illustrator
Rosemary Wells

Publisher
Penguin Publishing, 2000

ISBN
0140566678

kindergarten classroom. At home, children often ask parents to "read it again" when they hear a favorite story. In school, the teacher's multiple readings of emergent literacy books helps children become familiar with rich narrative, hear the inflection and pacing of storybook language, and learn to use detailed illustrations to assist them in remembering storyline.

After an emergent literacy storybook has been read to children at least four times, multiple copies of the book should be added to a basket labeled, "Stories We Love," or something similar. Children will have opportunities to return to these books at independent reading time. They will refer to the pictures and use their memory of the teacher's reading to recreate the story in their rereading. Given the opportunity to do this, children pass through different reading stages from simply "labeling" pictures on the page, to telling the story off the pictures, to using progressively more dialogue and storybook language, moving finally toward more "conventional" reading where they use the print. To go on this reading journey, it is important for children to hear the story read aloud many times, have a lot of opportunities to reread it to a partner and have a supportive teacher nearby who thoughtfully coaches into the reading.

Researchers Elizabeth Sulzby and Marie Clay, in their studies of emergent readers, have found that when children are given opportunities to do this type of "pretend" reading (referred to as "reading" or "rereading") they go through these stages of reading development. To support this process, teachers can select books with more text than readers can decode that can not be easily memorized, have elements of drama and suspense, and have characters to which young children can relate.

This book can be an inspiration for early writers because it tells about Max wanting desperately to write for a very important reason. Teachers may seize this as an opportunity to help youngsters understand authentic reasons to write. Max's stages of writing are similar to those that children go through. First he scribbles, then he writes a revised version of his scribbles, and finally he writes with the knowledge that there needs to be a real meaning behind what he writes.

Bunny Cakes is a great book to use as an interactive read aloud. It can be read aloud to the class with pauses at occasional places, inviting children to talk to their partners. Readers will generate things to talk and think about. A teacher may want to go from partner conversations to a whole-group conversation and say, "So, can someone get us started on a conversation?" The teacher can then expect one child to report on what he or she said in the partner talk. Children will not know the importance of talking back to each other until the teacher shows them this. After one child says, "Max keeps messing up," the next child might say something totally unrelated such as, "A worm cake is disgusting." This is an opportunity to emphasize to children the importance of listening to each other and talking back to each other. "So Brian noticed that Max keeps messing up. What do the rest of you think? Can you talk back to Brian?"

In this way, children may grow theories about the book including perhaps, the idea that Ruby wants to show Max how to do more grown-up things, but Max doesn't seem to be able to do them. This may lead to a text-to-text comparison of this story to others about Ruby and Max. It's also an opportunity for children to make text-to-self connections. Do they have bossy older brothers or sisters? The message of this story that writing and pictures can convey important information is one that will allow emergent writers to feel proud of how much they already know about written communication. Just like Max, they can write in ways that others can "read" and understand.

Genre
Picture Book

Teaching Uses
Read Aloud; Language Conventions; Partnerships

A Field Guide to the Classroom Library, Lucy Calkins and the Teachers College Reading and Writing Project, Heinemann, ©2002 Teachers College, Columbia University; http://www.heinemann.com/fieldguides

Buzz Said the Bee

Wendy Cheyette Lewison

Book Summary

The book opens: "Once there was a bee/ who sat on a duck." Soon she dances a jig and sits on a pig, who takes a bow and sits on a cow. As the pile of animals grows higher, each animal says, "Scat" but instead of scatting each animal, in turn, just sat. The turning point comes when the cow in the middle of the stack begins to weep, says "Moo," and somehow somersaults out of the stack. The bee reappears saying "Buzz-z-z!" And the story ends with the line, "And that's all there was."

Basic Book Information

This is part of the *Hello Reader* series published by Scholastic. Like other books in this series, this book contains a blurb inside the front cover that contains the first six lines of the book and serves as a prelude to the story.

This is a funny book; both text and pictures will make readers of all ages smile. The 29-page book consists of approximately fifteen sentences. Some sentences begin and end on the same page, and some pages have one or two sentences. Other sentences spread over two pages, and the second to last sentence spreads over five. The pictures support the text throughout, and the pages are not numbered.

Noteworthy Features

There are two patterns in the text. The first pattern tells the first part of the story. An animal sits on another animal, which protests by making its characteristic sound, saying "There's a _____ on me," "Scat." But the animal on top does not move. Therefore, the animal carrying the weight does something (weeps, dances a jig, etc.) and then proceeds to sit on top of another animal. As the pattern repeats itself, each animal takes on a larger burden because the pile grows.

By the middle of the book this pattern ends and another begins. After the cow weeps, *each* animal in turn makes his or her characteristic sound (*moo, oink,* etc.) and falls from the pile. This pattern ends after five pages when the bee buzzes and they all run away.

Much of the book is written in rhyming couplets, which are sometimes spread across several pages with one line on one page, and its rhyming line on the next page.

Teaching Ideas

It may take readers a while to realize how the pattern of the story goes, and then more time to see that the pattern switches halfway through the text, and the overall importance of being aware of patterns. How can patterns

Illustrator

Hans Wilhelm

Publisher

Scholastic, 1992

ISBN

0590907417

TC Level

4

help us, as readers, when we are confused or stuck on a word?

The teacher may challenge her students to find other rhymes in the story. Being alert to the rhyming pattern will help a reader realize that the (perhaps) challenging word *a-g-a-i-n* is one that rhymes with *hen*.

Youngsters will find that this book offers continued challenges as they read it, reread it, and reread it again. The first time through, a reader may not read the sound words: the *buzzes*, *moos* and *oinks* with much enthusiasm. Also, the dialogue may not sound very different from the narration, until the teacher points out that *CLUCK* is typed in all caps to emphasize the word, so as you read it your voice may get loud and excited.

In conferences or small group strategy lessons, a teacher may do a bit of teaching about reading dialogue, reading with expression, rereading for fluidity, and the importance of being aware of patterns.

Later in partnerships, young readers will delight in assuming the roles of various animal characters and reading with expression.

Genre

Emergent Literacy Book

Teaching Uses

Independent Reading; Partnerships; Small Group Strategy Instruction; Whole Group Instruction; Language Conventions

A Field Guide to the Classroom Library, Lucy Calkins and the Teachers College Reading and Writing Project, Heinemann, ©2002 Teachers College, Columbia University; http://www.heinemann.com/fieldguides

Call 911

Rebel Williams

Book Summary

This book tells the reader when 911 should be dialed: for fire (firefighters), accidents (paramedics), and kidnapping (police). Each example is displayed on a two-page spread. The final page summarizes it all and has all of the public servants pictured. All of the victims change from one scene to the next.

Basic Book Information

Call 911 has 22 words on 8 pages. The text is consistently located at the bottom of each page, below the picture. Each sentence begins on the left page and is completed on the right. This is a Wright Group book from the nonfiction *Twig* collection.

Noteworthy Features

The pictures and stories in this little book can be quite terrifying. First there is the image of the house burning down, then the woman seriously hurt and grimacing in pain, and then the kidnapper grabbing the child and pulling him into the car. While children certainly need to learn what to do in these instances, the graphic pictures of the situations may disturb some. Teachers will have to use some discretion about using this book in the classroom.

The repetitive text, "Call 911 and _____ will help" appears on each page. The numbers "911" and the word "and" appear on every page. Some of the language is difficult, for example, "paramedics" and "firefighters." The pattern changes at the end of the text.

Teaching Ideas

Children reading this will undoubtedly want to talk about the events in the story with a partner, speculating on what exactly has happened and what is likely to happen next. Picture details can be scrutinized to support the reading of the story. This work in constructing meaning from the words and pictures is critical for a good read of this story.

This book may trigger memories in readers of emergency events in their own lives. Teachers may use this topic in a mini-lesson as an opportunity to help children learn how to use personal responses to support and deepen their reading. How did the events in their lives and those in the book relate to one another? Can one inform the other? This too can be a discussion topic between partners.

Teachers may use this book help children learn how, why, and when to dial 911 for themselves. Do they know how to do it from home? From school? From a pay phone? Considering the tragic events of September 11th,

Illustrator
Cindy Spencer

Publisher
Wright Group, 1998

ISBN
0780290712

TC Level
2

knowing this skill might provide children with a sense of independence and security.

Genre
Nonfiction; Emergent Literacy Book

Teaching Uses
Interpretation; Critique; Content Area Study; Partnerships

A Field Guide to the Classroom Library, Lucy Calkins and the Teachers College Reading and Writing Project, Heinemann, ©2002 Teachers College, Columbia University; http://www.heinemann.com/fieldguides

Caps for Sale

Esphyr Slobodkina

Book Summary

Each day, a peddler walks carefully up and down the streets, balancing a huge pile of caps on top of his head and saying "Caps! Caps for sale! Fifty cents a cap!" He is very careful not to disturb any of the caps on his head, which are all in a particular color order. One morning, unable to sell a single cap, he walks out into the countryside, sits down under a tree, checks that all of his caps are in place and falls asleep. While the peddler is asleep, a band of mischievous monkeys steals every one of his caps, except for his own checked cap.

When he awakes, he checks for his caps but doesn't find them until he looks up at the tree. On every branch he sees a different monkey wearing one of his caps. Wondering how he is going to get back his caps, he begins talking to the monkeys. They repeat everything he says back to him. The peddler gets so angry that he throws his own cap on the ground and walks away. Not realizing that the monkeys are still copying him, they too throw the caps on the ground. The peddler picks up all of his caps and places them back on his head in the same color order as they were before and begins walking through the town again and saying "Caps! Caps for sale! Fifty cents a cap!"

Basic Book Information

Caps for Sale, subtitled *A Tale of a Peddler, Some Monkeys and Their Monkey Business* is a timeless classic picture book, in print for over fifty years and beloved by generations of readers. The author and illustrator, Esphyr Slobodkina, is a painter, designer, and sculptor as well as a writer and illustrator of children's books. Her paintings are in the permanent collections of the Corcoran Gallery, the Whitney Museum of American Art, the Philadelphia Art Museum, and many others. *Caps for Sale* was featured on the television show Reading Rainbow and it won a Lewis Carroll Shelf Award in 1958. Other works by the author include *The Wonderful Feast* (1955), *The Clock* (1956), *Pinky and the Petunias* (1959) and *The Long Island Ducklings* (1961). Slobodkina has also illustrated *The Little Fireman, The Little Cowboy* and *Sleepy ABC's*, all written by Margaret Wise Brown. *Caps for Sale* comes in both hard and soft covers. An audiocassette and a Spanish version of this book are also available.

Noteworthy Features

This book is filled with such warmth, humor, and simplicity that children will ask to hear it over and over again. Although *Caps for Sale* is relatively easy to read, the interest level is high because of its plot, drama, and suspense. The book contains illustrations on one page and text on the next.

Illustrator
Esphyr Slobodkina

Publisher
Scholastic, 1987

ISBN
0590410806

TC Level
6

In certain places in the story, the illustrations actually precede the text in their development of the plot, pushing the reader to notice the plot developments before they are described in the text.

The author also uses repetition and wonderful true-to-life dialogue such as when the peddler calls, "You monkeys, you, you give me back my caps." The book also contains onomatopoetic responses as when the monkeys retort, "Tsz, tsz, tsz."

Teaching Ideas

In the A library, the primary instructional purpose of *Caps for Sale* is for use as an emergent literacy read aloud. This instruction is based on the research of Elizabeth Sulzby, whose work with kindergarten children informed her of the importance of recreating parent-child interactions around the reading of books in the kindergarten classroom. At home, children often ask parents to "read it again" when they hear a favorite story. In school, the teacher's multiple reading of emergent literacy books helps children become familiar with rich narrative and to hear the inflection and pacing of storybook language. They also learn to use the detailed illustrations in picture books to assist them in their rereading of the story.

After *Caps for Sale* has been read to the class at least four times, multiple copies of the book could be added to a basket of "Stories We Love" (or some similar label). At independent reading time, children, in partnerships, are invited to read the book to each other "the best way you can." They should be given time to read quietly to themselves and then time to read to their partner. Children will refer to the illustrations, to their memory of the teacher's reading, and to their growing internalization of the story's plot and emotional content as they recreate the story in their rereading.

Given opportunities to hear and read many books that have a strong storyline, characters that they personally relate to, and supportive, detailed illustrations, Sulzby has shown how children move through different reading stages. They go from labeling the pictures on the page, telling the story off the pictures, using progressively more dialogue and storybook language, then moving toward a more conventional, print-based reading. To go on this reading journey it is important for children to hear the story read aloud many times, have many opportunities to reread it to a partner, and to have a supportive teacher nearby to thoughtfully coach into their reading.

Later in the year, *Caps for Sale* can be used as an engaging "accountable talk read aloud." Teachers might consider assigning read aloud partners who will sit together on the rug while the story is read. At significant, pre-selected moments in the reading, the teacher can ask the children to turn to their partner and "say something." This encourages children to remain anchored to the text and to make important personal connections to the characters and the story.

In *The Art of Teaching Reading*, Lucy Calkins writes, "We read aloud to demonstrate to children and to mentor them in the habits, values and strategies of proficient readers and to help them experience the bounties of thoughtful, reflective reading." *Caps for Sale* is the perfect read aloud book, and it can be reread often as we mentor children in different strategies. When teachers stop occasionally to think aloud as they read, sharing thoughts, reactions, or reading strategies, children are given a glimpse into the mind of a skillful reader. Doing so provides children with a powerful model of the kind of active and engaged reading that they can do during their own independent reading.

Book Connections

As of now, this book is not part of a series, but in March 2002 Esphyr Slobodkina will be publishing a new book titled *Circus Caps For Sale*.

Genre

Picture Book

Teaching Uses

Independent Reading; Partnerships; Language Conventions; Read Aloud

Chato's Kitchen

Gary Soto

Book Summary

A very cool cat named Chato invites his new neighbors, five mice, over for dinner. He and his cat friend cook all day, getting more and more excited about the feast of mice and salsa they are about to enjoy. When the mice come, they bring their friend-a dog. The group then enjoys a nice, vegetarian dinner together.

Basic Book Information

Renowned children's poet and author Gary Soto and illustrator Susan Guevara bring us this beautiful, fun and hip picture book. In jaunty English with a sprinkling of Spanish, Soto tells the tale of this cool, but hungry cat and his exploits with his "tasty" neighbors. The pictures are colorful and entertaining and support the content of the story. There are even subplots in the pictures that kids will be excited to discover (e.g., a mouse's phone conversation; the family of birds that goes to a wedding).

Noteworthy Features

The book opens with a short glossary of the thirty-some basic Spanish words and phrases used in the book-both conversational phrases like *no problema* and the names of the foods that Chato cooks for the mouse feast (e.g., *fajita*). Children who are not familiar with Spanish may want to glance over this list before they read-not to memorize the words, but to get a general sense of them. Remind children that this glossary exists for reference if they should later find that they cannot figure out a word from its context.

The language in the book is figurative and funny, which delights some readers and confounds others. "Chato," the first lines of the book reads, is a "low-riding cat" who hears a rhythm and "feels the twinge of mambo in his hips." This beginning can be a bit opaque for some readers, but if they push on with some idea of what is happening, the main plot soon unfolds and can carry them along with it.

Teaching Ideas

Some students have decided to chart the ups and downs of Chato's emotions as the story proceeds. This kind of plot analysis may be more fruitful here than character analysis. The characters aren't meant to be complicated. The plot and the emotions, however, run high and low, and can be followed and discussed in interesting ways.

Perhaps the most fun and important part of *Chato's Kitchen* is its setting in the barrio. If children are studying setting across books, this one may be a good one to add, as the setting sets the tone and adds a twist to this story.

Illustrator
Susan Guevara

Publisher
Scholastic, 1995

ISBN
0590897489

 A Field Guide to the Classroom Library, Lucy Calkins and the Teachers College Reading and Writing Project, Heinemann, ©2002 Teachers College, Columbia University; http://www.heinemann.com/fieldguides

The setting is well described in nearly every line, from the expressions characters use to the meals they cook.

As with many stories, there are a few simple, easily internalized, sequential questions that can help students get started assembling an interpretation: 1) What kind of person would the animal in the story be in real life? 2) What kind of action does the character take? 3) What would that choice or action be similar to in the real world? 4) What are the consequences of that action? and 5) What would the consequences be for the real-world action?

With answers to these questions, children could build an interpretation of the story. Certainly, there are many possible interpretations. It is also important to keep in mind that the goal is to help children understand how to arrive at an interpretation, not necessarily to find or agree with any one in particular.

Children may well decide that this story's message is that you have to have powerful friends if you don't want to be eaten by the predatory "Chatos" of this world. Or, they might decide instead that the message is that if you get into situations where you plan on "eating" someone else, you better watch out, because someone may be getting ready to "eat" you. Others may find that the message might be that nature balances things out, sometimes you get eaten, sometimes you eat, and sometimes no one eats anyone. In any case, if children disagree, that can be best for their learning, since each child, or group, has to support a particular interpretation with evidence from the book in order to prove it as a valid interpretation.

Genre
Picture Book

Teaching Uses
Read Aloud; Whole Group Instruction; Interpretation; Character Study

A Field Guide to the Classroom Library, Lucy Calkins and the Teachers College Reading and Writing Project, Heinemann, ©2002 Teachers College, Columbia University; http://www.heinemann.com/fieldguides

City Dog

Karla Kuskin

Book Summary

Noted poet and writer of *The Philharmonic Gets Dressed* (Harper, 1982), Karla Kuskin, tells the story of a city dog's first trip to the country in verse. This city dog is wild with freedom and glee as she experiences the country for the first time.

Basic Book Information

The book begins, "We took the dog to the country...." On each page, the dog is both befuddled by, and overjoyed with, the new experience of the vast countryside. The verse is a free-form rhyming scheme, which makes it a little hard to predict. The very last page holds the poem in its entirety, stanza by stanza.

City Dog has won numerous awards, among them, the John Burroughs Outstanding Nature Book for Children and the *New York Times* Notable Book of the Year. Karla Kuskin is the winner of the NCTE Award for Excellence in Poetry for Children.

Noteworthy Features

This is a 31-page book where the text averages from three words to eight lines on the page. Text usually runs along the bottom of each page, but is also incorporated. On a couple of two-page spreads the illustrations alone tell the story, especially on pages 28-29, as the moon rises and we watch City Dog chase after fireflies and play in a wide-open field.

Kuskin uses language to create imagery that readers may find unusual, refreshing and, possibly, a bit ponderous. Phrases such as, "...the melon yellow moon looked down at the pretty city dog..." combine so much imagery that some readers may need for it to be broken down.

Teaching Ideas

When used as a read aloud, *City Dog* can be used to show young readers how to use inference to develop understanding of a character in a story. You may first need to have a general discussion about ways in which the city and the country differ, in order to allow all students some understanding of the environments. One teacher remarked to her gathered class, "It's interesting that the story begins here, as they pack up the dog and leave the city. As readers, we don't really know what it was like in the city. It doesn't say, does it? The only way we can find out is by looking at City Dog and figuring out from the dog's behavior how different the city and the country are. What do we know about this City Dog?"

The class responded with exclamations of the dog's wild behavior as the

A Field Guide to the Classroom Library, Lucy Calkins and the Teachers College Reading and Writing Project, Heinemann, ©2002 Teachers College, Columbia University; http://www.heinemann.com/fieldguides

family drove to the country and when they arrived there. One student said, "I think that she [the dog] is acting out so much because she was kept inside so much in the city." The teacher, who had been waiting for this, replied with, "And that use of what you know about the world and the story is called an inference. You used what the book gave you and figured out the rest."

Teachers often like to use this book while teaching poetry. Kuskin uses alliteration (the repetition of the same beginning sounds, *crabs, crows*) and rhyming words *sea, me*. These techniques can be pointed out as being both intentional and important. The book may also be used as an example of vivid descriptive writing. Kuskin not only uses rhyme, but she also uses metaphor, personification (the countryside *rolls around*) and other figurative language to bring the dog in the country to life. In writing workshops, student writers may want to try using some of these techniques themselves.

This is a book that could also be used as an example of alternatives to the common "What I did on summer vacation" writing. City Dog goes to the country, very much like some children go on vacation in the summer. Rather than a humdrum listing of, "First we did this, then this, then this," the beginning, middle, and end of *City Dog* whirl around the emotions the new environment inspired.

When used in guided reading lessons teachers may call attention to the *-s* and/or *-ing* endings by asking, "What's the same about all of these words?" (e.g., *holes, bikes, toes* or *walking, barking, rolling*). If the children are able to do this, the teacher may generate other similar words to show how to link this information to solve other words.

Book Connections

City Mouse & Country Mouse by Isabelle Chantellard shows a similar contrast of setting with city and country.

Genre
Picture Book

Teaching Uses
Independent Reading; Read Aloud; Interpretation; Character Study; Teaching Writing; Small Group Strategy Instruction; Whole Group Instruction; Language Conventions

Come On, Rain!

Karen Hesse

Book Summary

This jewel of a book uses poetic language to tell the story of a little girl, Tessie, who lives in the sweltering hot city. From her apartment balcony, Tessie stares past chimneys and rooftops to see, way off in the distance, a bunch of gray clouds bulging under a purple sky. Tessie whispers, "Come on, Rain!"

Soon Tessie and her friends are in bathing suits, waiting for the rain, which finally comes after great longing. "The first drops plop down big, making dust dance all around us," Tessie says, and soon the Mamas have thrown off their shoes and stockings and joined the girls in a glorious dance through puddles. After their joyful rain celebration, Tessie and her Mom head home "fresh as dew."

Basic Book Information

Acclaimed author Karen Hesse wrote this exquisite picture book. As with her *Out of the Dust*, which won the Newbery Award, *Come On, Rain!* tells a story by means of a text that looks as if it were a poem. Hesse has also written *Sable* and *Just Juice*.

The illustrator of *Come On, Rain!*, Jon J. Muth deserves as much acclaim as does Hesse. His watercolor illustrations bring out the humanity and quirkiness of characters, and the oppressiveness of the setting, a sweltering summer day in the city. The illustrations are laid out in intriguing ways, often wrapping around the print.

Noteworthy Features

This book will take a reader's breath away. Every page has metaphor worth studying. Even the dedication is lovely, "To my mother... in celebration of all our summers." At the very end of the book, Hesse has a page of acknowledgments, which says, "A shower of thanks to..."

It is worth marveling over and discussing the way the pictures vary. Some are landscapes showing the big picture of a city horizon. Some zoom in and show just the arms and hands of children dancing among the raindrops, or their bare feet, or a flying shoe as a Mama sheds her weariness and stodginess and joins the celebration.

The illustrations are in yellow and gray until the end, when rain brings people to life, and that life is represented by the first presence of color.

Teaching Ideas

Many teachers approach the school year hoping that a few carefully chosen and dearly beloved books will become touchstone texts for their class. A

Illustrator
Jon J. Muth

Publisher
Scholastic, 1999

ISBN
0590331256

TC Level
6

touchstone text is a text that the class community adopts as a mentor text for everyone, together. Such a text is read and reread. A book such as this one can provide a lifetime of craft lessons for writers, and of comprehension lessons for readers.

But the first job is to fall head over heels in love with the text and the best way for a teacher to ensure that happens is to wear our love of the book on our sleeves. "I'm going to read you one of the world's most amazing books. This is a book that I've read a zillion times, and I adore it from head to toe." Saying this does a lot, but the more important thing will be to read the book well.

Probably a teacher will want to read it through without a lot of interruptions, knowing that if children come to love the book too there'll be lots of opportunities to revisit it. Maybe for a second reading, we'll ask children to listen for a part they love and we'll later recall and reread those parts, savoring them again without a lot of analysis. "Oh! I loved that too," we'll squeal and open the book to the page, rereading it again for everyone to savor.

On rereading the text, the class will need to get really close in and look with great care at a page or an issue. Perhaps the class will notice how Hesse made us *feel* the heat. She doesn't just *say*, "It was hot," she shows it-and of course the adage "show not tell" is a crucial one for writers. Teachers may point out how the verbs or action words are used. We see and feel how people move in the heat: Mother *sags* over her parched plants. Tessie *squints* into the endless sun. Mama *sinks* onto a kitchen chair.

Children who are writers will want to emulate what Hesse has done. "Let's remember how hurried we were yesterday when we got back late and had to rush for the buses," the teacher might say. "How can we pick *really* strong, exact action words like those Hesse uses to show how we hurried?" Perhaps to illustrate the teacher might add, "You didn't just pick up your backpacks, what did you do?" Soon the class may have begun working collaboratively to write a very short shared text in which they *grab* backpacks, *sling* them on, *slam* locker doors, and *throw out* goodbyes as they *race* towards the bus.

Teachers may also want to point out the overall structure of the story, and how the writer first tells about the everyday life of the city, and then about the one day in particular. This is an important structure for writers to try. Children will often skip the everyday part and zoom in on "One day it rained and we had a celebration" or "One day I got a bike." The "everyday" contextualizes this in ways that build anticipation and energy. Later, children will want to reread drafts they've already written during a writing workshop, finding and reconsidering their own action words.

This text may also be used to show writers the value of writing with focus. Hesse doesn't write about everything in her summer. She writes about the endless heat and then about one day when it rained. "She could have just said, 'It was very hot and dry. Then it rained and we were glad,'" the teacher might say, "But she wanted us to know just exactly how hot and dry it was, so that reading her book, we'd feel as if we were almost there with her. So I think what she did was she made a movie in her mind of that hot, hot day and she almost acted it out in her mind. She could feel the sweat and see her Mom sagging with the plants, and then she zoomed in and wrote with a whole lot of detail. That's what we're going to do today."

A Field Guide to the Classroom Library, Lucy Calkins and the Teachers College Reading and Writing Project, Heinemann, ©2002 Teachers College, Columbia University; http://www.heinemann.com/fieldguides

In class discussions teachers may point to the way feelings are shown. Good writers aren't apt to say, "She was very very happy." Instead writers show this in the text, showing also the character's particular kind of happiness.

Hesse also uses surprising words and invents new words, for example, "Rain *freckles* our feet." They dance in the "*Moisty green* air." *Moisty* isn't a word and air isn't really *green*, but Hesse's poetic language helps us feel the tone and mood of Tessie's rain-dance.

Genre
Picture Book; Poetry

Teaching Uses
Read Aloud; Interpretation; Whole Group Instruction; Teaching Writing; Small Group Strategy Instruction

A Field Guide to the Classroom Library, Lucy Calkins and the Teachers College Reading and Writing Project, Heinemann, ©2002 Teachers College, Columbia University; http://www.heinemann.com/fieldguides

Cookie's Week
Cindy Ward

Book Summary

Cookie is a cat that finds trouble to get into every day of the week, thus creating a pattern book for days of the week.

Basic Book Information

This is a 28-page book with full-color illustrations by Caldecott winner Tomie dePaola.

Noteworthy Features

The day of the week pattern is set up on page one as the story begins, "On Monday...Cookie fell in the toilet. There was water everywhere!" Each day of the week follows with a different kind of trouble for Cookie, but whatever the trouble is, it goes *everywhere*. This pattern is consistent until the last two pages where there is a twist.

Teaching Ideas

Some teachers like to use this book for guided reading and feel that a book introduction is particularly helpful to set the reader up for the days-of-the-week pattern. A teacher may choose to introduce this book by saying, "This is a book about a cat named Cookie. Cookie is on every page, and there is a page for every day of the week. It starts with Monday. What do you think will be the next page? Yes! It's Tuesday, and then Wednesday. You can count on this pattern. Find out what kind of trouble Cookie gets into each day. You'll have to look at the picture to help you."

The illustrations are very supportive of the text and should be used for crosschecking. One teacher began her introduction "This is a book about a cat named Cookie who gets into trouble every day. First, it's Monday and Cookie falls in the toilet. What do you think happened? Yuck! Yes, there was water everywhere! Every day Cookie finds more trouble. Remember Cookie is a cat and cats get *into* things. So every time Cookie finds trouble, the stuff that is inside comes out. What do you think comes out of a garbage can? I bet you know! Read and find out what happens with Cookie."

Although much of the vocabulary used won't be in the reader's sight vocabulary, it will be familiar because these are everyday items supported by the illustrations: *garbage, dirt, clothes, curtains.*

Cookie's Week is also a list book and can be used as such for writing and for reading. Having a particular structure, such as the list, can give a book a predictable pattern that young readers can depend on. One teacher introduced *Cookie's Week* to a group of first graders like this: "We've been thinking and talking about list books. What makes a list book, a list book?"

Illustrator
Tomie dePaola

Publisher
Penguin Putnam, 1988

ISBN
0698114353

TC Level
4

One little boy said, "It tells about one kind of thing, like ice cream. My ice cream list has chocolate, vanilla, strawberry and "chunky monkey" on it." The teacher continued, "That's right. Lists are usually about the same kind of thing, or for one particular kind of thing. In *Cookie's Week*, this is a list of what Cookie the cat does every day of the week. On Monday, Cookie falls in the toilet. On every other day of the week, Cookie does something else until we get to Sunday, then on Sunday, it changes a little. What Cookie does on Sunday isn't like what she's done on the other days. Think about that when you get to the last page." The teacher may then give copies of the book to each reader, asking students to make a prediction about what might happen next.

Genre
Picture Book

Teaching Uses
Whole Group Instruction; Independent Reading

Corduroy
Don Freeman

Book Summary

Corduroy is a teddy bear that lives in the toy department of a big store. He is waiting for someone to buy him so he can have a real home. One day Lisa and her mom are shopping. Lisa falls in love with Corduroy but her mom says that she does not have enough money to buy Corduroy that day. Lisa's mom also points out that Corduroy is missing a button from his overalls and therefore might not be a good choice. That night Corduroy searches the store for his missing button and ends up in the furniture department. When Corduroy tries to yank what he thinks is his lost button from a mattress, he knocks over a lamp and the security guard comes. He takes Corduroy back to the toy department. Sadly, Corduroy still has no button. The next day Lisa returns to the store with money from her piggy bank. She buys Corduroy and carries him home in her arms. She sews on another button, and hugs him. Corduroy knows that he has at last found a home and a friend.

Basic Book Information

Corduroy is regarded as a classic. Freeman has written many other favorites, including *A Pocket for Corduroy*, *Beady Bear*, *Mop Top* and *A Rainbow of My Own*.

Noteworthy Features

Corduroy is a Level 7 book-and as such, it's way too hard for most kindergartners and early first graders to read. But the story is so irresistible that children ask to hear the book read aloud again and again.

Teaching Ideas

In the A Library, this book is intended primarily for use as an emergent literacy read aloud. This instruction is based on the research of Elizabeth Sulzby, whose work with kindergarten children informed her of the importance of recreating parent-child interactions around books in the kindergarten classroom. At home, children often ask parents to "read it again" when they hear a favorite story. In school, the teacher's multiple readings of emergent literacy books helps children become familiar with rich narrative, hear the inflection and pacing of storybook language, and learn to use detailed illustrations to assist them in remembering storyline.

After the story has been read to them at least four times, multiple copies should be added to a basket of books called, for example, "Stories We Love." Teachers can give children opportunities to return to these books at independent reading time. They will refer to the pictures and use their

Illustrator
Don Freeman

Publisher
Scholastic, 196

ISBN
0140501738

TC Level
7

memory of the teacher's reading to recreate the story in their rereading. Given the opportunity to do this, children pass through different reading stages from simply "labeling" pictures on the page, to telling the story off the pictures using progressively more dialogue and storybook language, and then moving toward a more "conventional" reading which closely resembles the print on the page. To go on this reading journey, it is important for children to hear the story read aloud many times, have a lot of opportunities to reread it to a partner, and to have a supportive teacher nearby who thoughtfully coaches into their reading.

In the B Library, and later in the school year in the A Library, *Corduroy* can be used as an accountable talk read aloud. The first time a teacher reads it, he may want to think aloud in ways that model a response to the book. For example, the teacher might look at the cover of the book, while quietly saying, "I love to read the title of a book and look at the cover, don't you?" then something like, "I'm noticing this cute little bear. I wonder if his name is Corduroy because look, his overalls are made of corduroy? That's a funny name for a bear and for a book. I wonder if the book will be about his overalls? Let's read on. . . . " In a similar way, the teacher might demonstrate one of these reading behaviors during our read aloud sessions: pausing to show children that readers raise questions; speculating about what might happen next; connecting one page of the book with another, and so forth. Of course, teachers will want to be careful that they don't pause too often for these comments. For kindergarten children, especially, it's not advisable to offer weighty lectures about metacognitive processes. Children do, however, benefit from living alongside richly literate adults who sweep children up in their own literacy.

At another reading of *Corduroy*, the teacher might use her inflection to get children wondering, noticing, or anticipating. At passages, which the teacher expects will elicit a response, he might say, "Is your head full of ideas? Turn and talk with a partner." After children have been in school for a while, each child can be assigned a "turn and talk partner." We'll ask them to always sit beside this partner during the read aloud and soon they will have practiced this ritual enough that the logistics become smooth.

The first time a turn and talk is suggested, some children are likely to feel they don't have a lot to say. However, by getting onto the rug and conferring with one or two partnerships, teachers can help children to respond to text and share ideas with each other. It usually isn't advisable to have children report back on their partnership talks to the whole group, because the book is waiting. Creating long intervals for discussion can interrupt the thread of the story.

We might preface another reading of *Corduroy* by telling children that readers reread books often and each time they notice new things about the story. Perhaps the conversation will focus on, "What are you noticing that you didn't notice before?" Over time children's focus can be steered in a particular direction. For example, it could be suggested that readers pay attention to the characters in a story. "Let's really think about Lisa and what she's like," the teacher could say. Alternatively, the teacher might say, "Sometimes I read a book and think, 'Do I agree?' 'Do I disagree?'" This latter prompt could yield some interesting conversation because the teacher (or child) may say, "I disagree with the idea that Corduroy doesn't deserve to be chosen because he is missing a button! That's like saying you can't be adopted if part of you is injured. . . . And how come when Lisa gets Corduroy home, she quickly replaces his missing button and only then hugs him!" The point, of course, won't be to teach this or any other set of ideas about this book, but it is crucial to show children that, as Purves has said, "Books are tools to think with."

Book Connections

In talking and responding to books we can compare books by the same author or about the same characters. The book *A Pocket For Corduroy* would provide a natural opportunity for children to understand that knowing a character in one book may help us to better understand a character in another book.

Genre
Picture Book

Teaching Uses
Partnerships; Read Aloud; Critique; Interpretation; Language Conventions

Daniel's Duck
Clyde Robert Bulla

Book Summary

Daniel and his family live in a cabin in the mountains of Tennessee during frontier times. During the long winter, the father made Indian moccasins to bring to the spring fair in the valley and the mother made quilts. Both Daniel and his brother, Jeff, try to craft a wood carving, wishing they could carve as well as the famed Henry Pettigrew, whose birds look as if they could fly and horses look as if they could run. The day of the fair arrives and people laugh in response to the duck that Daniel has carved. Seeing this, Daniel grabs the duck and runs red-faced to the river to throw the duck in. But Henry Pettigrew comes after him, explains the laughter, admires Daniel's duck and asks if Daniel will sell it to him. He promises to show Daniel his carvings after the fair and the story ends as Daniel gives his duck to Henry Pettigrew.

Basic Book Information

Clyde Robert Bulla has written many books for children who are just beginning to read chapter books. Teachers will probably know his book, *The Chalk Box Kid,* and may want to search for his other titles.

This book is part of the HarperCollins, *I Can Read* series, which began with Else Holmelund Minarik's book *Little Bear.* That book paved the way for a host of other books to be written with short-enough chapters and a simple-enough plot to be suitable for readers who are just transitioning into chapter books. This is considered a Level 3 *I Can Read* book, designed for what Harper calls, "the newly independent reader."

Noteworthy Features

One of the unusual features about this book is that although it's titled *Daniel's Duck*, for the first half of the book Daniel doesn't stand out from his brother, Jeff, who also carves. It's only toward the end that the story zooms in to focus on Daniel.

This book looks like an early chapter book, but it doesn't have chapters. Thus, it would be much easier for children to read, if it did have chapters with explicit titles such as "The Long Winter," "The Spring Fair," and "Daniel's Duck."

The book is a bit more challenging because it is historic fiction, making the events a bit less accessible to youngsters. The activities Jeff, Daniel and their parents do aren't those that readers will be apt to do or may be familiar with. These characters make woodcarvings, Indian moccasins and warm quilts. The text alone doesn't convey all the information about the historic content; the pictures also "tell" of bathing in a tin tub and traveling by horse-drawn wagon.

Illustrator
Joan Sandin

Publisher
HarperTrophy, 1979

ISBN
0064440311

TC Level
6

Teaching Ideas

For a child who is just reading books of this level, *Daniel's Duck* poses a few special challenges. One comes from the fact that it isn't broken into chapters with stopping points, nor are children given a table of contents that previews each upcoming section of the book. A teacher might point these things out to a reader and say, "If you don't have chapter titles to set you up and let you know the main topic of a chapter, it can help to turn through the pages of the book and try to get a sense of what the main story will be." When doing this, it helps to turn rather briskly through the pages because any one picture could launch zillions of different possible stories. But if the reader continues to look to the next and next and next page, the array of possibilities narrows into a storyline that is discernible.

A teacher may suggest that children give themselves stopping places by putting Post-its on certain pages, and use these stopping places to make meaning: pages 5-15 tell mostly about the brothers and the hobby of wood carving, pages 15-30 tell about the long winter, pages 31-41 tell about the fair, and page 42-64 is the story of Daniel's duck.

If the children meet later with a partner to talk about the book, they may discuss any of these questions: How is life in Daniel's world different than it is now? Bulla often writes about the theme of children with artistic leanings who yearn to be recognized and supported in their artwork. Daniel is also an artist. What is Bulla saying about art? How this book is like and unlike Bulla's other books, particularly *The Chalk Box Kid*.

Book Connections

Another book by Bulla with a similar theme is *The Chalk Box Kid*. Whereas "The Chalk Box Kid" draws chalk-art in an abandoned city lot, Daniel carves a wooden duck in his Tennessee mountain cabin.

Genre
Historical Fiction; Short Chapter Book

Teaching Uses
Independent Reading; Partnerships; Author Study

A Field Guide to the Classroom Library, Lucy Calkins and the Teachers College Reading and Writing Project, Heinemann, ©2002 Teachers College, Columbia University; http://www.heinemann.com/fieldguides

Danny and the Dinosaur Go to Camp

Syd Hoff

Book Summary

Danny takes his friend, the dinosaur, to summer camp with him. They enjoy themselves running races, playing football, rowing, writing letters home and hiking. Danny's dinosaur adds a special twist to each activity, such as acting as Danny's boat, or carrying everyone when they're tired of hiking! All of the campers and the counselor, Lana, discover how great it is to have a dinosaur as a friend.

Basic Book Information

Danny and the Dinosaur go to Camp is part of the *An I Can Read Book* series. There are 32 pages with one to four sentences per page. Quotation marks and exclamation points are used simply throughout. There is a lot of dialogue but all of it is referenced. The references always come at the beginning or the end of the sentence. Each page is brightly illustrated and always matches at least one sentence of text on a page. The majority of the text is written with high frequency words, such as: *went, along, friend, said, you're, first, ever, had, here, let's, took, everybody, nobody, children, shouted,* and *wrote.* A few more difficult words may cause a problem for the emergent reader such as: *toasted, marshmallows, tight, vacation, carried* and *breakfast.*

Noteworthy Features

Children will love this simple funny tale of Danny and his dinosaur in the familiar world of sleep-away camp. Although the text is very simple, Syd Hoff does a good job of creating humor by placing the dinosaur in activities that are familiar for children, but silly for a dinosaur, and then matching them with cartoonish, yet effective illustrations. The story is simple, though not well developed. But, in developing the fantasy that many children have of having a dinosaur as a loyal pet, it will hold the interest of most readers at this level.

Teachers may need to do some instruction with children who are unfamiliar with the concept of going to sleep-away camp.

Teaching Ideas

Danny and the Dinosaur Go to Camp may be used as a read aloud, in a guided reading group, as an independent reading book for early readers, or as part of an author study of Syd Hoff.

The most obvious and strongest characteristic of books written by Syd Hoff is the humor. When introducing *Danny and the Dinosaur Go to Camp*, a teacher may say; "This is the story of a boy who has a dinosaur as a friend.

Illustrator
Syd Hoff

Publisher
HarperCollins, 1996

ISBN
0064442446

TC Level
6

A Field Guide to the Classroom Library, Lucy Calkins and the Teachers College Reading and Writing Project, Heinemann, ©2002 Teachers College, Columbia University; http://www.heinemann.com/fieldguides

They go away to sleep-away camp and do lots of funny things together. Can you imagine some funny things you would do if you could bring a dinosaur to camp? Do you think a dinosaur could go to camp?" Readers will enjoy discussing their fantasies of what that could be like. In this way, the teacher can also work on personal connections to the story.

Readers who have mastered emergent skills such as: one-to-one matching, directionality, checking the picture against the text, or "getting their mouths ready" for an unfamiliar word, can use this book to support those behaviors. At the same time, this book also enables children to attempt new skills. Some of these skills include: reading text that doesn't have pictures that match fully, reading longer sentences, reading in a character's voice (using quotation marks and punctuation), tackling harder high frequency words and reading with increasing fluency and sustainability.

Teachers may work with readers on developing self-checking skills, strategies for figuring out unfamiliar words (such as using context, rereading, looking for the unfamiliar word in other parts of the text etc.), retelling the story for fuller comprehension and how to talk about funny, interesting or confusing parts with other readers.

If used as part of an author study, teachers may discuss the ways in which most Syd Hoff books are alike. (For example, most Syd Hoff books have a child with an unlikely animal friend, and the animal characters talk. Also there are very few sentences on each page.) Readers might also discover and discuss recurring characters, like Danny and the dinosaur.

Book Connections

Danny and the Dinosaur Go to Camp is one of three books about Danny and his dinosaur. The other titles are: *Danny and the Dinosaur* and *Happy Birthday, Danny and the Dinosaur!* Other titles by Syd Hoff at a similar reading level are: *Sammy the Seal, Captain Cat, Oliver, Stanley* and *The Firehouse Cat.*

Genre
Emergent Literacy Book

Teaching Uses
Author Study; Whole Group Instruction; Independent Reading; Small Group Strategy Instruction; Interpretation; Language Conventions; Character Study

Fishing

Annette Smith

Book Summary

The book begins on Monday as the main character goes fishing with his mom. It continues to list the days of fishing with dad, a big sister and a big brother, and the whole family. On each of these days, the narrator doesn't catch a fish, then he goes fishing with his grandmother, catches a fish...and the next day fishes with her again.

Basic Book Information

The PM Readers is a series published by Rigby. The PM Readers tend to come in kits where every book looks exactly like every other book. Some teachers think this is less than ideal because at every level, a library should be full of books where each has its own individuality. On the other hand, the PM Readers are an important resource for teachers because first, there are many of these at the early reading levels and second, the publishers recognize the supports that early readers need and offer these. The PM Readers are especially good at providing a lot of easy text, full of high frequency words. PM Readers use complete sentences (e.g., "I see the cow./ I see the pig./ I see the horse.") to reinforce the repetition of high frequency words.

Finally, the PM Readers are special because a great many of even the earliest books are stories. It's nice to be able to also give beginning readers the opportunity to read stories that not only have problems and resolutions but also characters across a series.

Noteworthy Features

The text has large print, consistently placed throughout the text. The simple text, highly to moderately matched to illustrations, supports early reading behaviors such as one-to-one matching and directionality. The repetitive structure appears on each page with one simple pattern change on the second to last page. Sentences have natural language structure ("On __ I went fishing with my___."). The familiar words *On, I,* and *my* appear on most pages, helping to anchor children to the text. High frequency words include: *On, I, went, fishing, with,* and *my.*

Teaching Ideas

Teachers may want to introduce *Fishing* as a book where a boy lists the people he goes fishing with on each day of the week. On the first page, he says that on Monday, he went fishing with his mom. (The pattern can be elicited from the child, with the child working on the words *I* and *my*). Read to find out who else went fishing with the boy.

Illustrator
Karen Young

Publisher
Rigby, 1996

ISBN
0763541737

TC Level
2

A Field Guide to the Classroom Library, Lucy Calkins and the Teachers College Reading and Writing Project, Heinemann, ©2002 Teachers College, Columbia University; http://www.heinemann.com/fieldguides

Children who have not yet mastered one-to-one matching or who do not yet check the picture against the first letter may substitute *he* for *I*. "Check again," the teacher will say. Although the pattern is consistent, the three lines of text per page might make it difficult for the child to follow and stick with the story, particularly if one-to-one matching and return sweep haven't been mastered, or if the child does not yet have a bank of sight words.

Children may notice the different forms fishing takes depends on whether the child is accompanied by Mom and the sister (in which case they resort to the rather primitive method of using string with a hook) or with the father or brother (who have proper rods, nets or even an entire boat). The reader may comment, "This isn't fair" which suggests that the child is already learning the value of reading critically, and being able to say, "I see the world this author has created and I disagree." It might also generate some interesting book talk conversation with a partner.

Genre
Emergent Literacy Book

Teaching Uses
Independent Reading; Partnerships; Interpretation; Critique

A Field Guide to the Classroom Library, Lucy Calkins and the Teachers College Reading and Writing Project, Heinemann, ©2002 Teachers College, Columbia University; http://www.heinemann.com/fieldguides

Fun With Hats

Lucy Malka

Book Summary

Three girls put on different hats, and each hat gives them a new identity. One hat allows a girl to be a clown, another hat allows a girl to be a pirate, and finally, in the last hat, a girl is a magician. At the end of the book, the reader is invited to put on a hat and decide what to be.

Basic Book Information

Lucy Malka, a literacy specialist in New York, wrote this Mondo book. As with many of the books in this series, there is a one-line summary sentence on the back cover that introduces the young reader to the book.

Fun With Hats is an 8-page pattern book with 38 words. The title is on the first page. All pages contain one line of print. There is change in the pattern on the last page. The text is consistently placed below the picture. The print is amply spaced to permit children to point to the words. Colorful illustrations are on each page. The events are presented in list format. There is no story sequence.

Noteworthy Features

This may be a more challenging text than others in the series for some readers because of the narrower spaces between words, the more complex sentence syntax and the somewhat ambiguous pictures.

Although the book follows a natural speech pattern ("I put on a hat. Now I am a...."), children might have some difficulty with the word *now*. If the teacher does a book introduction, it may be important to guide the children in repeating the phrase, "Now I am a...."

Teaching Ideas

One way to enter the book is to use the cover to predict what the book might be about. The teacher might say, "This book is called *Fun With Hats*. The cover can help us know about the book. What do you see on the cover?" The picture and blurb on the back cover can also be introduced. The teacher might say, "Let's look at the back cover. What do you see in the picture? Why are there hats in the picture?" If this is the first time the reader is encountering a blurb, the teacher might say, "The words under the picture tell us about the book. Listen while I read them to you."

The topic of dressing up and pretending is familiar to many children. There are many details in the pictures such as a trunk, a variety of hats hanging on hooks, and the costumes the girls will use to become the "clown," the "pirate" and the "magician." The teacher may need to help children define these words and crosscheck the pictures. Readers will need

Illustrator
Melinda Levine

Publisher
Mondo, 1995

ISBN
1572550430

TC Level
1

to have the vocabulary to identify each costume and crosscheck the pictures. Children may also have to search the pictures to determine who is dressing up and who is talking. The assortment of hats on the last page allows children to make choices and entices them to reread the book.

A student who is reading this book should be able to point to the words as he is reading. This is a great book for the child who has been doing this for some time, because the spacing isn't as large as it is in other books. The pattern also becomes more sophisticated. Rather than one-line patterns that children may have come to expect, this pattern has two parts: "I put on _____./ Now I am a _____."

To encourage the use of crosschecking, a teacher might ask, "How did you know that the girl said, 'Now I am a magician'?" A reader might explain that she used the picture as a context clue. A teacher could follow up by asking a crosschecking question, such as, "What letter would you expect to see at the beginning of the word *magician*?"

Children who choose this book will enjoy talking about it. As they thumb through the book, the pictures can lead to great discussions. Because the pictures contain many details, much of the conversation may not center around the written story. On page3, for example, a child might talk about the poodle doing tricks rather than the girl in the hat. On alternating pages, there is a toy box loaded with different hats, and children love to imagine the chosen hat and what it represents. Children who are given many opportunities to have book conversations in partnerships will end up being much more successful when they do tackle the print.

The last page is where many readers experience the most difficulty. Suddenly the reader is invited into the conversation. Not only does the pattern break, but the sentence begins with *you*. A sentence that begins with *what* follows, which creates another possible difficulty. In a teaching lesson at the end, the teacher might want to show how the *-ow* in now is the same as the *-ow* in clown. But if the reader needs less support, then the teacher might say: "Readers have to pay close attention to the words on the page. Sometimes at the end of a pattern book, there is a change. You have to use the pictures and the letters to help you figure out what the words say."

Genre
Picture Book

Teaching Uses
Independent Reading; Small Group Strategy Instruction; Interpretation; Partnerships; Language Conventions

Good Night, Little Kitten

Nancy Christensen

Book Summary

It's time for Little Kitten to go to bed, yet that's the last thing that Little Kitten wants to do. Little Kitten would much rather play with the blocks, the fire engine, and the rocking horse. Little Kitten's Mama and Papa keep saying, "Good Night, Little Kitten." Little Kitten replies, " I want to stay up." Finally, Mama and Papa get no response. When they go to look, they find the kitten curled up on the window seat and fast asleep.

Basic Book Information

This is a 29-page book with colorful illustrations by Dennis Hockerman on every page. The pages are numbered. There is a controlled vocabulary consisting of 24 words in this book. The words are listed on the inside cover.

Noteworthy Features

The pictures in this book are very engaging. The whole cat family, Mama, Papa, and Little Kitten all live like humans. Talk about the cat's pajamas! This little kitten is fully decked out in polka dot jammies! Children love to look at the small details in the illustrations, like the hanging picture that Little Kitten drew and the abundance of toys in the bedroom. If young readers turn to the back cover, they'll find yet another scene with Little Kitten. The illustrations, as well as the sentences, are laid out across a two-page spread.

The sentences may seem a bit awkward to adult readers because of the controlled vocabulary. However, in the words of the publisher, "These 24 words are repeated through the story, so that young readers will be able to easily recognize words and understand their meaning."

Good Night, Little Kitten contains a lot of dialogue. All of the dialogue is referenced, which makes it easier for readers who are new to this literary device. Some children may find the dialogue a bit confusing. When Little Kitten's parents say, "Good Night, Little Kitten," they are implying that it is time for him to go to sleep. Children might not make this inference and wonder why Little Kitten's parents keep saying "Good Night, Little Kitten" repetitively, when it is clear that Little Kitten has heard them, has continued playing, and is not interested in going to bed.

Teaching Ideas

Because one sentence is continued over the course of two pages, it may make the phrasing of this book more difficult for early readers to follow. This can be an opportunity to demonstrate the importance of attending to punctuation. This book also presents a chance to introduce quotation marks

Illustrator
Dennis Hockerman

Publisher
Children's Press, 1990

ISBN
051605354X

TC Level
3

A Field Guide to the Classroom Library, Lucy Calkins and the Teachers College Reading and Writing Project, Heinemann, ©2002 Teachers College, Columbia University; http://www.heinemann.com/fieldguides

to students. Teachers may want to read aloud *Good Night, Little Kitten* to demonstrate how punctuation may affect the intonation of your voice as you read. In partnerships, readers will have fun practicing this.

As in all books for the very earliest readers, in *Good Night, Little Kitten* one-to-one matching may not come easily to the child. Teachers can remind students who still need to point under the words, to point crisply under each of the words. Students should also be monitoring to see if there are any words left to point to after they finish reading a line. If there are, students should be aware of this error and be able to self-correct.

There are a number of ellipses throughout *Good Night, Little Kitten*. For children in the upper-elementary grades, this book can be used in a writing workshop. It demonstrates one use of the ellipsis, and therefore, will present a clear message to children who want to begin using this punctuation in their writing. For children in the lower grades, it is important for teachers to explain what this kind of ellipsis means and to model how an ellipsis affects the reading of a text.

Upon inspection of this book, teachers may note the presence of gender stereotypes. Papa cat reads the newspaper while Mama folds the laundry, knits, and dons an apron. This is not a reason to ban the book from the library, but instead can be used by teachers to have discussions with children about other activities and roles moms and dads may take on, in a variety of family configurations. Teachers will want to make sure that their classroom libraries reflect the experiences of their student population.

Genre
Picture Book; Emergent Literacy Book

Teaching Uses
Independent Reading; Language Conventions; Read Aloud; Teaching Writing; Critique; Partnerships

A Field Guide to the Classroom Library, Lucy Calkins and the Teachers College Reading and Writing Project, Heinemann, ©2002 Teachers College, Columbia University; http://www.heinemann.com/fieldguides

Good-Night, Little Brother

Jenny Hessell

Book Summary

Big sister tricks little brother into going to sleep by having him perform each step of getting ready for bed just to "show" teddy how he puts his pajamas on, gets under his blankets and so forth.

Basic Book Information

This little book has 8 numbered pages. On each left-hand page, there are five lines of print. Little brother says he doesn't want to go to bed. Big sister responds that he does not have to, but requests that he performs one more step to show teddy. On the last page, big sister says good-night to little brother, who is sleeping.

Noteworthy Features

The pattern in this book supports readers from page to page, but there is little within each page on which the reader can lean. The pictures do illustrate the text, but they don't always lend clues to the reader for the new words on each page. While the sister is holding up pajamas on the page when little brother is supposed to get into them, there is no easy way to convey "get under the covers," or "close your eyes" with the illustrations.

Teaching Ideas

In addition to the print work support that this book offers, similar to that of other books at about this level, the book also offers some unique opportunities for thinking deeply about books. What is really going on in this little story? Kids have to try to figure out what big sister is really thinking, in opposition to what she says. Some readers may argue that the sister really does want to show teddy how to go to bed, while others may realize that she is using a clever trick to help her brother get to bed. If there is a disagreement on this matter, it will be a challenge for each reader to explain why she is right. In some cases, readers rely on evidence outside of the book to try to support their point. In some cases, children argue that little brother isn't asleep at all on the last page; he is only showing teddy how to close his eyes, just as his sister asked. The work of figuring out who is probably right is challenging reading work.

Sometimes, readers discuss whether the trick big sister plays is a nice one or a mean one. Is she being fair? Is she ignoring her little brother's feelings? Some kids wonder where the parents are throughout this nighttime ritual-why aren't *they* the ones putting the little boy to bed? Many children will notice that although there are books beside the bed, this child goes to sleep without a bedtime story. Imagine that!

Illustrator
Lyn Kriegler

Publisher
Rigby, 1989

ISBN
07010184X

TC Level
3

A Field Guide to the Classroom Library, Lucy Calkins and the Teachers College Reading and Writing Project, Heinemann, ©2002 Teachers College, Columbia University; http://www.heinemann.com/fieldguides

Book Connections

This book has interesting parallels to the PM Reader, *Ben's Teddy Bear,* and the other books about Ben. How is this little boy like and unlike Ben? He, too, keeps his clothes on the chair beside his bed. His teddy resembles Ben's teddy and both boys have a shelf of books beside the bed. This boy is much younger, less independent... and he has a big sister.

Genre

Emergent Literacy Book

Teaching Uses

Critique; Independent Reading; Character Study; Interpretation

A Field Guide to the Classroom Library, Lucy Calkins and the Teachers College Reading and Writing Project, Heinemann, ©2002 Teachers College, Columbia University; http://www.heinemann.com/fieldguides

Growing Colors

Bruce McMillan

Book Summary

Each right-hand page contains a full color close-up photograph of a fruit or vegetable plant. Each left-hand page has a smaller color photograph of the fruit in its natural habitat, and an extra large word in color, labeling the color of the fruit or vegetable (e.g., GREEN written in the color green). At the end of the book there are two pages full of reduced-size photographs. Each one is placed in between the word for its color and its name.

Basic Book Information

This informative nonfiction book about the colors, names, and parent plants of common fruits and vegetables is published by Mulberry. It's an oversized book that will stand out in many early libraries.

Noteworthy Features

Many Level 1 and Level 2 books are nonfiction books with a list structure, but this one is special because it looks like nonfiction books that more experienced readers will read.

Teaching Ideas

This basic nonfiction text has many features of more advanced nonfiction texts, and so it can be used to introduce children to the genre and to features of nonfiction. The two pages of reduced-size photographs and accompanying labels at the end of the book are like an index. Although this list doesn't have page numbers, readers can still learn that the back of nonfiction books often have listings of what the book contains. They can also learn to move back and forth between the reference page, with all its labels and reduced photographs, and the text of the book itself. This moving back and forth between pages while following one idea is a strategy readers of nonfiction must learn. Readers can learn the name of the fruit or vegetable and then turn back to the page on which it first appeared to get a closer look at it. Because the page numbers are not in this "index," readers must attend closely to the photograph or the color word.

Readers can also use these back pages-if they can maneuver between them and the main text of the book-to confirm or revise their guesses as to what the crops are. Are those round things oranges or apricots? What will the word look like if it is apricots? If children are reading in partnerships, they can check the back pages to verify their predictions.

This book stimulates thinking about its illustrations. In it, the reader has to figure out how the pictures relate to one another. Why is this picture of the tree put together with the word "purple" and the picture of the fruit?

Publisher
Mulberry Books, 1988

ISBN
0688131123

TC Level
1

Why are there these bushy plants near this picture of the yellow vegetable? And what are these tan things? The book shows pictures of the vegetables in various stages of maturity in some pictures, and children will have to figure out for themselves that it is the same plant and same crop. Some children who are familiar with basic fruits and vegetables may be surprised at the varieties of colors these crops come in. Brown peppers? The seemingly odd colors may also provoke questions as to the why's and how's of plants and crops. With a very small amount of text, the book creates fuel for a lot of thinking, wondering, and discussion about the plants it pictures. It may even provoke children to want to try to taste these fruits and vegetables, or grow some themselves if the climate is suitable.

In the A library, this book could be used as part of a reading center that is focused on books about colors. Teachers can introduce this center in a variety of ways. All of the mini-lessons can be centered on this genre. Then, children can choose from a variety of label books. (e.g., Label Books about Food, ABC Label Books, Label Books about Numbers, Label Books about Animals, Label Books about Colors, etc.). Another possibility is to do a nonfiction study as a whole class. Then, centers could have books on a variety of different nonfiction subjects.

Book Connections

In the A Library, this book could be paired in a center with Tana Hoban's *Is it Red? Is It Yellow? Is It Blue?* Ellen Walsh's *Mouse Paint* and Leo Lionni's *Little Blue and Little Yellow*.

Genre
Nonfiction; Picture Book

Teaching Uses
Content Area Study; Reading and Writing Nonfiction; Partnerships; Whole Group Instruction; Small Group Strategy Instruction

Harriet, You'll Drive Me Wild!
Mem Fox

Book Summary

In this delightful picture book, Mem Fox tells the story of a pesky daughter and a mother who doesn't like to yell, but eventually loses her temper. Harriet Harris doesn't mean to be pesky; sometimes she just can't help it. Her mother doesn't mean to lose her temper, but after a day of knocked-over juice, dribbled jam and a ripped feather pillow, the formerly patient mother just does. They both realize, in the end, that sometimes they just do things they wish they hadn't. Most importantly, the lesson we learn is that despite the yelling and tears, the mother and her daughter still love each other very much.

Basic Book Information

The 30-page book is filled with glorious illustrations that bring the daughter and her mother to life while complementing the writing. The use of dialogue and repetition in this book make it a cherished read aloud choice.

Noteworthy Features

This picture book by Australian writer Mem Fox is an excellent read aloud. With this text, it might be useful for the teacher to practice reading it aloud as it will be far more effective if the teacher is familiar with the text. Because Mem Fox is a true wordsmith, this book is filled with alliteration and other literary devices.

Teaching Ideas

When students read this grand book (and others like it) aloud, we will want to ask them to pay attention to parts of the text that sound good to their ears and feel good on their tongues. What has the author done to make our ears perk up?

This is an excellent book for helping students pay respectful attention to punctuation and to the way the text has been written, ie., the way it appears on the page. Students will note the italics of key words: *darling*, *you*, and *they* in the story, and the large or bold print. These things should change the voice of the reader.

When we read the book aloud a second or third time, or when students read it on their own, it will be important to pause and notice that the story takes place in one day, and how time is moving within the narrative. Movement of time, an important story element, is clearly demonstrated in this book.

At the beginning of a unit of study on the elements of story, this simple text could be used to point out all of the elements that authors use to

Illustrator
Marla Frazee

Publisher
Harcourt, 2000

ISBN
0152019774

A Field Guide to the Classroom Library, Lucy Calkins and the Teachers College Reading and Writing Project, Heinemann, ©2002 Teachers College, Columbia University; http://www.heinemann.com/fieldguides

construct stories. In this book, the story elements are quite straightforward. For example, there are only two characters, the mother and Harriet; the setting is clearly the house; and the movement through time is highlighted by words such as "At lunch...." and "Later that afternoon...." What is happening in the plot is clear both in the illustrations and in the words that tell of Harriet's constant disasters. Both Harriet and her mother are changed just a bit by the end of the story. The balance of narrative and dialogue helps the reader stay interested, and also moves the story along at a steady pace.

In class discussions, readers will have many responses to this book. Many will feel it reminds us that all relationships are filled with times of both tenderness and turmoil. Perhaps readers will respond to the text by reflecting on ways they deal with anger themselves. They may also talk about the regrets characters have in this story, and any they may have in their own lives. Students may want to talk or write about how they feel when they do something that they didn't mean to do.

Students who enjoyed this book might want to read other books by Mem Fox to compare and contrast characters, events and themes. Perhaps this book can be a part of a Mem Fox author study.

Book Connections

Harriet, You'll Drive Me Wild! is just one of Mem Fox's highly acclaimed books. She is also the author of *Tough Boris, Koala Lou, Possum Magic, Shoes From Grandpa, and Wilfrid Gordon McDonald Partridge*.

Genre
Picture Book

Teaching Uses
Read Aloud; Interpretation; Language Conventions; Author Study; Independent Reading; Teaching Writing

A Field Guide to the Classroom Library, Lucy Calkins and the Teachers College Reading and Writing Project, Heinemann, ©2002 Teachers College, Columbia University; http://www.heinemann.com/fieldguides

Henry and Mudge in Puddle Trouble
Cynthia Rylant

Book Summary

Henry and Mudge in Puddle Trouble is one in a series of books about a boy and his lovable 180-pound dog who do everything together. This is the second book of their adventures. There are three separate, yet connected stories in the book. In "The Snow Glory," Henry tries and tries to resist picking a beautiful flower in his garden. When he finally decides he can resist no longer, he confesses to Mudge, but Mudge eats it! At first, Henry is really angry, but quickly realizes that the flower never belonged to him anyway. In "Puddle Trouble," Henry and Mudge spend all afternoon splashing in a muddy puddle. Henry's father finds them in the middle of their adventure and it appears he is going to be really angry. At the last moment, when Henry is feeling remorseful, his father jumps in to play with them! In "The Kittens," Henry and Mudge are excited about, and then protective of, the kittens next door. Mudge "adopts" them. One day, while Henry is at school, Mudge saves the kittens from an uncertain fate, when a strange dog comes "sniffing around."

Basic Book Information

Henry and Mudge in Puddle Trouble is the second book in a series of books about the same characters, written by Cynthia Rylant. The book is 47 pages long, separated into three individual stories. The stories are listed in a table of contents. The stories do not rely upon each other, but they are connected by a subtle theme: it is a springtime book. Each story is between 12 and 15 pages long and is brightly illustrated. Some of the illustrations are full page, and some are at the top, bottom or middle of a page. Many of the sentences are short and straightforward, but there are several examples of longer, more complicated sentence structures and vocabulary. Simple question marks, exclamation points and quotation marks are used throughout the book.

This series focuses on the relationship between Henry and Mudge and their adventures together. The whole series does not necessarily have to be read in order. The books from the series that contain the character Annie, Henry's cousin, are best read sequentially because a storyline develops over the course of the three Annie books. Many of the books in this series have short stories connected by a theme such as winter, moving, or a birthday.

Noteworthy Features

The text of *Henry and Mudge in Puddle Trouble* is simply, yet beautifully written. There are many "big" concepts (of friendship, family, childhood fears, love, etc.) that are subtly woven into the text. For example, on page

Series
Henry and Mudge

Illustrator
Suçie Stevenson

Publisher
Aladdin, 1987

ISBN
0689810032

TC Level
6

18, the text states, "Henry knew it wasn't his snow glory. He knew it wasn't anybody's snow glory. Just a thing to let grow. And if someone ate it, it was just a thing to let go." There are many places in the series where these subtle themes are alluded to, but not directly written into the text. This adds to the depth and the interest level of these sweet stories. It also makes them great opportunities for discussions. There are many humorous sections in each story-usually something Mudge does-which are easily enjoyed and understood.

Teaching Ideas

The characters of Henry and Mudge (as well as other minor characters that appear throughout the series) are not particularly well developed. Also, the setting in many of the books stays the same throughout the book. This should make it easier for young readers to follow and enjoy the story. Some italics and capital letters are used for emphasis. Some young readers may need instruction on how to read those words.

Each story can be studied with a closer look at the story elements. All stories have characters, a setting, a plot, movement through time, and a change that's central to the plot and/or the characters. Readers may think about how much time goes by in each of the three stories. It's also thought-provoking to reread the stories looking to see if each one has a single turning point.

There are many other *Henry and Mudge* books that retain most of the same characters and introduce new ones, while maintaining the same level of vocabulary and content as the first few books. In book or partnership discussions, readers may compare and discuss ways in which the books are similar and different, how the author's voice is consistent from book to book, and whether the characters, settings and plots have changed or remained the same. For example, a teacher may say, "I notice that in the story called 'The Snow Glory', Henry starts to feel angry when Mudge eats the flower. But when he looks at Mudge with his soft brown eyes and his big head, he just feels full of love for him. Henry felt the same way in the first book, *Henry and Mudge*, after Mudge came back from being lost."

Book Connections

Henry and Mudge in Puddle Trouble is part of a large series of books about the same characters. Some other titles include: *Henry and Mudge Under the Yellow Moon*, *Henry and Mudge in the Green Time*, *Henry and Mudge and the Happy Cat*, *Henry and Mudge and the Careful Cousin*, and *Henry and Mudge and the Forever Sea*. Other books that are near the same level in vocabulary, content and theme are the *Little Bear* books by Else Holmelund Minarik and, at a slightly more advanced level, the *Oliver Pig* books by Jean Van Leeuwen.

Genre
Emergent Literacy Book

A Field Guide to the Classroom Library, Lucy Calkins and the Teachers College Reading and Writing Project, Heinemann, ©2002 Teachers College, Columbia University; http://www.heinemann.com/fieldguides

Teaching Uses
Independent Reading; Interpretation; Language Conventions; Partnerships;
Author Study

Hermit Crab

Beverley Randell

Book Summary

The book begins, "Hermit Crab is at home. She is inside a shell. She is too big for this little shell." Because she has outgrown her shell, she looks for a bigger one. She finds a big shell, but there is a crab in it. A hungry fish comes along and sees the hermit crab. Just in the nick of time, hermit crab finds a big shell and jumps inside. Hermit crab is safe in her new shell.

Basic Book Information

The PM Storybooks, developed in New Zealand and published by Rigby, place a priority on always including the traditional story elements. These texts include stories with characters, a problem and a resolution. The only exceptions are their very earliest books. The PM Readers are known for including a large number of high frequency words, and for controlling vocabulary so that in books of a comparable level of difficulty, the same high frequency words reoccur. The PM Readers use complete sentences to reinforce repetition of high frequency words and simple sentence syntax. But the fact that PM Readers include many high frequency words means that sometimes the resulting sentences seem stilted and unnatural.

Noteworthy Features

Though most stories are told in past tense, this text is written in present tense: "Hermit Crab is at home. She is inside a shell." Key words of significance are highlighted in bold type: **big, eat,** and finally, **safe.**

Teaching Ideas

A teacher may want to do a book introduction to support readers with this book. As the students look at the cover page, a teacher could say: "This is a picture of a hermit crab. Have you ever seen a hermit crab? This hermit crab has outgrown her shell, so she has to find a new one. She has to be careful when she takes her shell off because then she has no protection and another animal in the sea can easily eat her. Let's see if she can find a new shell."

This book is appropriate for readers learning to match one spoken word to one written one. The teacher can cue the reader to find a known sight word that will serve as an anchor for a one-to-one match. References can be made to the word wall in the classroom if the sight word is on it.

Teachers may also ask students to find an unknown word by using the initial letter. For example, "Can you find the word *home* on page 2? What letter would you expect *home* to start with?"

Opportunities to crosscheck are presented in this book. For example, there is a picture of a fish on page 8. A teacher might observe if the children

Sidebar

Illustrator
Julian Bruére

Publisher
Rigby, 1994

ISBN
0435066994

TC Level
3

use the picture as a source of information and then use the picture to check against the letters. The teacher can praise the children for doing this or show the children how to crosscheck one source of information with another.

The teacher may want to find opportunities in this book to teach for word-solving strategies. For example, the text uses the words *looking* and *going*. The teacher can call attention to the *-ing* chunk in one of these words and then turn to the other one and ask, "What do you notice?"

In addition, the teacher might focus on the compound words *today* and *inside*. Let the children know that they can solve a new word by thinking about a word or a chunk of a word that they already know.

A careful reader who checks for picture cues may notice that when Hermit Crab finds a large inviting shell, there is a bit of purple peeking out, foreshadowing the fact that the shell is already inhabited. It is interesting to see that the creature that has already moved into the bigger shell is another hermit crab. Although the bigger crab looks menacing, the big fish is portrayed as the real danger because he likes to eat hermit crabs.

A teacher may use the dramatic dialogue (typed in italics) on page 14 as an opportunity for a choral or shared reading of the text, or as an opportunity to extend the story through drama or a role-play.

Genre
Emergent Literacy Book

Teaching Uses
Independent Reading; Whole Group Instruction; Partnerships; Small Group Strategy Instruction; Language Conventions

Honey for Baby Bear

Beverley Randell

Illustrator
Isabel Lowe

Publisher
Rigby, 1994

ISBN
0435067192

TC Level
4

Book Summary

Baby Bear is busy eating some honey from a jar. He asks Mother Bear, "Who makes honey?" When Mother Bear replies that bees make honey, Baby Bear goes into the forest to look for bees. He sees them going into a tree and finds the honey, which he quickly eats. Baby Bear discovers that he is lost in the forest so he climbs up a big tree and sees Father Bear fishing in the river. Baby Bear shouts over to Father Bear that he is lost. Father Bear comes over to Baby Bear and takes him home to Mother Bear. Baby Bear tells Mother Bear that he got lost, but he is very proud that he found the honey.

Basic Book Information

The PM Storybooks, developed in New Zealand and published by Rigby, place a priority on including story elements. Even texts that at first appear to be lists are, in fact, stories with characters, a problem and a resolution. The only exceptions are their very earliest books. The PM Readers are known for including a large number of high frequency words, and for controlling vocabulary so that in books of a comparable level of difficulty, the same high frequency words reoccur. The PM Readers use complete sentences to reinforce repetition of high frequency words and simple sentence syntax. The fact that PM Readers include many high frequency words means that sometimes the resulting sentences seem stilted and unnatural.

Noteworthy Features

The book includes many high frequency words: *make, went, look, can, see, like, said, up, come, here,* and *go,* and the repetition of these will give readers a way into the new content on each page. This book will support early reading behaviors such as directionality, one-to-one correspondence, and monitoring of known and unknown words.

Illustrations provide moderate to high support. The author uses varied simple sentence patterns. One sentence has as many as thirteen words, but most sentences are short. Most pages have about six lines of print. The print is large and well spaced.

Teaching Ideas

This is a good book for a guided reading lesson. A possible introduction could be: "This book is called *Honey for Baby Bear.* What do you think Baby

Bear is doing on the cover? Baby Bear went looking for honey in the big forest and he got lost. Let's see what happens."

This book is appropriate for readers who have the early reading behaviors under control (i.e. directional movement, one-to-one matching, locating known and unknown words). The text will provide opportunities for readers to read longer text and make predictions. For example on page9, the teacher can ask the children to predict what Baby Bear might do now that he is lost.

The teacher can help the students practice putting together the process of using the information in the text: searching, checking, and using phonological information while reading on the run. For example on page 11, if the student read, "I can see the stream," the teacher might prompt the child to search by saying, "You said 'stream;' does that look right?" The teacher may then take the opportunity to observe if the child is crosschecking the picture with the word *river* or the teacher could also hold back support by saying to the child, "There was something wrong on this line. See if you can find what was wrong."

The teacher can use what she observes about the children's knowledge of letters, words, and use of strategies to plan for an extension of the lesson. She can select an example to teach for word-solving strategies. For example, the text uses the word *shouted* on page 13. The teacher can ask the children if there is anything that they know about the word *shouted* that would help them solve it. The teacher can also call attention to the *out* chunk by constructing it with magnetic letters and then add the *sh* blend to the beginning of *out*. If this is easy, other words can be generated to show the children how to link known information to solve unknown words: *out, shout, about, mouth, found*. A teacher may also want to talk about the *-ed* suffix and have the student add it onto the word *shout* with magnetic letters.

Teachers may also take the opportunity to teach the use of quotation marks, question marks, exclamation marks, periods, capital letters, and the use of bold print.

If the children have read *Father Bear goes fishing*, or *Blackberries*, the teacher and students might also have a discussion about the three books and the Bear Family. The author and illustrator may also be discussed.

Book Connections

Honey for Baby Bear is part of a series written by Beverley Randell. Other books in the series include *Father Bear goes fishing, Blackberries, Baby Bear goes fishing, Baby Bear's present, Baby Bear climbs a tree, Baby Bear's hiding place, House hunting* and *Father Bear's surprise*.

The theme of this book is strongly suggestive of Winnie-the-Pooh, and there are other interesting connections. For example, Baby Bear, like Winnie-the-Pooh, composes and sings a honey song.

Genre
Emergent Literacy Book

Teaching Uses

Independent Reading; Small Group Strategy Instruction; Whole Group Instruction; Partnerships; Language Conventions; Interpretation

I Love My Family

Joy Cowley

Book Summary

I Love My Family is narrated from the perspective of a young boy who talks about his love for each of his family members. ("I love my father . . . I love my mother. . . .") The story takes place at his sister's wedding. There is a twist ending, on the last page, when the boy finally talks about something that he does not love . . . his grandpa's whiskers.

Basic Book Information

This book contains 31 words spread out over 9 pages. There is one sentence per page, clearly printed in black font against a white background. The text can be found on the bottom of each page underneath a colorful illustration. Aside from the twist ending, each page begins with, "I love my . . ." There is only sentence that extends over more than one page, found on the last page of the book. For the most part, the illustrations support the text.

Noteworthy Features

The book is highly repetitive in structure and contains many high frequency words. Like many of the books in this library, the pattern of the book only changes on the last page. The last page of the book also varies from the rest of the text in difficulty level. The last page contains the first instance of a wrap-around sentence; a contraction (*don't*); a possessive (grandpa's) and the difficult and somewhat antiquated word, *whiskers*.

One of the most noteworthy features of this book is that the narrator must be inferred. The main character is never formally introduced in the text. Readers will probably deduce that the young boy's the narrator by looking at the illustrations. There is a young boy in each of them. And, if readers turn to the back cover, they will probably delight in finding a portrait of the young boy.

The change in the repetitive pattern and the location of the print on the last page offers chances to observe, and possibly teach, that the print carries the message.

Teaching Ideas

In a book introduction, the teacher may want to prepare the children by telling them that this is a book about a family. Elicit responses from students by asking, "What are some family words that we know?" In this way, the students will be thinking about words that they may face in the pages ahead. If a student suggests that the word *brother* is a family word, for example, a teacher can have the students in the group turn to page 5 and point to that word. The unfamiliar word *whiskers* and the contraction *don't* may also be

A Field Guide to the Classroom Library, Lucy Calkins and the Teachers College Reading and Writing Project, Heinemann, ©2002 Teachers College, Columbia University; http://www.heinemann.com/fieldguides

Illustrator
Robyn Belton

Publisher
Wright Group, 1996

ISBN
0780249070

TC Level
1

part of this book introduction.

The topic of family in books is a much-needed bridge between home and school in these early school years. Teachers might want to group books about families in their libraries. *I Love My Family* is about a traditional family. However, teachers should be conscious of the many different family structures that exist today, and try to find a myriad of books that represent this diversity. In this text teachers should also note that to some readers it may be confusing that the little boy's sister is an adult who is old enough to get married.

This book can serve as a valuable resource for teachers who are trying to develop early reading behaviors in their students. In a reading workshop, teachers can use this as a tool to teach children one-to-one matching because it contains a number of high frequency words kids may already know which will anchor their pointing fingers. Teachers may also coach children on fluency, self-correction and directionality using this text.

In reading partnerships or in small group discussions, encourage comprehension and book talk by asking children why the boy does not like his grandpa's whiskers.

I Love My Family's twist ending is representative of many of the books in this library. In a reading workshop or reading center, children may enjoy collecting examples of books with "surprise endings." It is important for children to know that many books in this library have such an ending. This anticipation will allow children to prepare themselves to tackle a page that is often more difficult than the rest of the text.

Genre
Emergent Literacy Book

Teaching Uses
Small Group Strategy Instruction; Partnerships; Interpretation; Whole Group Instruction

A Field Guide to the Classroom Library, Lucy Calkins and the Teachers College Reading and Writing Project, Heinemann, ©2002 Teachers College, Columbia University; http://www.heinemann.com/fieldguides

I Shop with My Daddy
Grace Maccarone

Book Summary

I Shop with My Daddy is the story of a girl who goes to the grocery store with her dad. The story begins with a drive to the store, getting the shopping cart, and then choosing the various foods that they put into the shopping cart. The reader learns all the different items that they buy, along with other foods that the girl asks for, but isn't allowed to get. The story ends with the girl and her dad buying ice cream cones as they leave the store.

Basic Book Information

This book is in the first level of a series published by Scholastic known as the *Hello Reader* series. Teachers will notice, perhaps with some concern, that Priscilla Lynch's balanced advice on the opening page of other *Hello Reader* books has given way to advice from Francine Alexander. Francine suggests the teacher first read the book to the child, and then read it again, this time having the child read one line at a time repeating after the teacher. During reading, if the child forgets what the teacher read and reread to the child, and for a moment, seems stymied, the teacher doesn't prompt the child to reread or to think, "What would make sense?" but instead directs the child to look at the words again asking, "Do you know the sounds?" The child is then asked to use phonic skills to sound out the word. This is rather troublesome advice on the opening page of a book that has been specifically designed to suit the child who is very, very new to reading.

Noteworthy Features

Text placement is usually at the top of the page but it is not consistent. It consists of one or two lines that are written in fairly large print.

There are at least three pattern shifts throughout the book. The first pattern begins with sentences always containing the word *take(s)*, listing what "we take" at the grocery store. The girl (who is the narrator of the story) changes from saying, "We take" to "I take" or "My daddy takes." At several junctures, the girl switches and asks, "Can we get some _____?" Now her dad responds, "Not today" which makes her "put it/them away." The third pattern shift occurs when she says, "I want a treat." The amount of picture support in the text varies, with the most picture support provided (oddly enough) when the language pattern is consistent.

The book includes many high frequency words: *I, we, and, my, to, the, take, open, put, get, some, today, so, them*, etc.

There is an erratic pattern of rhyme that creates an uneven rhythm. In the beginning of the text, sentences end with words that rhyme (*door/store*). There is more rhyme later in the text (*berries/cherries, cheese/please, today/away, meat/treat, pay/say*, etc.).

Illustrator
Denise Brunkus

Publisher
Scholastic, 1998

ISBN
0590501968

TC Level
4

Teaching Ideas

In a conference or small group, a teacher may decide to give an introduction to this book. One teacher said, "*I Shop with My Daddy* is about a little girl who tells what she and her daddy do when they go shopping at the grocery store. She and her daddy take many things from the shelves and place them in the cart and then at the end, they pay for all of their items. And there is one more thing they do before they leave...." It is not necessary for the teacher and child to turn through all the pages, but the teacher may want to point out some of the tricky words.

Another teacher used this book to point out the varieties of punctuation marks and how we read differently with our voices for different marks. Some children were overheard reading this in a partnership taking on different voices. One child took the role of reading the part of the daddy and saying "Not today." Another child took on the role of the little girl and said, "Can we get some _____?"

During writing workshop some students were using this text to study how writers use dashes and then tried it in their own writing. A teacher may also use this book to teach students who may want to start using dialogue in their own writing.

Genre

Emergent Literacy Book

Teaching Uses

Independent Reading; Language Conventions; Small Group Strategy Instruction; Teaching Writing; Partnerships

A Field Guide to the Classroom Library, Lucy Calkins and the Teachers College Reading and Writing Project, Heinemann, ©2002 Teachers College, Columbia University; http://www.heinemann.com/fieldguides

I Went Walking

Sue Williams

Book Summary

I Went Walking tells the story of a young boy who is on a walk. Along the way he meets many farm animals. There is a refrain throughout the book as the boy encounters each animal. The little boy says, "I went walking." An unidentified voice asks, "What do you see?" The little boy then responds, "I saw a _____ (e.g., brown cow) looking at me." At the end of the book the little boy turns around and finds that all the animals are following him. On the last page, the parade of animals and the young boy dance merrily.

Basic Book Information

This is a 30-page book with vibrant illustrations by Julie Vivas. The fantastical illustrations resemble watercolor paintings. The text is clearly printed in a black font against a white background. Text placement varies from page to page. There are a number of high frequency vocabulary words throughout the story.

Noteworthy Features

One of the most distinguishing features of this book is its three-phrase refrain, repeated throughout the book. The only two words that change each time the refrain appears, are the color and name of the animal (i.e., pink pig).

This book is representative of many other books in Library A. The book focuses on animals and colors, which are popular themes in this library. Like many other books, there is also a twist at the end. The last page of the book, reads, "I saw a lot of animals following me!"

Another way in which this book is like many others in Library A, is its cumulative structure. Throughout the book, as the boy meets the animals, they add onto a parade following the young boy on his walk.

There is one feature of *I Went Walking* that is somewhat puzzling. There are wrap-around sentences throughout the book. But the part of the sentence that appears on the second line, has initial capitalization (i.e., first line: "I saw a green duck" second line: "Looking at me."). Children who have learned that only the start of a new sentence or proper names should appear in caps may be confused. Teachers can perhaps present a disclaimer and explain to children that it is incorrect to use capital letters in the middle of a sentence.

Another slightly confusing element of the story is its colors. The "red" cow could easily be identified as "brown." Children who are using the pictures to figure out the colors of the animals might easily misidentify the color. Checking the initial consonant will help them self-correct.

Another noteworthy feature of this book is its unidentified narrator. The

Illustrator
Julie Vivas

Publisher
Voyager Books, Harcourt Brace, 1989

ISBN
0152380116

TC Level
2

A Field Guide to the Classroom Library, Lucy Calkins and the Teachers College Reading and Writing Project, Heinemann, ©2002 Teachers College, Columbia University; http://www.heinemann.com/fieldguides

boy says, "I went walking." A voice responds, "What did you see?" There is no reference as to who this speaker may be throughout the book.

Teaching Ideas

I Went Walking provides a lot of support for young readers. It is highly repetitive. There are only 4-lines throughout the entire book. The only words that change in the refrain are the color and name of the animal. These words can be decoded by using the corresponding pictures that depict the animal.

When the teacher pulls alongside readers who are reading this book she may want to coach one child by prompting him to reread when he encounters difficulty and encourage another to look at the picture and get her mouth ready to look at the sound. All students should be encouraged to check for meaning.

I Went Walking is a wonderful book to use in reading partnerships. The question and answer format lends itself to readers taking on the different roles of the speakers. One student might say, "I went walking." Then the other student would reply, "What did you see?" Children have a lot of fun with this playful back and forth. This type of reading should sound more conversational and will help to develop students' fluency with reading text, an important factor in building comprehension.

The illustrations in *I Went Walking* are really spectacular. They help to create a sense of suspense that young children can enjoy. On the pages that say, "What did you see?" there is a small part of the animal peeking out (e.g., the tail of a black cat sticking out from a basket). Children will probably be yelling out, "It's a black cat!" but until they turn the page, they won't find out if they guessed right.

Teachers who want to use this book as a basis for a related phonics lesson might want to work on the *-ing* ending: *looking, walking* and *following* are all words in this book that use this ending. If teachers wanted to add *-ing* words on a word wall, they should make sure that every student in the class is able to read these words. Every student should feel that the words on the word wall are ones they are confident reading and using in their writing.

Genre
Picture Book

Teaching Uses
Independent Reading; Partnerships; Small Group Strategy Instruction

In a Dark, Dark Room and Other Scary Stories

Alvin Schwartz

Book Summary

This is a collection of seven short, scary stories that Schwartz retells from familiar folktales and ghost stories. They are humorous, with just the right touch of mystery, to make young readers think "Wow!"

"Teeth" tells of a young boy who meets strangers who smile at him. Each stranger has teeth longer than the one before, until the boy meets the last stranger and runs home. "In the Graveyard" is about a stout woman who sees very thin corpses. She wonders aloud if she will some day be that skinny. When the corpses answer her, she screams. "The Green Ribbon" tells the story of a young girl, Jenny, who always wears a green ribbon around her neck, but refuses to tell her friend, then husband Alfred, why. Finally, when she is old and close to death, she tells him to remove the ribbon. When he does, her head falls off.

"In a Dark, Dark Room," the title story, follows a pattern, taking us to a dark, dark box, inside of which is "A GHOST!" "The Night It Rained" is the story of a driver who, passing a cemetery, gives a young boy a ride home in the rain. The driver lends the boy a sweater. The next day, when he stops by his house to pick up the sweater, he learns from the boy's mother that her son died a year ago. The driver returns to the cemetery, finds the boy's grave and, on the top of it, the sweater. In "Pirate," we meet a young girl, Ruth, who searches everywhere in the room for a pirate ghost that supposedly haunts it. Satisfied that she is the only one in the room, she says aloud "There is no one in this room but me" and a voice answers "And *me*."

"The Ghost of John" is a humorous six-line poem which ends with the lines, "Wouldn't it be chilly/ with no skin o-n?"

Basic Book Information

This is a 60-page *I Can Read* collection of stories written in short, simple sentences with an uncomplicated syntax. Zimmer's cartoon-like illustrations bring humor to each piece. A seated black cat, looking through an open doorway is illustrated on the dedication page, possibly Calliope, to whom the book is dedicated. Here and there the same black cat appears throughout the illustrations as an observer. There is a "Foreword," and an end-of-the-text note on "Where the stories came from." A final page includes information "About the Author" as well as "About the Illustrator." Each chapter is complete in itself, unrelated to the other stories. While the stories are meant to be "scary," they are told in a way that lets children see the underlying humor. The titles only hint at the content of the story. Schwartz's *Scary Stories* book series are very popular with older readers. This

Illustrator
Dirk Zimmer

Publisher
HarperCollins, 1984

ISBN
0064440907

TC Level
6

A Field Guide to the Classroom Library, Lucy Calkins and the Teachers College Reading and Writing Project, Heinemann, ©2002 Teachers College, Columbia University; http://www.heinemann.com/fieldguides

book brings similar stories to the younger crowd.

Noteworthy Features

In addition to the seven stories in this collection, there is a brief foreword that introduces the reader to the style of the stories and an afterword that gives the source for each story. Because they are stand-alone, these tales can be read in any sequence. The simple sentence structure Schwartz uses makes them easy to comprehend. Vocabulary words, such as *corpse, graveyard*, and *cemetery* may challenge some readers. Of the seven stories, two are told in first person, the rest in third person narration. The dialogue is common and free of dialect. The surprise endings make the stories entertaining.

Teaching Ideas

Teachers might want to discuss the foreword with the children to prepare for reading. In it, Schwartz points out that scary stories are meant to be fun because when there is no real danger, we *like* feeling scared. Since some timid children might take these stories to heart, teachers might want to stress that none of these stories is true, but only tales to read, recite and enjoy.

The collection of tales also provides teachers with an opportunity to discuss the difference between realistic stories and fantasies. Teachers might ask students to read through the stories, looking for evidence of actions or events that could not happen in real life (corpses talking, ghosts haunting, men with hideous long teeth, for example). Students might make connections between the stories in this book and other books they have read.

For teachers who may want to try out a choral reading with a group or in partnerships, the author gives some solid advice. Schwartz advises the reader to tell the stories "s-l-o-w-l-y and quietly and everyone will have a good time." A teacher may model how various punctuation marks, italics, words in bold or caps may be read by raising or lowering her voice to highlight humor, fear or surprise: "Ooooooh!"

The author "retold" the stories from a variety of sources himself. These short tales lend themselves to oral retellings. Readers can read these during independent reading time and then meet with partners during partner reading time to retell them. Alternatively, the teacher could read one story to the class, and the class as a whole or in partnerships might retell the stories either orally or in writing.

Book Connections

Students who enjoy this book might want to read other *I Can Read* books that the author has written: *I Saw You in the Bathtub and Other Folk Rhymes*, *There Is a Carrot in My Ear*, *Busy Buzzing Bumblebees*, and *Ghosts! Ghostly Tales from Folklore*.

Genre
Short Chapter Book; Anthology of Short Stories; Fairy and Folk Tale; Poetry

A Field Guide to the Classroom Library, Lucy Calkins and the Teachers College Reading and Writing Project, Heinemann, ©2002 Teachers College, Columbia University; http://www.heinemann.com/fieldguides

Teaching Uses
Whole Group Instruction; Independent Reading; Partnerships; Read Aloud;
Independent Reading; Language Conventions

A Field Guide to the Classroom Library, Lucy Calkins and the Teachers College Reading and Writing Project, Heinemann, ©2002 Teachers
College, Columbia University; http://www.heinemann.com/fieldguides

In the Woods
Annie-Jo

Book Summary

This book begins by saying, "A snake is in the woods," and then continues for six or seven pages, switching the animal who is in the woods. The final page asks the reader what else is in the woods.

Basic Book Information

This book is published by Mondo. Over the last few years Mondo has become one of the leading publishers of nonfiction books for early readers. Mondo is an Australian-based company, and its publications reflect a knowledge of early readers and an awareness that a collection of early books should look more like a library than a kit. Mondo books are made in a wide variety of shapes and sizes and each has its own individuality.

Noteworthy Features

Large and beautiful photographs of the forest and of woodland creatures grace the pages of this book. Most of the photographs come from the Audubon Society.

Inside the front cover there is a beginner version of an index. It lists, for example:

page 2: Corn Snake
page 3: Cottontail Snake

On the back cover, there is a little blurb (a feature one finds in chapter books). The back-cover blurb, like the index, is a beginner version of such blurbs. This contains a photograph and just a few words, all meant to direct a reader to the text. These words, however, will be more challenging for the reader than the actual text.

The reason this book belongs in Level 2 instead of Level 1 lies on the final page. We assume that many of the books in a classroom lending library will be read independently by children, without an introduction. A child who is reading Level 1 books will be ill equipped to read the last sentence of this book. On this last page, there are two lines on the page, and the second line breaks the pattern of the rest of the book and begins with a fairly difficult word, *What,* and then says *else* (an even harder word!) *is in the woods?*

For a reader who is ready to move on past the earliest books, this book offers wonderful challenges; and the index and back cover are more challenging still.

A reader of this book will probably still be pointing under the words, and this book has been written in a way that makes pointing very easy. There is wonderful spacing between the words (unlike, for example, in *Brown Bear, Brown Bear*) and the font is very recognizable. Sometimes publishers use the "typewriter *a*" which is different from the *a* children use as writers, or they

A Field Guide to the Classroom Library, Lucy Calkins and the Teachers College Reading and Writing Project, Heinemann, ©2002 Teachers College, Columbia University; http://www.heinemann.com/fieldguides

Publisher
Mondo, 1998

ISBN
1572555386

TC Level
1

have tails on the *T* or *D*. The font in this book is similar to that which children use in their writing and it will probably match the classroom alphabet chart.

Teaching Ideas

A teacher who pulls alongside a child who is reading this book will notice right way that each page of this book gives the child more opportunities to use words this child probably already knows-these can be called sight words or high frequency words. Almost every page, for example, begins with the word *A* and reading experts say this "offers the child a great way into the page" because immediately the child can hook onto a word she knows and begin matching known words with print on the page.

On every page, the next word the child encounters will probably *not* be a known word and the child could stop, paralyzed, and appeal to the teacher for help. The teacher will want to keep his or her gaze steadily *on the text* so that the child's instinct to glance up for help isn't rewarded. We want readers to come to realize that the help they are looking for is *on the page*. If we are looking at the book, the child will follow our gaze and look there as well. We may go so far as to point at the picture, but it is subtler and more instructive to do less and leave more work in the hands of the child. A teacher can try just looking at the picture and saying nothing. Many children will say, "Snake?" If we avoid responding we can help to make readers independent of us. Usually the child who has asked "snake?" and gets as a response our continued silent focus on the text will return to the text, rereading the sentence with the new word in it. Luckily, the child's returning attention to the book will be supported because the next three words-*is, in, the*-will probably be known words.

When the child reaches the word *woods*, we might decide to just say the word. If the child follows the strategy of studying the picture, the child could produce lots of options: *grass, mud, dirt*, and we would want to support the process the child will have used. The problem will be that none of the words fit the bill. The option of having this child "sound out" or word-solve, or chunk the word, may not be the best option here because this child is ready to use initial consonants but the /w/ alone won't get most readers to the word *woods*.

Rereading the first page should carry the child through the remaining pages. If the child miscues on *rabbit* and reads *bunny*, that should not be of big concern or if the teacher would like to see the child self-correct, the teacher might say, "Could it be rabbit?" and then say, "Check," nudging the child to check the first letter.

The child will probably read, "a owl" not "an owl" and again, many teachers know this probably isn't something worth fussing over in a first reading of the book. The child will reread the book many times and maybe this miscue will resolve itself (or become a teaching point) in a later reread. If the child *does* stop and realize *an* is not *a*, that would be very good news indeed, suggesting the child is really attending to print.

The final page is the big challenge in this book. In shared reading and reading mini-lessons, we will probably have talked about how the last page often is the funny part, or the page that changes the pattern, or the tricky page. In this book, the last page is almost a transition last page because it

A Field Guide to the Classroom Library, Lucy Calkins and the Teachers College Reading and Writing Project, Heinemann, ©2002 Teachers College, Columbia University; http://www.heinemann.com/fieldguides

starts with the pattern but then there is a very different final sentence. Readers who read this independently will do lots of good work trying to solve this sentence but they will probably end up just guessing what it might say. If a teacher is near, the wisest thing to do would be to tell the child the first two words, "*What else...*" pointing under them as we say them.

After a child has worked through the last line, a teacher might say, "Sometimes it helps me to reread it to make it smooth. Why don't you try that?" At every level of reading a child should be putting words together so they sound like normal talk, not like robot-talk. If the child's finger pointing leads to exaggerated spaces between spoken words, we will want to say "Say it faster" or "Say it like you are talking." The fact that the finger pointing can lead to robot reading is the reason why, before very long, we are going to ask children to read without pointing at the words.

The reader will have done a lot of work and will profit from reading the text with independence, putting all that she knows together into something that is approximately what an experienced reader might do with the text.

Genre
Nonfiction; Emergent Literacy Book

Teaching Uses
Independent Reading; Language Conventions; Small Group Strategy Instruction; Partnerships

A Field Guide to the Classroom Library, Lucy Calkins and the Teachers College Reading and Writing Project, Heinemann, ©2002 Teachers College, Columbia University; http://www.heinemann.com/fieldguides

It Could Still Be A Fish

Allan Fowler

Book Summary

This is a nonfiction book that first asks the question, "How do you know if it is a fish?" The reader is then presented with fish that have features and behaviors that are not very fish-like, and the book ends by stating various facts about the fish that people keep as pets and those that people eat.

Basic Book Information

This 32-page book features full-color photographs of many beautiful fish. It starts with the identification of the parts of a fish that all fish have like gills and scales, setting up the "same as" structure. For the remaining pages, Fowler details some different kinds of fish like eels and sharks, showing how they are the same but different. There is a photograph on almost every page; those that have text only hold one or two lines of text. The "Words You Know" section acts as a glossary. There is a photograph of a fish with its parts identified, and there's an index on the very last page.

The Rookie Read-About Science books are clearly laid out with photographs on each page. They are visually appealing and are very easy to hold and look through or read. The texts vary in difficulty somewhat: some rely on more text, while others are more list-like. All of the books have the same structure of beginning with a question, and the rest of the text then explains the answer to that question with a variety of examples. Each book also has two sections at the end: "Words You Know," a picture glossary, and an index to familiarize young readers with noteworthy features of common nonfiction texts. The books cover a variety of science topics such as: rocks, trees, rivers, and mammals, etc. It may be more supportive, however, to use the easiest books in the series with more struggling readers or those new to nonfiction.

Noteworthy Features

Allan Fowler has written *It Could Still be a Fish* with a repeating pattern that is also present in his other books: *It Could Still Be Water*, *It Could Still Be a Desert*, *It Could Still Be a Lake*, *They Could Still Be Mountains*. Within these books, Fowler uses a compare-contrast approach, showing that fish (or mammals, etc.) can look different from each other and have slightly different features, but they are all still fish (or mammals, etc.). Although these books are set up in a similar structure, they do have different levels of difficulty. *It Could Still Be A Fish* is the easiest of the books in this series.

Although this book lacks a table of contents or chapter headings, it can serve as a worthwhile introduction to some common features of nonfiction writing. It does include photographs, a picture glossary called "Words You Know," and an index in the back.

Publisher
Children's Press, 1990

ISBN
0516449028

TC Level
7

Teaching Ideas

In too many schools, children read only novels during the independent reading workshop, relegating nonfiction to the social studies and science curriculum. But some children, like some adults, prefer nonfiction to fiction. These children-and research suggests they are often boys-are denied their own best avenue into the life of being avid, passionate readers. Then, too, children who read mostly fictional books don't develop the broad repertoire of reading skills and strategies involved in how to read nonfiction texts that will put them in good stead in the world. As we go through our days, most of us read nonfiction texts constantly-and children benefit from an early start on reading this type of text. Nonfiction and fiction books, therefore, should be equally accessible to children in classroom libraries containing books on interests we know children already have, and books that will even further pique the curiosity of our student readers.

Anyone who has ever visited an aquarium knows that fish come in a dazzling array of shapes, sizes and colors. This book highlights some of the weird and exotic ways fish look, and children will want to browse through it, skimming and scanning until they find intriguing sections which they'll want to read. It's important for teachers to welcome this less-than-thorough approach to nonfiction reading, because that's how readers skim and scan to decide what to zoom in on, and to read in more depth.

Teachers will want to encourage children to talk back to what they see and read. Children will at first make exclamations such as "weird" or "cool" and we'll want to encourage them to say more, and to pay attention to their own responses. For example, a child might, on page17, exclaim that the eel is ugly. If we encourage him to say more, he may say, "I think the eel is the ugliest fish in this book," and this theory, of course, can launch a guided reread to check again which other fish are contenders for the "most ugly" prize. A child might see that the water in the tuna picture looks blue, and in the trout picture, it looks black or that the trout seems twice the size of a tuna. Any of these noticings can begin inquiries if children know that one key goal for reading a book like this is to launch inquiries which lead to directed rereads, to conversations with others, and to other texts.

One of the most striking features of this book is that the text is very much divided into categories of information, but these aren't marked off for readers by subtitles, chapter headings or even paragraphs. This makes the book much harder to read. A child can't skim a table of contents and head to a specific page with a specific purpose in mind, nor does the child have bold print to read which essentially says, "A new part begins right here,"or "It's *mainly* about...." But the fact that these features are missing from the book provides a great teaching opportunity. A teacher could point this out to a child and challenge the child to use Post-its to create his or her own version of subtitles. This, of course, teaches the child to read asking, "What is this mainly about?" to summarize, and to attend to the rhetorical devices an author uses to turn corners in the text.

In reading centers, teachers may collect a variety of texts on the same subject area for readers to compare and contrast. As readers become more familiar with the topic, they may want to do some simple "cross-referencing" to discover what all books about that topic have in

A Field Guide to the Classroom Library, Lucy Calkins and the Teachers College Reading and Writing Project, Heinemann, ©2002 Teachers College, Columbia University; http://www.heinemann.com/fieldguides

common, or what a particular book lacks or adds to their study of the topic.

As readers become more familiar with their research topic, they may use this book as a model for writing their own books. They may write a simple "research report" about what they've learned. They may also want to write a book based on their questions, hypotheses, etc. that may lead them to more research and to attain even more information about the topic than was included in the book read. Writers may want to try including a simple index or glossary in their books.

Genre

Nonfiction; Picture Book

Teaching Uses

Independent Reading; Content Area Study; Reading and Writing Nonfiction; Teaching Writing; Partnerships; Interpretation; Small Group Strategy Instruction

A Field Guide to the Classroom Library, Lucy Calkins and the Teachers College Reading and Writing Project, Heinemann, ©2002 Teachers College, Columbia University; http://www.heinemann.com/fieldguides

It Could Still Be a Mammal

Allan Fowler

Book Summary

This nonfiction book outlines the definition of what a mammal is and shows photographs of a variety of mammals. The book clearly explains the differences among mammals for early readers.

All of the *Rookie Read-About Science* books are clearly laid out with photographs on each page. They are visually appealing and are very easy to hold and look through or read. The texts vary in difficulty somewhat: some rely on more text, while others such as *It Could Still Be a Mammal* are more list-like. This text has many pages that are just pictures of the animal with the words "or a dolphin" or "like a sea lion" below the photograph. All of the books have the same structure beginning with a question like, "How do you know it's a mammal?" The rest of the book then explains the answer to the question with a variety of examples. Each book also has two sections at the end: "Words You Know," a picture glossary, and an index to familiarize young readers with noteworthy features of common nonfiction texts. The books cover a variety of science topics such as rocks, trees, rivers, fish and mammals, etc. It may be more supportive, however, to use the easiest books in the series with more struggling readers or those new to nonfiction.

Basic Book Information

It Could Still Be a Mammal has 31 pages without chapters. The photographs in the book are outstanding and clearly show the animals that are being written about. After the initial question of "How do you know it's a mammal?" the book outlines the defining features of each mammal and concludes by asking if the reader knows who the smartest mammal in the world is: "You are!" In the "Words You Know" section, there are small-sized pictures of each mammal in the book, labeled with its name underneath, that corresponds to the larger photographs found within the body of the text. This serves as a visual glossary for young readers. This end section also gives the "definition" of a mammal by repeating its characteristics in complete sentences echoing the text.

Noteworthy Features

The simple setup of this text is a nice introduction to young readers of nonfiction. The index is short and lists animal names. The narration speaks to the reader through the device of asking a question, then answering it with many examples; thus, it speaks directly to the reader, pulling the reader in. The sentence structure is supportive to young readers. Many sentences are short and clear: "Dogs are mammals. Cows are mammals. Horses are mammals, too" (pages 5-7). The title of the text *It Could Still Be...* supports this structure as it explains how each mammal is different in its own right,

Publisher
Children's Press, 1990

ISBN
0516449036

TC Level
7

yet is still a mammal. This can be the beginning of a young reader's understanding of species and categories in science.

Young readers will be familiar with many of the animals described. But there are a few challenging vocabulary words for readers to conquer: *backbone*, *warm-blooded*, *ocean*, *covered*, *pouch*, *spines*, as well as some animal names. Animal names are listed again in the index. The photographs make it easier to identify the animals, and the "Words You Know" glossary reinforces the vocabulary needed to read the book independently. The simple structure and layout of the series encourages readers to use the book in many different ways and come to "memorize" both the animal names and more sophisticated vocabulary words.

Teaching Ideas

Teachers in all grades will find it helpful to introduce nonfiction text with this series, or to talk about the various forms a nonfiction text may take, and the features that make it distinct from fiction. The simple format allows early readers to gain independence in reading nonfiction and learn new information about interesting subjects.

This series can also be used in guided reading groups for a variety of purposes: introducing nonfiction; learning about how an index, glossary or table of contents is used; reading more sophisticated science vocabulary; understanding words within the context of a book; and categorizing new information learned in a nonfiction text.

The book also offers an opportunity to raise awareness of punctuation. In several places, sentences begin on one page and continue on the next (pages 11-12). A teacher may use this to demonstrate that a reader's voice does not stop at the bottom of each page, but that punctuation determines our pace.

Struggling readers can read the *It Could Still Be A...*series independently or in partnerships and look across the series as they become more secure in their vocabulary and gain confidence with the scaffolding patterns in the series. The picture support and repetitive nature of the text can also encourage struggling readers to feel successful.

One of the most striking features of this book is that the text is very much divided into categories of information, but these aren't marked off for readers by subtitles, chapter headings or even paragraphs. This makes the book much harder to read. A child can't skim a table of contents and head to a specific page with a specific purpose in mind, nor does the child have bold print to read which essentially says, "A new part begins right here," or "It's *mainly* about...." However, the fact that these features are missing from the book provides a great teaching opportunity. A teacher could point this out to a child and challenge the child to use Post-its to create his or her own version of subtitles. This, of course, teaches the child to read asking what the main ideas are, to summarize and to attend to the rhetorical devices an author uses to turn corners in the text.

In reading centers, teachers may collect a variety of texts on the same subject for readers to compare and contrast. As readers become more familiar with the topic, they may want to do some simple "cross-referencing" to discover what all books about that topic have in common, or what a particular book lacks or adds to their study of the topic.

As readers become more familiar with their research topics, they may use this book as a model for writing their own books. They may write a simple "research report" about what they've learned. They may also want to write a book based on their questions, hypotheses, etc. that may lead them to more research and to attain more information about the topic than was included in the book read. Writers may want to try including a simple index or glossary in their books.

Book Connections

After becoming familiar with these texts, young and struggling readers can move on to more challenging nonfiction texts such as the *Sunshine Books* from the Wright Group or texts by Gail Gibbons. They can also study one subject area, such as mammals, and collect a variety of texts that support their content reading. Using magazine articles from such young juvenile publications as *Cricket* or *Ladybug* may also be a nice connection as readers become stronger nonfiction readers and encounter a broadening variety of formats.

Genre
Nonfiction; Picture Book

Teaching Uses
Whole Group Instruction; Language Conventions; Small Group Strategy Instruction; Independent Reading; Content Area Study; Reading and Writing Nonfiction

A Field Guide to the Classroom Library, Lucy Calkins and the Teachers College Reading and Writing Project, Heinemann, ©2002 Teachers College, Columbia University; http://www.heinemann.com/fieldguides

It Didn't Frighten Me

Janet Gross; Jerome Harste

Book Summary

This book begins with a picture of a child sitting up in bed after his dad had turned out the light for the night. The child sees an orange alligator in the tree outside his window. Then the next page shows the view outside the child's window and says, "But . . . that orange alligator didn't frighten me!" The text continues like this with the child seeing a purple witch, a pink dinosaur, and a lot of other scary and funny things. On the last page, the child sees a big brown owl saying, "Whooo me?" and the refrain changes to "And did it ever frighten me!"

Basic Book Information

This book was written by Janet Gross and by the renowned language arts researcher Jerry Harste who is known for coauthoring *Creating Classrooms for Authors and Inquirers*, with his colleague, Kathy Short.

This is a 23-page book with vivid, humorous illustrations. Each double-page spread has consistent text placement with the poem/refrain repeated on the left hand side of the page, and text supporting the picture of each new "creature" on the right hand side of the page.

Noteworthy Features

The book is a pitch black book with letters in white print, making a striking effect and matching the content and theme of the story.

The book reads like a song. Each verse in that song begins with a phrase that many of us know from scary stories, "One pitch black, very dark night. . . ." Like many early books the text is repetitive, but the unit that repeats is larger in this book than in many other books for beginning readers. In this book, the entire four-line "poem" repeats, with each stanza containing two words that vary-those words identify the new creature that is in the window frame.

Teaching Ideas

Because of its rhyme, song-like, and literary qualities, this would make a good choice for a shared reading text. If readers who are reading books at lots of different levels all hear this book read aloud to them and all join in chorus-like shared readings of the text, then this book need not be reserved only for Level 3 readers. If it's been a shared reading text, all children should feel they have it "under their belts." Even readers who cannot yet unlock the puzzle of unknown words using graphophonics may choose to read this book relying on the memorized refrain and the strong picture support just as they have done with easier but somewhat similar books such as *Brown*

Illustrator
Steve Romney

Publisher
Mondo Publishing, 1986

ISBN
157255097X

TC Level
3

Bear, Brown Bear What Do You See? or *Five Little Monkeys Jumping on the Bed.*

The teacher may decide to do a book introduction to offer an independent reader some support. If a teacher has access to additional copies, a book introduction could also be given to a small group of readers. In her introduction, one teacher said, "This book is arranged a little differently than many. It is kind of a song or poem. Once you've read the first page through one time, go back and read it again so you can pull it all together and make it sound like a song."

The sheer quantity of print on page 2 may intimidate a reader. A teacher therefore, may decide to scaffold the child through the first page. If, on the other hand, she's done an introduction with a group, she might say, "Why don't the four of you work on this first page together? Read it through and help each other. Then, when you have got it, go back and reread it to make it smooth." When giving an introduction to a single reader or a partner pair the teacher might say, "I'll stay here while you read this first page. I don't think you are going to need my help, but I'll be here." She wouldn't say, "I will be here just waiting to help" because she always want to be teaching toward independence.

A reader who is ready for this text will be able to use phonics knowledge to work out an unknown word, looking not just at the initial and final letters, but looking all the way across the word. The reader should also be cross-checking one cue against another, as well as self-correcting and monitoring for meaning.

It is very important to resist the urge to pre-teach a word like "pitch" to a Level 3 reader. Some teachers might be tempted to do this simply because the word "pitch" is sure to challenge a reader-but the word should be within the grasp of these readers and especially so if we encourage them to word-solve together. Human beings learn words best by using them in meaningful contexts and once the child reads this page with intonation, the child will probably recall the phrase "pitch black night."

Whether or not the teacher does an introduction, she will listen to children read and encourage them to "put the words together to make it smooth." This is a great book for teaching fluency and phrasing and readers, when they get to books with more text like this, often get bogged down and begin to read word by word. This is especially common for children reading at this difficulty level because when readers get to Level 3 and 4 books, the texts require them to slow down and chunk across words.

The book is full of literary language. A perfect example is the phrase, "I looked out my window only to see a . . ." a seven- or eight-year-old is unlikely to actually say "I looked out my window only to see," or even to say, "One pitch black, very dark night. . . ." The book is as challenging as it is because of this literary language, and readers of Level 3 and Level 4 books benefit when we tell them that the words in books sound like a story, and that writers often use literary or storybook language. This is a new feature of books at this level and beyond, and children benefit from being encouraged to feel and delight in and enjoy the sounds of a story. Because there are few challenges in this text other than the use of literary language, the book is a great one for this purpose.

A Field Guide to the Classroom Library, Lucy Calkins and the Teachers College Reading and Writing Project, Heinemann, ©2002 Teachers College, Columbia University; http://www.heinemann.com/fieldguides

Genre

Emergent Literacy Book; Poetry

Teaching Uses

Independent Reading; Partnerships; Small Group Strategy Instruction; Read Aloud

Jamaica's Find

Juanita Havill

Book Summary

Jamaica, while playing alone in the park, comes across a red sock hat and a cuddly, stuffed gray dog. Instead of placing both items in the lost and found at the park house, Jamaica returns only the hat and takes the stuffed animal home. At home, Jamaica shows off her dog to her family, which is not thrilled about having a dirty stuffed dog sitting at the dinner table. Once Jamaica is asked to take it out of the kitchen area, she begins to think about whether she did the right thing by keeping the dog. She overhears her mother mention, "It probably belongs to a girl just like Jamaica." While sitting in her room and talking to her mother, Jamaica feels empathy for the owner and decides that she wants to return the dog to the park house. After bringing back the stuffed dog, Jamaica meets a girl named Kristin, the original owner of the stuffed animal. As Jamaica happily reunites Kristin with her missing dog, the girls exchange smiles and become friends.

Basic Book Information

This picture book is a winner of the 1987 Ezra Jack Keats New Writer Award and a Reading Rainbow Selection. This 32-page picture book has at least one illustration for each pair of facing pages. The text in the book can be found on both sides of the page and superimposed over some pictures. The watercolor illustrations in the book closely represent the written text.

Noteworthy Features

The text itself has been placed to fit around the illustrations. As such, words are not in any consistent place on the page. The illustrations, however, support the text carefully. The characters' expressive faces and postures can help children understand the emotions the text on each page describes.

Teaching Ideas

This book is about honesty, compassion, and making good decisions. Jamaica's moral dilemma of dealing with right and wrong is a thread woven from the beginning to the end of the book. In and outside the classroom, there are many ways in which children can learn from this book.

The book can be a mentor text for children who are trying to write their own personal narratives. Many children retell incidents in their own lives without consciously shaping them as stories. They would benefit from a reminder of the features of narrative, and from examples of successful, cohesive stories.

This book also lends itself to teaching the strategy of prediction. Readers could use prior knowledge and looking at the cover to predict what the story

Series
Jamaica series

Publisher
Houghton Mifflin Company, 1986

ISBN
0590425048

TC Level
5

will be about. Throughout the text, they can predict what will happen next and explain the textual basis for their predictions.

Book Connections

Juanita Havill has written two other books with the same main character, *Jamaica and Brianna* and *Jamaica Tag-Along*. In this text, as well as Rod Clement's *Grandpa's Teeth*, the main characters deal with issues of honesty, making choices and attending to their consciences. *Believing Sophie*, by Hazel Hutchins, and *Fanny's Dream*, by Caralyn Buehner, both address the major themes presented in *Jamaica's Find* and show how characters resolve similar problems.

Genre
Picture Book

Teaching Uses
Independent Reading; Teaching Writing; Character Study; Critique

A Field Guide to the Classroom Library, Lucy Calkins and the Teachers College Reading and Writing Project, Heinemann, ©2002 Teachers College, Columbia University; http://www.heinemann.com/fieldguides

Jessica

Kevin Henkes

Book Summary

Ruthie Simmons is an only child who has an imaginary friend named Jessica. This friend goes everywhere and does everything with Ruthie. Anything that Ruthie does wrong gets blamed on Jessica. When Ruthie goes to Kindergarten, Jessica follows her. Ruthie displays her feelings of apprehension through Jessica. The turning point in the book comes when Ruthie lines up to march to the lavatory and needs a partner. Ruthie feels that Jessica, her imaginary friend, suffices, but she soon finds that another little girl is inviting her into a partnership. Ruthie says she will be the little girl's partner, only to find this new friend of hers is named Jessica. The book closes as the two walk hand-in-hand down the hallway. This story is about growing up and making new friendships.

Basic Book Information

The illustrations in this picture book are beautiful and match the text perfectly. The text is varied throughout the book and can be found in different sizes and places on the page. The book begins and ends with the same words: "Ruthie Simmons didn't have a dog. She didn't have a cat, or a brother, or a sister."

Noteworthy Features

This story articulates a lot of feelings many young children feel on the first day of school. Children will relate to Ruthie's worries about finding a partner in line, about the first day of school, and about not wanting to take responsibility for a mistake such as spilling juice.

Although the text and illustrations roughly go together, the text can be found in different sizes and different locations on the page, which will be tricky for readers. Otherwise, the text is relatively straightforward.

The most confusing part of the book may be the ending. Some students may not understand that Jessica, the imaginary friend and Jessica, the real friend, are two different entities. This may create some misunderstanding, and it will be important for children to reread for clarification if the ending does not make sense to them.

Teaching Ideas

This would be a perfect book to read aloud to children in primary grades on one of the first days of school. This text could spark conversations about how the class members feel about the start of a new year and this could help children understand that many others, too, are anxious.

Because *Jessica* follows a classic story structure, the text could also help

A Field Guide to the Classroom Library, Lucy Calkins and the Teachers College Reading and Writing Project, Heinemann, ©2002 Teachers College, Columbia University; http://www.heinemann.com/fieldguides

Illustrator
Kevin Henkes

Publisher
Mulberry Paperback Books, 1989

ISBN
0688158471

TC Level
5

children develop a sense for the elements that reoccur in all stories. Readers could read or listen to the text with an eye toward noticing the characters, setting, and plot. Readers could talk about a change that happens in the book, one that is central to the characters and the plot. Readers could also notice the passage of time in this book. The book especially dramatizes the changes that occur in Ruthie, who begins the novel with an imaginary friend and moves on to meeting a true friend.

Readers will probably be confused by the first pages of the book. The text tells us that Jessica went wherever Ruthie went, but the picture shows just one girl, alone. "Huh?" the engaged reader will ask. It is important for children to learn that the first pages in a book are often a bit confusing, and that's okay. By reading forward, one begins to see things more clearly. The dawning realization that Jessica is an imaginary friend is important to the story, and the wise teacher won't ruin the surprise by previewing this for the reader.

The font in this book invites readers to take great pleasure in reading the book with expression. Ruthie's parents are not unlike the parents in *The Carrot Seed* who say over and over, "It won't come up." Her parents are also reminiscent of the sister in Bernard Waber's *Ira Sleeps Over* who firmly suggests that Ira not bring his blanket to the sleep over.

Book Connections

Kevin Henkes also wrote *Chrysanthemum, Chester's Way*, and *A Weekend with Wendell*. If students enjoy this story, they will enjoy his other works.

Genre
Picture Book

Teaching Uses
Author Study; Read Aloud

Just Like Daddy
Frank Asch

Book Summary

This story is written in first person by a young bear who retells his day from waking up until he catches a big fish. After every episode, he says "...Just like Daddy." The story begins, "When I got up this morning, I yawned a big yawn...Just like Daddy." There is a surprise ending when the bear catches the fish "...Just like Mommy!" On the final page the illustration alone tells the ending of the story: the family frying fish over a campfire.

Basic Book Information

Some texts are narratives that contain a central character and move through time. Other books are lists, stringing equal episodes together. This book is a combination of the two structures. The young bear is retelling the chronological sequence of the day he went fishing, but because he adds the chorus of "Just like Daddy" after every event, the text also reads as if it were a list of what the young bear does in a day that is just like what Daddy does.

Noteworthy Features

The structure and repetitive refrains in this book, which are described above, provide support that readers need as they tackle the linguistic complexity of this book. For most readers, the challenge of this text lies not in accumulating the text into a cohesive whole (the patterns and steady progression through time make that easier), nor do they lie in the words themselves (although there are tough words here). Instead, the challenge lies especially in the syntax of those long, rich and varied sentences. Many of the sentences include clauses. The episodes do not occur in a simple next, next, next fashion. Instead there are passages such as "On the way, I picked a flower" and "When we got to the lake...."

Even in books that move chronologically through time or through a catalog of different topics, there are often repeating elements that tie the text together and provide unity to it. These repeated elements might be a metaphor or color. In this relatively simple book, there are several repeating elements; the repeating text is one. Another is the little red bird who visits every page.

Teaching Ideas

As children read this book, they can become more accustomed to reading long, complex sentences that contain adverbial clauses. The children will receive support in this from the very simple chronological structure of the book and its repeating refrains, because both of these elements will help readers have the confidence to tackle the challenges the book poses.

Illustrator
Frank Asch

Publisher
Simon & Schuster, 1981

ISBN
0671664573

TC Level
4

A Field Guide to the Classroom Library, Lucy Calkins and the Teachers College Reading and Writing Project, Heinemann, ©2002 Teachers College, Columbia University; http://www.heinemann.com/fieldguides

Teachers may want to use the text as a model for writing by asking: "What do you like to do that is 'just like Mommy or Daddy'or somebody else in your family?"

Book Connections

Frank Asch has written many books about Little Bear. Teachers may want to collect them in a reading center so that students may follow the character (and Little Bird) through several adventures.

Genre
Emergent Literacy Book; Picture Book

Teaching Uses
Independent Reading; Language Conventions; Small Group Strategy Instruction; Character Study; Interpretation

A Field Guide to the Classroom Library, Lucy Calkins and the Teachers College Reading and Writing Project, Heinemann, ©2002 Teachers College, Columbia University; http://www.heinemann.com/fieldguides

Leo the Late Bloomer

Robert Kraus

Book Summary

Leo, the young tiger, is a late bloomer. He can't do the things the other animals around him are doing. His father is worried and watches him for any sign of blooming. Leo's mother isn't worried and just says to Leo's father, "Patience." Leo's father keeps watching him, discreetly, but Leo doesn't bloom. Then one day, several seasons later, Leo blooms and can do everything the other animals around him are doing. When Leo speaks, he even says a whole sentence "I made it!"

Basic Book Information

This is a large picture book with warm, silly line drawings as illustrations. It is a favorite in classrooms around the country.

Noteworthy Features

Many children like this story and its warm, colorful, line drawings.

The book is also an easy read for most kids without being a "babyish" book. Many of the pages have only one line, and that line is often short, for example, "He couldn't read." The small amount of dialogue is tagged, and the text is patterned with small bits of repetition. The vocabulary employed is fairly common. Despite these characteristics of an easy, simplistic book, this one presents (and implies) issues that are challenging and emotionally complicated, so kids have fuel for interesting and contemplative discussions.

Teaching Ideas

The topic of children learning to do things at different stages is one often talked about in classrooms, and teachers warmly welcome a gentle book on this topic. This book can initiate a productive whole-class conversation about different kinds of learners, and the ways in which we should show respect to, and patience for, one another.

When children begin trying to figure out how Leo might be feeling throughout the book, it often happens that they also begin to think about how Leo's father and mother might be feeling. Children ask each other whether that's the father they see in the pictures watching Leo, even when the text says he isn't watching. They try to figure out how he is feeling and they ask why he isn't talking to Leo about his feelings. They discuss what the father's worry might mean to Leo, and sometimes children discuss why Leo's father asks Leo's mother questions about their child, as if the mother were the expert on Leo. How could his mother be so sure that Leo will bloom, and his father, so unsure? These conversations, not only about parental worry and pressure, but also about gender roles and assumptions in

Illustrator
Jose Aruego

Publisher
HarperCollins, 1971

ISBN
006443348X

a family, can easily stem from this book, especially when kids are working on it with an angle toward personal response or character study.

When kids have had lots of conversations about the most obvious topic in the book, Leo's late blooming, they may point out that Leo and his parents could have been focusing on the things that Leo does do well, and not just on the things he couldn't do, or on the things all the other animals can do. His parents could have been helping him learn, or telling him not to worry, or telling him that he was doing a great job trying or that they loved him even if he never "bloomed" at all. The discussion could end up being a discussion of different strategies friends and parents can use when kids are worried about things they can't yet do. If this isn't a discussion that kids are ready to have, teachers may want to pose these questions in order to add alternatives to the way the situation is handled in *Leo the Late Bloomer*.

Book Connections

Teachers have set this book alongside Ruth Krauss' *The Carrot Seed*. Others have set this book alongside other books that also demonstrate the importance of persistence.

Genre
Picture Book

Teaching Uses
Read Aloud; Independent Reading; Critique; Interpretation; Partnerships

M and M and The Bad News Babies

Pat Ross

Book Summary

Mandy and Mimi are best friends who do everything together. They have the same straight brown hair, the same missing tooth, and they live in the same apartment building. Sometimes they even pretend to be twins. The two friends decide to take their first babysitting job so they can earn money to buy fish for their fish tank. They babysit for their neighbors, the twins, Richie and Benjie. The girls try their best to keep the twins occupied and out of trouble, but before long, they've lost them! They find the twins admiring the fish tank and all is well. Mandy and Mimi spend their first earnings buying new fish for their tank.

Basic Book Information

M & M and The Bad News Babies is part of a series of books about the two best friends Mandy and Mimi. It has 41 pages with 3 untitled chapters 10-13 pages long, with 5-8 sentences on a page. There are black-and-white illustrations on every page that support some part of the text. The story takes place over several days and is set in Mandy's or Mimi's apartment, as well as out in front of the apartment building. There is simple referenced dialogue throughout the text. The text is straightforward and simple.

Noteworthy Features

M & M and The Bad News Babies is a good example of a chapter book that is more difficult than very early chapter books, but not quite as difficult as the chapter books one finds often on library and bookstore shelves which tend to be longer, more complex and mostly all text. Here the sentences are slightly longer, the font is slightly smaller and the concepts are slightly subtler than what one sees in very early chapter books such as the *Frog and Toad* or *Oliver Pig* series.

There are several examples where the author uses italics for emphasis, which may be unfamiliar for readers at this level. The illustrator also uses word balloons in the illustrations, which may be foreign for some readers.

Teaching Ideas

M & M and The Bad News Babies can be used as a read aloud, a partner reading book or an independent reading book, and teachers may use this book to model good reading behaviors for any of these uses.

M & M and The Bad News Babies is a great book for children who are ready to develop and practice strategies that enable them to read longer books in a fluent and sustained way. Some of the many "jobs" children can practice while reading this book include: paying attention to punctuation in

Series
M and M

Illustrator
Marylin Hafner

Publisher
Puffin Books, 1997

ISBN
0140318518

TC Level
7

longer sentences, and using it to promote understanding; reading more quickly and smoothly without the help of a "pointing finger" or bookmark under each line; as well as *not* reading out loud. Readers may also practice putting words together so they read phrases with fluency and phrasing; reading dialogue in a character's voice; and self-correcting miscues by asking themselves "Does this make sense to me?" Teachers can do a mini-lesson with the whole class or confer with independent readers in order to help readers practice any of these strategies.

Teachers may say to readers: "Before you begin reading today, look through the part you are about to read and put a Post-it or bookmark on a good place to stop for a moment and practice the strategy we learned today. If you are reading with a partner, discuss with your partner where would be a good place to stop and talk."

As a read aloud, a teacher may do a short mini-lesson on how to use your voice appropriately when reading text that is italicized, or text inside word balloons. In a shared reading lesson, a teacher may show part of the text on an overhead projector or photocopy enough copies for children to look at individually. While reading the text aloud, the teacher can ask the readers to listen to how and when her voice is changing. Children can practice reading alongside the teacher or in partnerships with their copies of the text.

In class or partner discussions, teachers may use this book to teach about feeling a personal connection to a story and/or character. *M & M and The Bad News Babies* is based on two universal experiences of childhood: having your first "paying job," and the nervousness, responsibility and pride that goes along with it; and the challenge and fun of having babies around the house! Readers who have earned money in their own lives may be able to relate to Mandy and Mimi. Children who have baby brothers and sisters will also find plenty of places in the story where they will feel a sense of personal connection to the story of the two bigger girls. In either case, engaged readers will have a lot to talk about.

Book Connections

There are many other books about Mandy and Mimi, including: *M & M and The Haunted House Game, M & M and the Mummy Mess, M & M and the Big Bag,* and *M & M and the Santa Secrets.*

Genre
Short Chapter Book

Teaching Uses
Independent Reading; Read Aloud; Partnerships; Small Group Strategy Instruction; Language Conventions; Whole Group Instruction; Interpretation

A Field Guide to the Classroom Library, Lucy Calkins and the Teachers College Reading and Writing Project, Heinemann, ©2002 Teachers College, Columbia University; http://www.heinemann.com/fieldguides

Madeline in America and Other Holiday Tales

Ludwig Bemelmans

Book Summary

Madeline's grandfather leaves her a fortune upon his death, and the whole Paris boarding school travels to Texas to hear the reading of the will. The girls enjoy adventures and sights in Texas, from visiting oil wells and eating chili to seeing a huge department store and riding horses through a cattle stampede. Madeline gets lost and the Texas rangers come out in full force to find her, in the depths of the department store. Everyone celebrates her return with lavish gifts on Christmas day. When Madeline says she will quit school because of her newfound wealth, the lawyer reveals grandfather's wisdom-the money is not hers until she turns twenty-one. The girls all return to boarding school, excited from their recent Texas adventure.

Basic Book Information

This large-scale book contains several stories about Christmas, some about Madeline, some about author's memories of Christmas, others about general good will and peace at Christmas time.

Noteworthy Features

This story is illustrated in the style of Ludwig Bemelmans by his grandson, so the pictures are slightly different then in other *Madeline* books, and all in full color. In this story, the pictures are less crucial to the understanding of the plot than they are in others, but they are still necessary to understanding the tale.

Understanding a bit about Texas (or at least its stereotypes) may help readers appreciate this story, although it isn't necessary, as the story introduces these elements gradually.

Teaching Ideas

There are a couple of possible conversations a teacher could support after reading this book aloud. Some teachers don't like the portrayal of Christmas in this story as simply a time to get lots and lots of presents from the wealthy. In this tale, there are no talks of feelings, or of generosity or of the joy of giving, there is only a depiction of the girls getting clothes and shoes and new hats and all kinds of toys for Christmas, all being rolled into the room by the delivery boys. This might be the basis for a conversation, even a teacher-started conversation. What do you think the delivery boys are feeling about all this? What do you think the girls are missing when

Series
Madeline

Illustrator
John Bemelmans
Marciano

Publisher
Scholastic, 1991

ISBN
0590043064

TC Level
7

hristmas, or any holiday celebration, becomes only about getting as many gifts as possible?

There are also possibilities for discussion in Madeline's comment that "there'll be no more school, that is the best part, for who is rich is already smart." Children often take this comment at face value without thinking through if they agree or disagree with Madeline. Some usually wonder what she means by this. Children also often have a lot to say about the reasons Miss Clavel could have for asking Crockett, the Lawyer, to stop spoiling the girls. What could possibly be wrong with giving them so many toys?

Book Connections

Other books in this series include *Madeline and the Bad Hat, Madeline and the Gypsies, Madeline's Rescue, Madeline's Christmas* and *Madeline*.

Genre
Picture Book; Anthology of Short Stories; Memoir

Teaching Uses
Independent Reading; Interpretation; Critique

Making a Memory

Margaret Ballinger

Book Summary

A little girl reflects on special memories that are represented through artifacts that are displayed on a shelf. Each object elicits a memory, beginning when she was five years old, and, in descending order, ending with a memory from when she was one year old. On each page, the little the girl discusses things she bought, drank, and so on at a given age. The book culminates with the little girl "making a memory"-a drawing for her father, so he too, will be able to have artifacts.

Basic Book Information

There are seven pages in the book, each with one line of text. A "memory bubble" illustration appears on each page, providing the reader with more information about the details of the memory.

Noteworthy Features

On each of the seven pages, there is one line of text that is consistently placed under the illustrations. Sentences switch between past and present tense. Pictures provide moderate support with the exception of the first and last pages. Each page begins with "I" followed by an action verb, and then followed by the word "this" (i.e., I bought this, I found this, I made this, etc.). The text contains many high frequency words including: *I, on, my, this, was, when, got, from, made, am, for,* and *dad.*

Teaching Ideas

A child who is reading this book will need to be able to read and make sense of the word "memory" in order to comprehend the text. A teacher might give a book introduction by saying, "*Making a Memory* is a story about a girl who thinks about her memories from the time she was little. She remembers special times when she was five, and four, and three, and so on. And then at the end, she makes a gift of memory for someone special."

This is an excellent book to use in a writing workshop, to support children in understanding that authors often write about childhood memories. Some primary teachers use this book as a touchstone text in a study of family stories. In a kindergarten or first grade class, children quickly notice the memory bubbles and relate them to speech bubbles. Sometimes, children borrow the memory bubbles and use them in their own writing. One child made a memory bubble about when he was three. In the center of his memory bubble was a little figure, which he said was his baby sister, and around the figure was what he said was his crib, his toys and all his clothes. In approximated spelling, he wrote that when his sister was

A Field Guide to the Classroom Library, Lucy Calkins and the Teachers College Reading and Writing Project, Heinemann, ©2002 Teachers College, Columbia University; http://www.heinemann.com/fieldguides

Publisher
Scholastic, 1996

ISBN
0590237926

TC Level
3

born, because he was a big boy, he gave her a lot of his things. Some teachers even use paper with "memory bubbles" as a paper choice during a memoir genre study.

Children who have studied list books will quickly recognize this as fitting into that genre though it's more sophisticated than most early list books. Children will recognize this as a list of memories and see this text as an example of a sophisticated list book.

If the class is using reading centers, this book might be included in a basket of books about personal memories. In these centers children read and talk across books, finding similarities and differences among them, and making text to life connections. A group of young readers took turns pretending that they were the little girl. Each child "told" her story by reading the words and the memory bubble.

Book Connections

Other Library A books in a center with this one might include *Birthday Presents* by Cynthia Rylant, and *When I Was Five* by Arthur Howard. *Wilfrid Gordon McDonald Partridge* by Mem Fox would be another good addition to such a center, and in the writing workshop both can serve as a model of the way in which objects can trigger memories.

Genre
Emergent Literacy Book

Teaching Uses
Partnerships; Small Group Strategy Instruction; Independent Reading; Language Conventions; Teaching Writing

Market Day

Lois Ehlert

Book Summary

This simple story of going to the market is beautifully told with both carefully chosen words and folk art. The story begins as a family that lives on a farm prepares to go to the market for a day. The animals awaken and are fed and then the family is ready to go. Lois Ehlert slows down the family's journey to the market to let the reader see and hear all the beautiful, but simple things that they see along their journey. The family then arrives at the market and spends their day both working and playing. Finally, the work is done, the day is over and the family returns home, only to pass again and notice the beautiful birds and snakes along their journey.

Basic Book Information

Lois Ehlert is the acclaimed author of a number of books for children including *Feathers for Lunch* and *Fish Eyes*. Lois Ehlert has always been fascinated by the beauty of handmade objects and has collected folk art, primitive art, and textiles from around the world. She used her passion for folk art to help her tell the story of going to the market. The design of her illustrations truly takes your breath away and helps to portray how extraordinary the simple things in our lives can be.

Noteworthy Features

At first glance this book seems to be a perfect choice to support early readers. The print is large and amply spaced and there are never more than four lines per page. The text rhymes and is supported by large, clear illustrations. But the book is more complicated than it looks. Although the text rhymes, the rhyming forces the author to use some complicated sentence structures such as, "past the birds that perch in the trees, past the snakes that sun in the breeze, past the fish and frogs that swim near the bridge, and past the sheep that graze on the ridge." The book also has a lot of vocabulary that would require background knowledge such as, "load up the truck, past the trees, wheels turning fast, past the fields-we're home at last."

On the other hand, many early readers are drawn to this book because of its large illustrations and playful language. Ehlert's books seem more like literature than like teaching tools, and this makes them a valuable addition to a classroom library.

A page at the end of the book gives additional information about each piece of art depicted and how it was made. For example, you learn that the vegetables featured in her book were created using papier-mâché and paint originated in Mexico.

Illustrator
Lois Ehlert

Publisher
Harcourt, 2000

ISBN
0152021582

Teaching Ideas

Teachers will want this book first and foremost to exist simply as a great book to read aloud. Also many students will want to linger with this book, marveling at the gorgeous pieces of folk art. They'll be sure to want to read and reread the last page of the book that gives additional information about the folk art. They will be eager to learn about living on a farm and going to the market and/or share their own experiences about these subjects.

This book is especially powerful to use in writing workshop where children can read and study what Lois Ehlert does as a writer and craft their own writing in similar ways. Children can learn many fine qualities of writing by using this book as a mentor or model text. They might notice how Lois Ehlert has a page that gives additional information at the end and they might want to structure one of their own books in this same fashion. Ehlert does a beautiful job playing with time in her book. She slows down and describes everything the family passes on the way to, and on the way home, from the market. Children could learn how to slow down time in their own books by describing in great detail one scene of their story, while quickly passing over another part.

This book is particularly appropriate for readers who might be doing a market study in the social studies curriculum.

Genre
Picture Book; Nonfiction

Teaching Uses
Independent Reading; Read Aloud; Teaching Writing; Author Study; Content Area Study

A Field Guide to the Classroom Library, Lucy Calkins and the Teachers College Reading and Writing Project, Heinemann, ©2002 Teachers College, Columbia University; http://www.heinemann.com/fieldguides

Meanies

Joy Cowley

Book Summary

The book begins: "Where do meanies sleep?/ Meanies sleep in garbage cans." This line is repeated several times, both exactly and with slightly different sentence structure. The rest of the book uses the same repetitive format to talk about where meanies wash, drink, eat, drive, and what they do. The text finally asks who would want to be a meanie. To which, at the end, children emphatically yell "NOT ME!" The author answers each question with disgusting things that meanies do to which readers usually grimace but also giggle at.

Basic Book Information

Meanies is a Wright Group *Story Box* publication. It's a singsong type of book with a lot of repetition that may appear to be easier for readers than it actually is. This particular book is much larger than the 5" x 6" size that most *Story Box* books come in.

Noteworthy Features

Although the text is repetitive, many students get a bit overwhelmed at first by the sheer amount of print on each page. Once readers realize that most of the print is a repeat of the same line three times, they can usually move through the book with more confidence.

This book is easier than many other Group 4 books because of the repetition and the patterned question/answer format. The pictures in this book add more support for the text than many other Group 4 book illustrations do; however, it offers less picture support than earlier levels. For example, on the page "Meanies drive old tin can cars," the reader will need to use graphophonic cues more than picture cues to figure out what the meanies are doing on that page.

Teaching Ideas

As teachers we benefit from looking over our books and knowing in advance the source of difficulty a child may encounter. This way, we can be ready to teach into the struggles a child does encounter.

In this book, we can anticipate that a child may find the question words *where*, *what*, and *who* to be difficult. All three words are at the beginning of sentences, and at the beginning of the text that is on a particular page, so there will not be a lot of opportunity for readers to get a running start on the text before they meet these rather abstract and hard-to-solve words. Since the question words in general are not easily decoded, they are learned from repeated encounters (as sight words), but until this point, many

A Field Guide to the Classroom Library, Lucy Calkins and the Teachers College Reading and Writing Project, Heinemann, ©2002 Teachers College, Columbia University; http://www.heinemann.com/fieldguides

readers will not yet have encountered these words in a text often.

If a teacher were to introduce this book either in a guided reading session or to an individual or partnership, the teacher might introduce the question/answer format of the text and then have the students locate the question words in the text before they begin reading.

Another minor text challenge that may crop up is the contraction *that's*. At this level the teacher will want to refrain from going into a discussion around contractions and give the reader time to monitor his reading by returning to the word *that's* and looking to the end of the word for the *s*. Most readers at this level will figure out what the word is on their own.

Many teachers want to use this book as a text where children can practice putting their words together and reading with fluency. Teachers seem to feel that the repetition in the book makes fluency easier. This is a very important thing for children to practice, but we haven't found that this particular text works all that well for fluency, and we're not quite sure we can really put our finger on why it doesn't. The reading often becomes choppy when children read the repeated part and then it only comes back together when they finish with, "That's what meanies...." It could be that the book isn't suited to fluency and phrasing because the lines are simply repeated sentences. Lines like these don't provide the rhythm or natural syntax that truly supports a fluent reading: "Meanies drive / Old tin can cars. / Meanies drive / Old tin can cars. / Meanies drive / Old tin can cars.

Genre
Emergent Literacy Book

Teaching Uses
Independent Reading; Partnerships; Small Group Strategy Instruction; Language Conventions

Messy Bessy

Patricia McKissack; Fredrick McKissack

Book Summary

The story is told by a narrator who talks to the main character, an enterprising and spirited girl named Bessy. The book begins with an illustration of Bessy gleefully painting an elephant and the words, "Look at your room, Messy Bessy." Bessy sees paint on the walls, books on the chair, toys in the dresser drawer, and games everywhere. Then she sees gum on the ceiling and jam on the window! The narrator tells Messy Bessy to get the soap and water and soon she's mopped and scrubbed and shoved stuff in her closet so the room is clean.

Basic Book Information

This book is a *Rookie Reader*, part of a series published by Children's Press, a division of Grolier. It is one of many *Messy Bessy* books written on a range of levels. These books have all been written by Patricia and Fredrick McKissack, whose awards include the Coretta Scott King Award, the Jane Addams Peace Award, the Newbery Honor Award, and the Catholic Library Association's Regina Medal.

Noteworthy Features

In this day and age when many children play only video and computer games, it's refreshing to see that Bessy's bedroom and life spill over with projects of all sorts. She's painting an elephant that she later pins onto her wall. Her chair is filled with a towering pile of books, and her bureau seems to hold more stuffed animals than clothes. She's got toys everywhere: a robot, a model of the planets, a drum and a horn, a dinosaur puzzle, a few games, and a doll house.

There is just one line of print on most pages, but the book is more challenging than it might seem at first glance. Although there is a bit of repetition here, readers can in no way assume that being able to read one page will help them read the next. Even the repeated refrains vary often in ways that require readers to stay on their toes.

The sentences are long, often encompassing three pages. This text pushes readers toward fluency and phrasing in a way that is helpful. There is some rhyme that acts to support readers taking in bigger chunks of the text as they read.

The story can be thought of as having two parts. Pages 3 through 19 show the narrator urging Bessy to look closely at the mess in her room. On page 21, the narrator's voice changes: "So Bessy rubbed and scrubbed . . ." which tells of Bessy's actions in the past tense.

Series
Messy Bessy

Illustrator
Richard Hackney

Publisher
Children's Press, 1987

ISBN
0516270036

TC Level
4

Teaching Ideas

Children will read this book many times, doing different kinds of work each time. The first challenge will be to look over the text and the pictures in preparation for reading comprehension. The book opens with familiar sight words. Here, the text isn't supported by the pictures, but most children who can read a book at this level will recognize *look, at,* and *you* so the reader will be able to get started with the text.

One can anticipate that a reader might be stymied by the text saying, "See *colors* on the wall." A reader may expect the sentence to say, "See *paint* on the wall" or "See *hand prints* on the wall" but the reader should see from the print that neither alternative works. The phrase, "See gum on the *ceiling*," may also pose difficulties. If a teacher wants to offer some help before the child reads, one option is to do a book-walk together and to mention the colors on the wall and the gum on the ceiling in a conversational way as we look at the pictures. *Busy* is another word that could use similar support. All of these sources of difficulty could simply be left for the child to tackle, and if the child is reading with 90 to 95 percent accuracy and with understanding, the child should have resources for tackling difficulty (and ultimately should be able to bypass it for a bit, if need be).

When a child reads this text, a teacher who observes can gain great insight. If for example, the student reads on page 18 "get the mope," the teacher will see the child using phonics and not meaning. To highlight meaning, the teacher will respond, "You said, 'Get the *mope.*' Does that make sense?" The teacher might also say, "Check the picture, what could it be?"

Another example would be if the child read on page 9, ". . . hat on the floor," the teacher might prompt the child. "You said, '. . . *hat* on the floor.' I'm glad that you made sense and that you looked at the picture, but do the letters look right?" The child will probably be able to correct the word *hat* to *coat.* In cases such as this, children are probably relying on the picture, not the print.

If a reader is encouraged to reread, thinking deeply about the text and expecting to grow ideas, the reader may: notice paint on the girl's overalls and on the closet walls; comment that the set-up of stuff in the room changes from one picture to the next ("On page 9, it almost looks like the turtle is playing checkers."); and wonder who is talking to Bessy.

Book Connections

It would be interesting to put this book alongside others that are similar. *Tidy Titch* would be a great comparison text, as would *Poppleton in Spring.*

Bessy can be contrasted with other characters as well. A contrast with Jamie Lee Curtis' character in her book, *When I Was Little,* would yield an interesting discussion about gender stereotyping.

Genre
Picture Book

A Field Guide to the Classroom Library, Lucy Calkins and the Teachers College Reading and Writing Project, Heinemann, ©2002 Teachers College, Columbia University; http://www.heinemann.com/fieldguides

Teaching Uses
Independent Reading; Language Conventions

Mine's the Best
Crosby Bonsall

Book Summary

Before the words even begin, readers see two boys come nose-to-nose on the beach, each carrying a blow-up serpent-like toy. Then the two boys argue about whose toy is best and why. This continues, with the boys squeezing and tugging at their balloon-like creature as they each argue that theirs is bigger, can stand up more, etc. As the argument continues, the creatures become more and more deflated till the boys see that their toys have been ruined by the competition. A friendship somehow grows out of all this, and in the end the two boys are arm-in-arm, pointing to other people's balloons and reminiscing, "Ours was the best."

Basic Book Information

This isa *My First I Can Read* book published by HarperTrophy. On its back cover, the book is inaccurately leveled as a preschool book. Like other books by Crosby Bonsall, this story is carried entirely by dialogue, with the left-hand side of the two-page spread always representing the voice of one boy, and the right-hand side the other boy. The book has no chapters, although a thoughtful reader could say there are parts to it.

Noteworthy Features

Although there are only 105 words in the book, and many of the words are repeated often, the text is harder than it looks because the words don't make reference to anything concrete and their meaning can't be conveyed in the pictures. The text is always inside quotation marks, with each boy's comments fitting into a single page. A few words appear in capitals for emphasis.

The wording switches from *mine* to *my, mine* to *mine's, you* to *your, your* to *yours,* and *she* to *she's,* which requires looking across words and self-monitoring for syntax. Most of the meaning throughout the text must be inferred from the pictures.

There is a blurb on the back cover that culminates in a question, but neither the blurb nor the question set children up to approach this book well. It says, "Two boys. Two balloons. Each boy thinks his balloon is the best. What do you think?" The goal is not for readers to join in on the squabble over whose balloon is the best. Instead, one hopes that readers will see how silly it is for these boys to squabble in such a manner. A better starter question might have been, "Why does it matter?"

Teaching Ideas

It's impossible to read this book without cracking a smile and even laughing

Publisher
HarperCollins, 1973

ISBN
0064442136

TC Level
4

A Field Guide to the Classroom Library, Lucy Calkins and the Teachers College Reading and Writing Project, Heinemann, ©2002 Teachers College, Columbia University; http://www.heinemann.com/fieldguides

out loud. How pleased young readers will be to find their reading skills have grown to a place where they can actually read-all by themselves-books which make them roar with laughter! A teacher may want to avoid previewing this book for young readers (except perhaps in the most modest way possible) so that children will be able to discover the very clear, obvious but surprising structure of two children talking back and forth to each other and encounter the funny parts all on their own.

If a teacher wants to help without taking away any of the surprises and the challenges of this book, they might suggest children read *Yo! Yes?* by Chris Raschka (also about two boys who talk and gesture back and forth) first, and only then progress to this book. Of course, it's easy to question whether we can really be there for each child's every book choice. Some teachers find it helps to put several books together in a plastic bag so that children who are beginning to read choose a collection of three books rather than making individual choices. If a teacher did this, we could imagine a bag of books that would contain *Yo! Yes?* labeled #1, this book labeled #2 and perhaps Bonsall's *And I Mean It, Stanley* as #3.

When a child brings this book to his or her partnership, the obvious thing to do will be to reread the book with each partner acting out one boy's part. Later children may talk about the book. One obvious topic to discuss is the ending. How did it happen that these two warring lads became fast buddies?

Book Connections

Books that are similar to this one include, *Yo! Yes?* by Chris Raschka, *Where's the Bear?* by Charlotte Pomerantz, and *The Chick and the Duckling* by Mirra Ginsburg.

Genre
Emergent Literacy Book

Teaching Uses
Independent Reading; Small Group Strategy Instruction; Interpretation; Partnerships

A Field Guide to the Classroom Library, Lucy Calkins and the Teachers College Reading and Writing Project, Heinemann, ©2002 Teachers College, Columbia University; http://www.heinemann.com/fieldguides

Mouse Soup
Arnold Lobel

Book Summary

A weasel captures a mouse with the intention of making him into soup. In order to distract the weasel the mouse convinces him he must put stories in his soup, which the mouse proceeds to tell him. When the weasel goes out to collect ingredients from the mouse's stories, the mouse escapes.

Basic Book Information

This short book for early readers has the look of the Frog and Toad books.

Noteworthy Features

The story of the mouse's capture acts as a frame for the four stories he tells. The stories are set apart as separate chapters with headings.

The text is of varied length, the majority of which is dialogue. The color pictures illustrate the main action of each scene, which makes comprehension easier.

Teaching Ideas

This book is appropriate for readers familiar with dialogue, readers ready for books that include a table of contents and chapters, and readers learning to predict text from pictures.

One possible way to introduce the book is to say, "This is the story of a mouse who uses his imagination to get out of a dangerous situation." Children will be interested in the clever way the mouse tricks the weasel into letting him escape, a theme that is repeated in the first of the four stories the mouse tells.

In a conference, a teacher might ask a reader to identify the "moral" of the remaining three tales the mouse tells. The child will probably talk about the fact that all the stories tell different ways of turning something sad or frustrating into something positive. A child could also be asked to discuss the "moral" of the book as a whole. The child might say the moral is that the reason the mouse is able to save himself is because he reads books, and therefore had stories to tell the weasel.

Book Connections

If students are engaged in an Arnold Lobel author study, they might be glad to know some of his other books include *Frog and Toad Are Friends, Frog and Toad Together, Frog and Toad All Year* , and *Days with Frog and Toad.*

Illustrator
Arnold Lobel

Publisher
Harper Trophy, 1977

ISBN
0064440419

TC Level
6

A Field Guide to the Classroom Library, Lucy Calkins and the Teachers College Reading and Writing Project, Heinemann, ©2002 Teachers College, Columbia University; http://www.heinemann.com/fieldguides

Genre
Picture Book

Teaching Uses
Independent Reading; Partnerships

A Field Guide to the Classroom Library, Lucy Calkins and the Teachers College Reading and Writing Project, Heinemann, ©2002 Teachers College, Columbia University; http://www.heinemann.com/fieldguides

Mr. Popper's Penguins

Richard Atwater; Florence Atwater

Book Summary

Mr. Popper's Penguins is the comic story of a semi-employed house painter whose passion for Admiral Byrd's polar adventures leads him (and his surprised family) to become caretaker of, at first one, and thentwelve, mischievous penguins.

With the help of practical Mrs. Popper and their children, Janie and Bill, Mr. Popper ingeniously creates a proper polar home in the basement of their house. It isn't long before the financial strain of a large, fresh-fish-eating family leads the Poppers to a brief career on the stage, and to a solution that pleases everyone.

Basic Book Information

This Newbery Honor book has 132 pages and 20 numbered, titled chapters of between four and nine pages each.

Noteworthy Features

Mr. Popper's Penguins is a rare combination of humor, science, history and fantasy. Although the slapstick antics of the Poppers and their penguins are in the foreground of the story, a reader also gets a taste of the 1930s atmosphere, learns something about the explorer Admiral Byrd, and gets information on penguin diet and behavior.

Set in a small town during the 1930s when Admiral Richard Drake was exploring Antarctica, *Mr. Popper's Penguins* contains what might be unfamiliar vocabulary and settings (e.g., "Pullman" train and "vaudeville" stage shows), but its delightful wackiness should keep readers involved. Engagingly comic illustrations, chronological narration, and short chapters will be assets to less patient readers. In general, there are fewer reading challenges (in terms of vocabulary, structure and dialogue) than in other books in this grouping.

Teaching Ideas

Mr. Popper's Penguins makes a good read aloud, but is also appropriate for independent reading.

Mr. Popper's Penguins can accompany other nonfiction research on the 1930s, penguins and the Antarctic. This research may help with comprehension of the book. For example, if readers collect information on penguins, they can then discuss how Mr. Popper accommodated the penguins' needs.

Kids can work on interpreting the message of the story. Commonly, students decide one message is that with enough enthusiasm, one can

Publisher
Little Brown, 1938

ISBN
0590477331

TC Level
12

A Field Guide to the Classroom Library, Lucy Calkins and the Teachers College Reading and Writing Project, Heinemann, ©2002 Teachers College, Columbia University; http://www.heinemann.com/fieldguides

accomplish nearly anything. Mr. Popper's eccentricity and passion, while bringing strange looks from the plumber, are assets to himself, his family and the penguins. Other readers decide on different messages, for instance, that odd people learn more. As long as kids are supporting their interpretations with textual evidence all of the messages they point to are fair game, and should generate lively discussion.

The characters of Mr. and Mrs. Popper are well drawn. Mr. Popper remains an irrepressible dreamer while Mrs. Popper is an utterly down-to-earth woman who ends up sharing Mr. Popper's love of the penguins. Students may want to study these characters and come to these conclusions about Mr. and Mrs. Popper's natures. Some students even do little character studies about the individual penguins!

Genre
Chapter Book; Fantasy; Historical Fiction

Teaching Uses
Read Aloud; Independent Reading; Character Study; Content Area Study

A Field Guide to the Classroom Library, Lucy Calkins and the Teachers College Reading and Writing Project, Heinemann, ©2002 Teachers College, Columbia University; http://www.heinemann.com/fieldguides

Mrs. Brice's Mice

Syd Hoff

Book Summary

Mrs. Brice's Mice is the story of an elderly woman who lives very contentedly with her twenty-five mice. Mrs. Brice does everything with her mice. She cares for them, sings at the piano with them, does her daily exercises with them and shops with them. One day, on a shopping trip, the littlest mouse saves them all from being eaten by a cat! On their return home, all the mice and Mrs. Brice share the finest cheese in celebration.

Basic Book Information

Mrs. Brice's Mice is in the *An Early I Can Read Book* series. There are 32 pages with an average of one to four sentences per page. The text is mostly comprised of simple sentences and dialogue that is referenced at either the beginning or the end of the sentence. Each picture matches at least one sentence on each page. Most of the story is carried by high frequency words such as: *she, had, behind, their, always, when, played, little, very, small,* and *between.*

Noteworthy Features

Many children love this simple, funny tale of Mrs. Brice's mice sharing her world so companionably. Though the text is simple, Syd Hoff is a master at creating humor and lovable characters with his words and cartoonish illustrations.

Although the story is simple, it develops the fantasy that many children have of having their pets share all the daily aspects of their lives and coming along with them wherever they go. Many children will love looking very closely at the pictures and seeing that the one very clever mouse who saves the day, is always out-of-step with the other twenty-four mice. He is a lighter gray than the others, and seems to have a special closeness with Mrs. Brice.

Teaching Ideas

From the first page on, the child who reads this will be an active reader. The book begins, "Mrs. Brice had twenty-five mice," and it's an unusual child who doesn't stop to count, confirming that yes, indeed, there are twenty-five mice. Soon an observant reader will spot that one mouse stands out from the rest, and this, of course, is how stories go. Here, the one very small mouse isn't named, but he does have a particular personality. He seems more cautious, more vigilant, and more anxious (e.g., he was afraid to fall between the keys of the piano and he slept on the clock so he'd know what time it was). This makes it all the more impressive when he jumps from his

Illustrator
Syd Hoff

Publisher
HarperTrophy, 1988

ISBN
0064441458

TC Level
5

A Field Guide to the Classroom Library, Lucy Calkins and the Teachers College Reading and Writing Project, Heinemann, ©2002 Teachers College, Columbia University; http://www.heinemann.com/fieldguides

safe perch atop Mrs. Brice's hat to lure the cat this way and that, wearing him out so much that everyone gets away safely to the supermarket.

The structure of this story is a bit unusual. The entire first half of the book is structured like a list, showing all the things Mrs. Brice and her mice do together. These things aren't usual or predictable-they dance on the piano keys and do exercises, stretch, bending to touch their toes. Then comes the "one day" event and it *is* a predictable one. A cat arrives on the scene. Once the mice escape, the story continues predictably with a celebration in which the mice eat "a nice big" cheese.

Book Connections

Mrs. Brice's Mice is very similar to other books written by Syd Hoff. Some of these books include: *Sammy the Seal, Danny and the Dinosaur, Danny and the Dinosaur Go to Camp* and *The Firehouse Cat.* In most of Hoff's books, a person befriends an unusual animal. Sometimes the animals talk, and sometimes they don't. This book has lots of interesting parallels to *Madeline* by Ludwig Bemelmans as well.

Genre
Picture Book

Teaching Uses
Independent Reading; Whole Group Instruction; Small Group Strategy Instruction; Language Conventions

Mrs. Wishy-Washy's Tub

Joy Cowley

Book Summary

Mrs. Wishy-Washy has a tub filled with animals. On each of four pages of this story we meet the animals: the cow, the pig, the dog, and the duck. What good would a tub be without water and soap? On the fifth and sixth pages, we learn these two items are also in the tub. And what did Mrs. Wishy-Washy do with all of these animals and the soap and water? Why "wishy-washy" them of course. This is a delightful nonsense story that a beginning reader can read while learning about print as well.

Basic Book Information

The book has 7 pages of text, six of which use the same sentence: "The ___ is in the tub," substituting the subject of the sentence. The text on the last page is in two lines: "Wishy-washy! Wishy-washy!" The single sentence on each page is consistently at the bottom of the page. Fuller's humorous illustrations add to the fun and provide a clue, as each animal is added to the ones already in the tub. The pictures are framed with a thin black line, separating them from the text and making reading easier. The narration is a simple list rather than a problem/solution story.

Noteworthy Features

This is a simple list book, told in third person narration. The sentence structure is simple. There is no dialogue. The pictures are tightly tied to the text, providing understanding to the implied meaning of the sentence.

Teaching Ideas

The main purpose of this story is to provide a humorous setting to a simple list. Teachers might want to introduce the book by discussing the title and illustration on the front cover. Students might suggest what Mrs. Wishy-Washy will do with this tub. On the title page, the four animals are depicted.

Students might speculate on what the animals are all looking at. Teachers might also comment on the existence of the name of the author, Joy Cowley and the illustrator, Elizabeth Fuller. Students should understand that names of authors and illustrators, those who write the stories and draw the pictures, are usually listed on the cover as well as the title page.

Teachers might have students "walk-through" the story; as students look at each picture, teachers might point out that the sentence at the bottom tells us who is in the tub. For each subsequent page, students can respond to the question: "Who else is in the tub?" Teachers might point to each word in the sentence on that page as the students respond. When they reach the last

Illustrator
Elizabeth Fuller

Publisher
Wright Group, 1998

ISBN
0780272609

TC Level
1

page, students should recognize "wishy-washy." If they do not recognize the words, teachers might direct their attention to the title on the cover, *Mrs. Wishy-Washy's Tub* .

Teachers might invite students to do a shared reading of the book-that is, reading along with the teacher, pointing to each word as they pronounce it, to practice matching one spoken word to one printed word. This might be followed by a silent reading of the book.

Teachers might have students act out the story. The teacher might hold up each sentence (or project it, using an overhead projector). A chorus of students might recite the sentence together while one student acts out the animal and "goes" into the tub. A student, acting as Mrs. Wishy-Washy, might pretend to "scrub" the animals as the chorus chants "wishy-washy, wishy-washy."

Book Connections

Joy Cowley has written a number of books published by The Wright Group and categorized as Level 1 books. Later, as their reading level increases, students might also enjoy reading *Mrs. Wishy-Washy* and *Splishy-Sploshy.*

Genre
Emergent Literacy Book

Teaching Uses
Partnerships; Interpretation; Independent Reading

Nicky Upstairs and Down
Harriet Zeifert

Book Summary

Nicky is a cat who plays in the basement and upstairs of his house. Every time his mother calls for him, he runs up or down the stairs. When his mother calls for him, he hides underneath the sink. Finally, he comes out of hiding and runs halfway up the stairs. Nicky triumphantly tells his mother, "I'm not upstairs! I'm not downstairs! I'm right in the middle."

Basic Book Information

This is a picture book with cute illustrations that are particularly loved by cat-owners.

Noteworthy Features

It is noteworthy that *Nicky Upstairs and Down* contains many wrap-around sentences. In addition, there are some sentences that continue across two different pages (you must turn the page for the continuation). The punctuation in *Nicky Upstairs and Down* is quite sophisticated and includes quotation marks, commas, exclamation points, and ellipses.

The illustrations in the book do not fully support the text. For instance, on one page it says, "Nicky's house has a downstairs." The corresponding illustration shows Nicky lounging on a chair in his living room.

Teaching Ideas

Nicky Upstairs and Down contains wrap-around sentences. Teachers may need to work with readers on following one idea across two lines. Even more challenging, are the sentences that are continued over the course of two pages. It is essential that students retain the initial idea of the sentence as they turn the page.

One of the ways that this book indicates a continuation on the following page is through the use of ellipses. If appropriate, ellipses may be something that a teacher decides to focus on during their teaching points (in a guided reading session) or reading mini-lesson.

Nicky Upstairs and Down contains a number of compound words, such as *upstairs, downstairs,* and *everywhere.* For readers who are still working on one-to-one matching, it is important for teachers to ensure that children are pointing only once under these compound words. For children for whom these words are somewhat unfamiliar, chunking may be a powerful strategy. Children feel like empowered readers when they discover that if they know the words *up* and *stairs,* then they also know they word *upstairs.*

This book elicits much discussion around different themes in whole class readings, partnerships, or independent work. Children may relate to the fact

Illustrator
Richard Brown

Publisher
Penguin Group, 1987

ISBN
0140368523

TC Level
4

A Field Guide to the Classroom Library, Lucy Calkins and the Teachers College Reading and Writing Project, Heinemann, ©2002 Teachers College, Columbia University; http://www.heinemann.com/fieldguides

that Nicky's mother always needs to know where he is. Young readers might want to speculate about why Nicky's mother is always asking, "Nicky, where are you?" Another point of discussion might be centered around Nicky's response. Children might also envision alternative solutions to Nicky's.

Another teaching option might be to compare animal characters in various books that talk and act like people against those that don't.

Genre
Picture Book

Teaching Uses
Independent Reading; Language Conventions

A Field Guide to the Classroom Library, Lucy Calkins and the Teachers College Reading and Writing Project, Heinemann, ©2002 Teachers College, Columbia University; http://www.heinemann.com/fieldguides

Our Skeleton

Brian and Jillian Cutting

Book Summary

Our Skeleton answers the repeated question: *"What bones are in here?"* with photographs and simple sentences about the most basic and obvious bones in the human body. It begins with leg and foot bones; continues on with arm, hand, skull, neck and backbone; and concludes with a full-page picture of the whole skeleton.

Basic Book Information

Our Skeleton is part of The Wright Group, *Sunshine Books* series. There is a table of contents and an index. There is an average of one line of text per page. The text is very simple and each page contains the repeated question: *"What bones are in here?"* and the answer. The names of the bones are used throughout the book.

Noteworthy Features

Although the book is virtually a pattern book, about half of the text is made up of very difficult, unfamiliar words for readers at this level (e.g., *tibia*, *thigh*, and *humerus*).

The photographs are very supportive of the text.

Teaching Ideas

This book may be used for several different reading experiences. *Our Skeleton* can be used as part of a genre study of nonfiction. Teachers may use this book to introduce readers to the features of nonfiction texts: an index, or table of contents, or to introduce them to "skimming and scanning" nonfiction texts to find specific information, read labeled diagrams, notice the format and/or layout of the book. Finally, teachers may help students find other books in the same series that may be like the one they are reading.

Teachers may model for children how we read nonfiction differently from fiction books. Readers can practice reading in smaller chunks, rather than from start to finish. Readers can practice generating a list of questions based on the title, skimming the book, or skimming the small chunk they've read, and then reading for informational answers to their specific questions.

This book can be used to develop the nonfiction reading skill of formulating hypotheses *after* reading, which will lead students to do more research, either by rereading this text, or finding other texts like it for further research.

Our Skeleton can be used in a reading center as one of a group of books about the skeleton, the human body, bones, etc. for readers to compare and contrast. As readers become more familiar with the topic, they may want to

Illustrator
Alan Gillard

Publisher
Wright Group, 1992

ISBN
0780202570

TC Level
3

do some very simple cross-referencing to discover what all books about skeletons have in common, or what this particular book lacks or adds to their study of a chosen topic.

As is the case with most nonfiction, this book presents many opportunities for relevant, meaningful discussion. Readers will need ample time to discuss their questions, their hypotheses based on questions they have, or information they've gathered; and their speculation about the topic. These discussions will enable readers to understand more of what they read, as well as possibly introducing them to a topic they might feel really excited by.

As readers become more familiar with their research topic, they may use this book as a model for writing their own book about skeletons. They may write a simple "research report" about what they've learned. They may also want to write a book based on the questions and hypotheses that have led them to more research and more information about the topic than is included in the book. Writers may want to try including a simple index, table of contents or glossary in their books.

This book may be used as part of a science curriculum devoted to the study of the human body and/or bones and skeletons.

Genre
Nonfiction; Emergent Literacy Book

Teaching Uses
Independent Reading; Content Area Study; Reading and Writing Nonfiction; Small Group Strategy Instruction; Interpretation; Partnerships

A Field Guide to the Classroom Library, Lucy Calkins and the Teachers College Reading and Writing Project, Heinemann, ©2002 Teachers College, Columbia University; http://www.heinemann.com/fieldguides

Owl Moon

Jane Yolen

Book Summary

In this Caldecott Award-winning picture book, a young boy goes out on a winter night to go owling with his father. The two walk quietly through the dark forest, the father occasionally whoo-whooing to call the great horned owl. Finally one answers the call and flies to a nearby branch. The boy's father catches the owl in the beam of his flashlight, and they look at the magnificent creature in the eye for a moment before it flies away. They walk home together silently, full of the warmth of excitement and wonder.

Basic Book Information

This large picture book is a breathtakingly wonderful Caldecott Medal-winner.

Noteworthy Features

This is an enormously popular book among children and teachers alike. Because of its quiet excitement and slow pace, and because teachers tend to like it so much themselves, many teachers choose to read the book aloud, and to return to the book often.

Teaching Ideas

Reading the book aloud helps set the pace of the story for subsequent independent readings. Although the text is laid out in short bits at a time, like short lines of poetry, some children do not take this cue to read slowly, and instead read at their usual rapid clip. When this is done, the line breaks only succeed in making the sentences and meanings choppy. When it's read aloud first, at a slow pace, children can hear the elegance of the words and the story.

For some children, the scene and ideas may be difficult to take in. Many children have never gone for a night walk with their father. Many have never walked through the country in the snow. To some, this event may seem as strange and hard to imagine as an exotic ceremony in a faraway land, and readers may need just as much support in envisioning it. Still, the many metaphors will pull the reader in, and the pictures certainly help set the mood.

Many readers and teachers prefer not to work on interpreting a book like *Owl Moon* because it feels like too technical a thing to do to such a beautiful book. However, if children are thinking about the messages that the book sends, work on interpreting may help them come away feeling that the book is even more beautiful. They may find that the book sends messages about patience and hope and other things that are important in life.

Illustrator
John Schoenherr

Publisher
Scholastic Inc., 1987

ISBN
0590420445

TC Level
10

As in any book, exotic setting or not, some readers will feel a personal response related to *Owl Moon* that may need an avenue for expression. Others will read the book and say, "What's the big deal, they saw an owl!" This very comment can reveal a great deal about the particular child and his or her reading and writing. It may also mean that *Owl Moon* is not a book that the child can easily connect with. Instead, another kind of book may be needed to help the child learn to appreciate literature. Later, the child may come back to books like *Owl Moon* and love them.

After the content has been discussed, the pace of the story might be a worthwhile conversation topic, whether the children have heard the book read to them or they've read it on their own. Why the line breaks? If the line breaks do indeed slow the pace, why the slower pace? Some children will point out that the beautiful language is more easily appreciated that way, and others may notice that the pace of the reading matches the pace of a walk in the deep snow, when you are on the lookout for the wonders around you.

Children writing their own stories or poems might well find help in referring back to this book to guide them when they make their own decisions about line breaks, use of metaphors, etc.

Genre
Picture Book; Memoir; Nonfiction

Teaching Uses
Read Aloud; Teaching Writing; Small Group Strategy Instruction

A Field Guide to the Classroom Library, Lucy Calkins and the Teachers College Reading and Writing Project, Heinemann, ©2002 Teachers College, Columbia University; http://www.heinemann.com/fieldguides

Papa's Spaghetti
Joy Cowley

Book Summary

Papa makes spaghetti for lunch. When he serves it, Mama notices a fly in it. Papa sends in a spider to catch it, and when someone notices the spider, he sends a bird to catch that. Larger and larger animals jump into the spaghetti until everyone calls "no more," and the spaghetti is all gone.

Basic Book Information

This book has 18 numbered pages with, on average, ten lines every two pages. Excluding the first and last pages, the text of each page is almost entirely the same with the only variations being who notices the creature in the spaghetti, the name of that creature, and the name of the larger creature Papa will send to chase it away. The text is written with dialogue, using quotation marks and naming the speaker.

Noteworthy Features

Within the patterned text that is repeated six times, there are several repeating lines that give the words a singsong or chant-like feel.

The pictures show the animal already in the spaghetti, but not the new animal that Papa names to chase that animal away. Although if the reader figures out the pattern of the book well enough, she may realize that to figure out the new animal, she can take a peak at the next page. The illustrations also do not give a hint about who is speaking, thereby offering no clue about that particular character's name.

Teaching Ideas

Because of the repeating lines, this may be an excellent choice for two readers to read together in a partnership. If the stronger reader reads a few lines first, that may leave the weaker reader with the echoing lines to read, making the job much easier for him. Or instead of alternating lines, readers might also alternate reads, since this book is so strongly patterned that it is memorable, even for a struggling reader.

Partners may also work on reading with expression, or taking roles in the text, as there is a different person speaking along with Papa on each page.

Readers will probably spend some time talking about how gross and disgusting it is to see the hairy spider crawling around in the lunch of spaghetti, and the crazy father who keeps sending more creatures into the pot. Sometimes, readers even wonder where the Papa gets these exotic animals so quickly. Is he a zookeeper? And why didn't Mama, or some other more reasonable member of the family, just get the fly out of the pot with a spoon or something?

Illustrator
Marie Low

Publisher
Rigby, 1989

ISBN
0790101491

TC Level
4

A Field Guide to the Classroom Library, Lucy Calkins and the Teachers College Reading and Writing Project, Heinemann, ©2002 Teachers College, Columbia University; http://www.heinemann.com/fieldguides

The very last page of the book usually takes some figuring out by the readers. When the characters call out "No more!" do they mean that Papa shouldn't keep calling these increasingly dangerous and large animals into their kitchen? Or do they simply mean that there is no more spaghetti for their lunch? What do you think?

Book Connections

There are several books and songs that are similar to this one, notably *There Was an Old Lady Who Swallowed a Fly*. Sometimes when several of these types of stories are gathered together, children have an easier time doing interpretation work. What do all these stories have in common? What are they saying or joking about? Do they teach us about ways to solve problems? Do they teach us ways not to?

Genre
Picture Book

Teaching Uses
Independent Reading; Language Conventions; Partnerships; Interpretation

Peter's Chair

Ezra Jack Keats

Book Summary

Peter has a new baby sister, and things have changed. He has to play more quietly, and his parents are using all of his old things for her. His high chair is getting painted pink, like the crib and the cradle. He finds his old chair and decides to run away with it. When he tries to sit in it, though, he realizes it is too small. By the time mother calls him inside for a special lunch and a hiding game, Peter feels differently. As he sits in the adult chair around the table, he asks his father if they can paint the little chair pink for his sister Suzie.

Basic Book Information

Caldecott award-winning author and illustrator Ezra Jack Keats offers this picture book, illustrated in his usual collage format, set in a city with the character of young Peter and his small dog Willie, both of whom are featured in many of his other stories. This picture book has about thirty pages. On each double-page spread, there are from one to five lines of print, always on only one of the pages. There is some dialogue, all of which is referenced with a "speaker tag." The book is not based on patterns or repetition, but is instead a story told in chronological order of one afternoon in Peter's life.

Noteworthy Features

As in many of Keats' books, in order to understand the full story, the reader will need to examine the pictures closely. Sometimes the text refers to events described in the illustrations, as when Peter's mother thinks she has found Peter, but it is only his shoes he has placed at the foot of the curtains.

This story begins in the middle of the action. While some readers find this type of opening to be a great hook because it draws them into the book, others find it disconcerting because they begin reading without knowing who, what, where, why, and when.

Teaching Ideas

The primary instructional purpose of *Peter's Chair* in Library A, is as a read aloud. This instruction is based on the research of Elizabeth Sulzby, whose work with kindergarten children informed her of the importance of recreating parent-child interactions around books in the kindergarten classroom. At home, children often ask parents to "read it again" when they hear a favorite story. In school, the teacher's multiple readings of emergent literacy books helps children become familiar with rich narrative, hear the inflection and pacing of storybook language and learn to use detailed

Illustrator
Ezra Jack Keats

Publisher
Penguin, Puffin, 1967

ISBN
0140564411

TC Level
6

illustrations to assist them in remembering storyline.

After the story has been read to children at least four times, multiple copies of the book should be added to a basket of "Stories We Love." Children will have opportunities to return to these books at independent reading time. They will refer to the pictures and use their memory of the teacher's reading to recreate the story on their own. Given the opportunity to do this, children pass through a series of predictable reading stages from simply "labeling" pictures on the page, to telling the story off the pictures, to using progressively more dialogue and storybook language, and then moving toward a more "conventional" reading where they use the print. To go on this journey, it is important for children to hear the story read aloud many times, have a lot of opportunities to reread it to a partner and have a supportive teacher nearby who thoughtfully coaches into their reading.

To support this process, teachers can select books that contain more text than emergent readers could decode on their own, that can not be easily memorized, that have elements of drama and suspense, and that have characters that many young children can relate to.

After children have heard *Peter's Chair* and *The Snowy Day*, teachers might want to create an Ezra Jack Keats reading basket. This would be a good time to also introduce *Whistle for Willie*, another book with Peter as the main character. A few of the books together would make excellent material for a character study of Peter. In each of the books, including this one, Peter has some unvoiced, and unexplained, emotions and conflicts that he works through by the end of each book. Readers sometimes like to put these events together to show how Peter has grown. Readers also sometimes like to put the books in chronological order as best they can, based on the kinds of things Peter is doing in his life in each book. In which books does he have his dog Willie? In which books doesn't he? Clues of this sort add to the puzzle of the correct order for the stories.

In classrooms with older children, this book can serve other purposes. Because there are so many similarities between Keats' books-recurring characters and settings, style of illustration and their interdependence with the text and the story structure-he makes a great author to study and this book makes a good addition to such a study. Through read aloud, partner and independent reading, or even in a reading center, readers can build collective knowledge about Keats and his style. What tends to be similar about his books? How is each unique? What can we say about his writing style? His choice of language and setting?

A few of his books together would also make an excellent character study of Peter. In each of the books, including this one, Peter has unvoiced, unexplained emotions and conflicts he works through by the end of the book. Readers sometimes like to put these events together to show how Peter has grown. Readers sometimes put the books in a chronological order as best they can, based on the kinds of things Peter is doing in each book. In which books does he have his dog Willy? In which books doesn't he? Clues of this sort add to the puzzle of the correct order for the stories.

Since the books never explicitly state how Peter is feeling or why, readers need to infer these emotions based on Peter's behavior and their own personal experience. This book is good to read aloud, even in the upper grades. It helps students build their ability to infer and to understand books based on their own experience. Since nearly everyone has experienced a reluctance to share or a discomfort with change, many readers in a class should be able to bring their personal experiences to this story.

It's helpful for readers to look for places in a story when a character really changes. Why does the character change? In this case, why does Peter suddenly feel okay about letting his baby sister have the chair? At first, many readers say it is because the chair no longer fits him, but with further discussion, they come to a deeper understanding of Peter's changing feelings about himself and his role in his family. This type of discussion, both with the whole class and between partners, can teach children to ask these questions when they read on their own.

Book Connections

Ezra Jack Keats has written many great books for children, including *The Snowy Day*, *A Letter to Amy*, and *Whistle for Willie*.

Genre
Picture Book

Teaching Uses
Author Study; Interpretation; Small Group Strategy Instruction; Language Conventions; Character Study; Read Aloud; Independent Reading; Partnerships

Polar Express
Chris Van Allsburg

Book Summary

This extraordinary book begins one Christmas Eve a long time ago. A little boy lies in bed awaiting the sound of ringing bells from Santa's sleigh and "hissing steam and squeaking metal." Instead, he hears and sees a train outside his window called *The Polar Express*. The train whisks him and the reader far away to the North Pole, a magical *city of lights* where dreams are realized and Santa will give away the very first gift of Christmas. The boy is chosen to receive the gift and out of all the gifts in the world, he requests one of Santa's silver bells from his sleigh. Before the next page is turned, his wish comes true. The clock strikes midnight and the boy puts the precious silver bell into his pocket. But when the other children on the train ask to see the silver bell, it is gone-nowhere to be found until the miracle of Christmas morning when wondrous things can happen and often do for those who believe.

Basic Book Information

When asked how he comes up with ideas, Van Allsburg says he uses a "what if" and "what then" method (e.g., What if a young boy were to find himself aboard a train to the North Pole? What then?). From there, he works to weave his images together into a story line. He is well-known for his imaginative use of light and perspective to portray everyday objects in extraordinary, mysterious and mystical ways.

His text is filled with mystery and words of wonder just like his pictures. This brilliant author and illustrator feels that his books are surrealistic and he gains inspiration from Degas and Hooper. The words compliment the pictures, which in turn compliments the text and will intrigue readers of all ages. Chris Van Allsburg is the author of 15 books, most recently *Bad Day at Riverbend*. *The Polar Express* and *Jumanji* both won the Caldecott Medal.

This picture book is 30 pages long. The pages are not numbered. With the exception of the last page, text is written in a column, either on the left or right hand side of each spread. The remaining space on each spread is covered by Van Allsburg's classic pastel illustrations. The last page, simply illustrated with a small picture of the sleigh bell, serves as an epilogue explaining the bell's jingle, "Though I've grown old, the bell still rings for me as it does for all who truly believe." The book is often sold as part of a gift set, including an audiotape of the story and a sleigh bell.

Noteworthy Features

This book provides students with the outstanding quality of what good stories do-transport us to different worlds, make us question and wonder and want to reread the book over and over again. It is a simple story told in

Illustrator
Chris Van Allsburg

Publisher
Houghton Mifflin

ISBN
0395389496

first person but one filled with such rich language (most especially metaphors), and an air of mystery that it can be read over and over again as readers discover deeper meaning.

This is a text that raises many questions during and after reading and is a wonderful way for teachers to encourage students to question, wonder, and reflect. Why did the boy ask for the silver bell? Can we go back into the text and notice where we have clues that he will ask for the bell? There is a lot of evidence in the text that would need to be explored. (However, since the book does not have page numbers, teachers may want to attach very small post-it notes to the bottom of the pages so children can cite page numbers.) Also, the rich text enables teachers to explore with children making inferences, such as why the parents thought the bell was broken. [Ed: please check edits so that meaning is still intact. Original paragraph was: This is a text which that raises many questions during and after reading and is a wonderful way for teachers to encourage students to question, wonder, and reflect. Why did the boy ask for the silver bell? Can we go back into the text and notice where we have clues that he will ask for the bell? There is a lots of evidence from in the text work that would need to be doneexplored. (Hhowever , , since the book does not have page numbers, so teachers may want to post attach the very small very small post- it notes on to the bottom of the pages so children can cite page numbers..) Also, it the rich text enables teachers to explore with children making inferences, such as why the parents thought the bell was broken.]

This is a terrific read aloud with poetic language and metaphors that can help children understand how authors carefully craft their words by showing not telling the reader. An example is the line, "Lights look like a strange ocean liner sailing on a frozen sea." The illustrations are all works of art and readers will want to jump aboard The Polar Express. While many teachers may want to use this book as a read aloud during the holidays, it is really one that can be read all year round. Although certainly, teachers may not want to miss the opportunity that this book provides to discuss the deeper meaning of gifts and why this little boy preferred the bell to any toy or video game. Children may want to share their own personal stories about gifts they received that have great meaning to them not because of the gift but because it holds a special place in their hearts.

Teaching Ideas

The teacher might open a read aloud by showing the cover to the children sitting on the rug and asking them to look carefully, examining the picture as an entire spread (front and back contain the picture) for some noticings and wonderings. If children are familiar with some of the other books by the same author, they may predict that this book will have a sense of mystery like in *The Garden of Abdul Gazasi, The Wreck of the Zephyr,* and of course the beloved *Jumanji.* The book provides plenty of rich opportunities for inference work and questioning which aids comprehension. Young readers may come up with many questions like, "How would the other children feel who came all that way and did not get a gift and this kid who gets one loses it?" Children with older siblings may question, "Why didn't the boy take his little sister Sarah along?" "Why doesn't the young boy have a name?" "Why do we never see the conductor at all in any of the pictures?" (Readers can cite evidence from the pictures by researching picturesthe text mentions the conductor but there are never any pictures of him.) Some astute children, especially those who ride the subway may pose the question, "How can it be an express? It made lots of local stops to pick up all those children." Further questioning may explore, "What would I have asked for if Santa was going to give me the first gift of Christmas?" There are many opportunities for inference work especially at the end, "Why did the parents think the bell was broken?" "Where is the young boy now?" "How old is he?" "How come he can hear the bell but his sister and friends cannot?" "What do you have to believe in to hear the bell?" Some smart students may even raise the question to their teacher that even though she is a grown up, would she hear the bell?

The rich language and the way that the words are put together enables children to really listen in throughout the text to the beautiful imagery and create a movie in their minds such as the sounds of "hissing stream and squeaking metal" of the train. And "the train was wrapped in an apron of steam." (The teacher can pose, "Is the train really wrapped in an apron?) "Climbed mountains so high, it seemed as if we would scrape the moon." The teacher could pause for a turn and talk, "Turn and talk to your partner, what do you think that means, 'Looked like the lights of a strange ocean liner sailing on a frozen sea.'" When Van Allsburg uses language such as "broke my heart"-the boy's heart doesn't really break like a dish would break. The teacher can ask, "What does that feel like to the boy to have a broken heart?" Turn and talk opportunities abound throughout the read aloud as teachers can also ask, "What do you think figurative language is? Literal language?"

Students can also be encouraged to study the mood of the book. Van Allsburg's books are often described as "mysterious." Students can discuss how the use of light and shadow, color, figure placement, perspective, and so on work together to create a sense of mystery. Such conversation can lead to a discussion on reality versus fantasy in the text. Did the journey to the North Pole really take place? Or was it just a dream? How do you know? Students can discuss how and why the author blurs the line between reality and fantasy through changes in scene and perspective. Things look so normal-the boy's bedroom, the train, the forest, the mountain-until the train enters the North Pole. The distant lights viewed from the shadows of the bridge look somewhat dreamy as they are reflected in the icy water, yet the village itself looks like any other typical winter wonderland lined in outdoor lights and dusted with snow. Santa's reindeer look just as real as the wolves in the forest.

Teachers can also have children explore Van Allsburg not just as a writer but an artist and how he made his decisions on what to draw with what corresponding words. Do children think the pictures came first or the words? (Van Allsburg says he sees pictures in his mind so it could be that at times pictures come first then the text tags along.) Many children may notice the use of light and dark, "Where is the light in this picture? Why did Van Allsburg use only dark colors here? The sense of the magical stays with us long after we finish the book and gives plenty of rich opportunity to linger, reflect, talk, and go back to the text and rediscover.

There are so many more teaching ideas with this book such as following

A Field Guide to the Classroom Library, Lucy Calkins and the Teachers College Reading and Writing Project, Heinemann, ©2002 Teachers College, Columbia University; http://www.heinemann.com/fieldguides

the big idea and talking back to text. Ask children, "What is your theory about this story?" (Theory charts can be created.) Let children know that their theory may change as they get more and more information from the text.

Students could compare and contrast other books by Van Allsburg-some are all in black and white while some are all in color while some have a combination of both. Teachers can ask, "Why do you think he does that?" Van Allsburg repeatedly has the same character in many of his books. The character's name is Fritz from *The Garden of Abdul Gazasi* and he is hidden in most of Van Allsburg's books including *The Polar Express*. Children will love trying to find him in his other books. (In *The Polar Express,* Fritz is the puppet on page one on the bedpost.)

Readers could discuss story elements. Besides plot they could discuss character. What do we know about the character? Why do you think the author left out the boy's name but told us his sister's name? What kind of person is this boy? Where is he today? Movement through time could be examined. Until the last page the children will be able to understand movement through time but then there is a gigantic leap. A discussion of how the book jumps ahead so many years and where the evidence is can be very challenging, as children become movement-in-time researchers. A teacher might use the text to have children note the progression of time from the beginning to the next to last page and then the leap at the last page.

Setting plays an important role in this story. As students hear the story over and over again, they will have new wonderings and noticings. Teachers can suggest that children pay attention to setting since the story shifts to several settings, the bedroom, outside his bedroom, outside the train, inside the train, over mountains, wilderness, to the North Pole, and back inside the comfort and safety of his family living room. Where is the last page that is boxed taking place? Where can we imagine he is now? This can lead to a discussion of change. A teacher might ask, "How has the character changed from the beginning to the end of the story? Is he still a little boy?" Children can think about how old he may be now.

Book Connections

Introducing this book is a fabulous way to begin an author study on Van Allsburg and all his incredible books that have poetic text and pictures that could be in an art museum. Children can compare and contrast his work and find a basic theme that may underline his books and spark a reader's imagination. How does he do this? What are some of his crafts? There are fifteen books to choose from but children should not compare more than three. Children individually may become Van Allsburg fans and want to read all his books during independent reading time. Children with artistic interests may wish to explore his drawings and study the work of surrealistic artist, too.

Genre
Picture Book; Fantasy

A Field Guide to the Classroom Library, Lucy Calkins and the Teachers College Reading and Writing Project, Heinemann, ©2002 Teachers College, Columbia University; http://www.heinemann.com/fieldguides

Teaching Uses

Teaching Writing; Read Aloud; Author Study; Character Study; Independent Reading

A Field Guide to the Classroom Library, Lucy Calkins and the Teachers College Reading and Writing Project, Heinemann, ©2002 Teachers College, Columbia University; http://www.heinemann.com/fieldguides

Ramona The Brave

Beverly Cleary

Book Summary

Ramona Quimby, the main character of all of the *Ramona* books, is six years old and struggling to be brave as she begins first grade in this chapter book.

Basic Book Information

Ramona The Brave is the third book in the *Ramona* series. This book is 190 pages long. It is divided into 9 chapters that build upon each other; they cannot be read as individual stories. Each chapter has a title, which gives the reader a clue as to what the chapter is going to be about. There are a few illustrative pictures but they do not directly support the text.

Each of the *Ramona* books deals with the trials and tribulations of being a little girl. Ramona is always the hero and she ages as the series goes on. However, the *Ramona* books may be read out-of-order because they have separate plots and are all on the same reading level.

Noteworthy Features

Throughout this particular book, the passage of time is made clear as Ramona's new room is being built. The sentences in the book are short and easy to comprehend, and the setting should be familiar since it involves a family, friends, a pet, a teacher and school. There are, however, many big words such as *indignant*, *humiliation*, and *persistence*. Still, readers should be able to grasp the meaning from the context. The dialogue is usually referenced, and it should be clear who is speaking.

Although the book was written in 1975, the reader will see it as happening in present day. Each chapter leaves us wondering what will happen next.

Teaching Ideas

It may be helpful to first introduce the book by saying a little about Ramona. For example, one teacher said, "Ramona is a little girl who does not like being just a little girl. She desperately wants to be grown up and brave. That is why she finds herself in some funny and frustrating situations. She wants to be grown up like her big sister Beezus, but she also wants to be back in kindergarten where everything was fun and easy."

First-grade teachers often read this *Ramona* book aloud because it is written about a six-year-old. It is too hard for most six-year-olds to read on their own, yet if they wait and encounter this book much later, they may not identify with Ramona because to them, she'll be acting like a baby. If readers are older than Ramona, a teacher may want to remind them how hard it was to be that age, and how unfair things often seemed.

Series
Ramona

Illustrator
Alan Tiegreen

Publisher
Avon Books, 1975

ISBN
0380709597

TC Level
9

A Field Guide to the Classroom Library, Lucy Calkins and the Teachers College Reading and Writing Project, Heinemann, ©2002 Teachers College, Columbia University; http://www.heinemann.com/fieldguides

Book Connections

Children may want to start at the beginning of the series with *Beezus and Ramona*, then *Ramona The Pest*. Students who enjoy the *Ramona* series books may also enjoy Beverly Cleary's other series books like *Henry Huggins* and *Ralph S. Mouse*, which are also on the same reading level.

Genre
Chapter Book

Teaching Uses
Read Aloud; Character Study; Interpretation

A Field Guide to the Classroom Library, Lucy Calkins and the Teachers College Reading and Writing Project, Heinemann, ©2002 Teachers College, Columbia University; http://www.heinemann.com/fieldguides

Red Leaf, Yellow Leaf

Lois Ehlert

Book Summary

This is an enchanting nonfiction story of a sugar-maple tree, the young child who planted it, and their relationship. Through exquisite illustrations in vibrant colors and language that evokes strong images, readers are immediately brought into the story. They are provided with a sense of the child and the tree growing up together, while at the same time they follow the journey of a little seedling as it grows into a tree. Readers are left to imagine the process beginning all over again. Though it is written in narrative form, from the point of view of the child telling the story of his tree, many facts are embedded within the context of the story. The story of the maple tree comes to an end, with the little child inviting the reader to become an active participant in the text with the question, "That's my favorite time. Can you guess why?"

Basic Book Information

In this 32-page picture book, illustrations span two pages and the text is written in large black print. The black font set against the brightly colored background supports the reader in attending closely to the print.

Noteworthy Features

As in many of her books, Ehlert's illustrations have a playful feel to them. On the first and last pages, a cut out shape of a maple leaf allows the reader to visualize the leaf with an added dimension. Many pages contain labels and captions that give the reader additional information (e.g., black-capped chickadee, a sugar-maple description, maple seeds). The last four pages form an appendix that gives the reader additional information about this topic. The first part provides a detailed description of the parts of the tree (leaves, buds, roots and sap, seeds, bark, tree flowers) and the last part provides an in-depth description of how to go about planting a tree. The size of the print is significantly smaller on these last four pages.

Teaching Ideas

This text provides an excellent introduction to more complex nonfiction. The print is fairly large and well spaced, but the more complex vocabulary will provide some challenges. The first part of the book is a fairly straightforward story, but as the story deepens, some familiar words are used in ways that will be somewhat tricky (e.g., crown of leaves, winged seeds). The young reader, who for the most part no longer needs to point to

Illustrator
Lois Ehlert

Publisher
Harcourt Brace, 1991

ISBN
0152661972

TC Level
5

words as he reads, may need to in some of the trickier places. As a result, teachers may find themselves coaching children to read and reread to increase fluency.

If a teacher chooses to provide a book introduction, he might begin by saying, "This is the story of a sugar maple tree and the girl who planted it. The girl is going to tell us how the seed started on the ground and then all the different things that happened to it that allowed it to grow into a big wonderful tree. Let's read this and find out how this seed became a maple tree." As the teacher flips through the pages, he would want to call the child's attention to the places that might be somewhat tricky.

This book can also be useful when teaching about the features of nonfiction texts, including how and when to read them. The book includes labels, captions, a glossary of terms (leaves, buds, roots, sap, seeds, bark, and tree flowers), and a how-to page (i.e., how to plant a tree). This is also an example of nonfiction writing in which information is embedded in the context of a story. Children who are familiar with nonfiction features will probably be aware that reading the glossary and the how-to pages will provide them with additional information and a deeper understanding of the concept. They may also know that they can decide to read them either before or after the rest of the text. Unlike those special nonfiction features, however, the story part of this nonfiction book will need to be read from the first page to the last.

Teachers can also take advantage of this text as an opportunity to demonstrate another purpose for rereading. Not only do readers reread to see if something makes sense, but also to gain more information that they might not have caught the first time. Ehlert has embedded a great deal of information in her illustrations that go beyond what's in the text. This leaves the book, and the topic, open to deeper conversations. The labels alone can open meaningful doors. Readers might wonder for example: How do people decide what information to put in the labels and what information to put in the body of the text? Who is meant to be reading these labels? What are the different buds and what type of traits do they have? Teachers should make sure that children immersed in a study of nonfiction texts see a wide variety, including some that are not in a narrative form, and others that contain nonfiction features that aren't found in this book (e.g., a table of contents).

A class engaged in a study of Lois Ehlert would find her books to have a number of similarities. In many of her other books, she offers the reader a gift even before the story begins (i.e., "I've been saving this little leaf from my sugar maple tree so I could show it to you."). Many of Ehlert's books are nonfiction, and most of them contain similar features (e.g., labels, a glossary, or index of words). Her illustrations are imbued with information that goes far beyond what's included in the body of the text.

One teacher used this book in a writing workshop to show students one example of the various ways authors invite readers into the story. In this book, Ehlert ends her story by directly asking the reader a question: Can you guess why? Writers may also want to try that technique in their own writing.

Genre
Nonfiction; Picture Book

A Field Guide to the Classroom Library, Lucy Calkins and the Teachers College Reading and Writing Project, Heinemann, ©2002 Teachers College, Columbia University; http://www.heinemann.com/fieldguides

Teaching Uses
Author Study; Partnerships; Independent Reading; Small Group Strategy Instruction; Language Conventions; Content Area Study; Reading and Writing Nonfiction; Teaching Writing

A Field Guide to the Classroom Library, Lucy Calkins and the Teachers College Reading and Writing Project, Heinemann, ©2002 Teachers College, Columbia University; http://www.heinemann.com/fieldguides

Rockabye Crocodile: A Folktale from the Philippines

Jose Aruego; Ariane Dewey

Book Summary

Two boars live in the jungle. One boar, Amabel, is "cheerful and kind," and the other, Nettie, is "mean and selfish." Amabel goes through her daily chores and because she is so courteous, the bamboo tree gives her fish. Then, the mother crocodile asks her to take care of her crying baby. Amabel does such a good job that the crocodile gives her a huge basket of fish. She shares her bounty with Nettie. The next day, Nettie demands fish from the bamboo tree and is rude to the crocodile and her baby. The mother crocodile sends her home with a sealed basket that Nettie is determined not to share. The basket turns out to be filled with stinging, creepy things. Nettie is upset, but realizes how foolish she's been. From then on she changes and the two boars take care of the crocodile baby and the bamboo tree and so "the crocodile supplies them with all the fish they could eat."

Basic Book Information

This 30-page book has two to four lines of text per page in black font, usually set on a white background. The location of the print varies, appearing sometimes above, more often below, the colorful cartoon-like illustrations. The text includes challenging vocabulary and dialogue that carries a large part of the story.

Noteworthy Features

For readers who are just learning to try to make sense of what they read, this book would probably best be avoided. The bamboo tree that rains down fishes for no clear reason, the mother crocodile who doesn't eat the boars, but instead weaves baskets and wants them to baby-sit, the sudden change of heart of the mean boar Nettie, all may be not exactly predictable or sensible events to the reader.

This story is about two boars that are markedly different from each other. Teachers might challenge student readers to tell how the characters are different and to find evidence in the text (marking them with Post-its) to support their views. Character webs or a Venn diagram would be a visual way to show these differences.

Teaching Ideas

This is a humorous tale, a fable in which boars stand in for people. It's also an easy tale to discern the moral of the story, or the lesson to be learned.

Illustrators
Jose Aruego; Ariane Dewey

Publisher
Greenwillow Books, 1988

ISBN
0688123333

TC Level
6

Therefore, children may use this one to get practice for stories where the lesson or moral is not so easily extracted. A teacher may want to use this story to launch a study on fables or folktales, especially folktales from various nations and cultures (starting with this one from the Philippines). When comparing the two genres (fables and folktales) in class discussions, teachers may want to lead their students through a series of questions about the fable, which should result in rich book talk: What kind of characters would the animals be if they were people? What kind of behavior does their behavior equal in the real world? What are the real world equivalents of the consequences of this behavior in the story?

Book Connections

The Talking Eggs by Robert San Souci is basically the same story as this one, but with daughters instead of boars and golden eggs instead of fishes. Children might enjoy seeing the two versions of the story together, comparing and contrasting them, and thinking through the author's decisions (*e.g.,* in *The Talking Eggs*, the evil sister never reforms, whereas in this story, the mean boar does).

There are probably more versions of this tale in Grimm's collection; perhaps the story of the swineherd is the most similar.

The pictures may send children to the better-known *Leo the Late Bloomer*, which is illustrated by the same author-illustrator team.

Genre
Fairy and Folk Tale; Picture Book

Teaching Uses
Character Study; Teaching Writing; Interpretation; Independent Reading; Read Aloud

A Field Guide to the Classroom Library, Lucy Calkins and the Teachers College Reading and Writing Project, Heinemann, ©2002 Teachers College, Columbia University; http://www.heinemann.com/fieldguides

Rosie's Walk

Pat Hutchins

Book Summary

As Rosie the hen goes for a walk, a fox follows behind her. Seemingly by accident, the hen manages to get the fox caught up in obstacle after obstacle as he pursues her. She arrives home for dinner without incident, with the traumatized fox nowhere in sight.

Basic Book Information

This book has detailed pictures and a short prepositional phrase in the midst of some white space on each page. The font is larger than most books at this level and has no serifs.

Noteworthy Features

The story in this book is played out not only in the words but also in the pictures. The pattern of the story is the hen that walks obliviously around the farmyard with the fox trailing behind her, encountering hazard after hazard. First the text explains where Rosie walked, using a prepositional phrase that is fully illustrated in the picture. Then, the illustrations on the wordless pages that follow, show the trouble the fox gets into as he tries to follow her.

Teaching Ideas

Many teachers like to have this book on hand when they are working with children on making predictions based on clues in the text and pictures. The kinds of things that happen to the fox are based on a predictable pattern; one page shows clues of what could happen to the fox and the next page shows what actually does happen. To figure out what will happen to him, students have to think about the physical evidence presented in the picture, and put that together with what they know has happened to the fox in the past.

Just as this book is good for helping students work on prediction, it is also good for helping students make meaning out of a text in ways that go beyond the words. If a student merely reads the text and does not pay attention to the pictures, the story is boring and pointless-in fact it doesn't make much sense at all. As teachers confer with students about their reading of this book, they may want to be sure that they are monitoring their own comprehension closely enough that they'll pick up on the connection. In most cases, if two students are reading the book together, at least one will notice something is happening in the pictures and soon they will both be involved in the fuller story.

This book can also help those students who are just learning English with

Illustrator
Pat Hutchins

Publisher
Simon & Schuster, 1968

ISBN
0020437501

TC Level
4

prepositions. In the pictures, it is very clear what Rosie is doing, and once students can read the words, the graphic illustration of where Rosie is may stick in their minds better than abstract concepts of "through" and "over."

Book Connections

Other books by Pat Hutchins include *Goodnight Owl, Titch, You'll Soon Grow Into Them, Titch,* and *The Doorbell Rang.*

Genre
Picture Book

Teaching Uses
Author Study; Teaching Writing; Partnerships

Sail Away
Donald Crews

FIELD GUIDE

B **C**

Book Summary

The book takes you through the trials and tribulations of a day of sailing. As the book begins, it looks like a great day for sailing. It is bright and beautiful, and there is just enough wind to enjoy the day. Halfway through the day, however, the sky turns cloudy and gray, and the sea turns rough. Finally, the sails come down and the boat returns home.

Basic Book Information

Donald Crews captures the sights and sounds of a day of sailing by creating illustrations that are large and captivating and by placing a few carefully chosen words next to these beautiful pictures. The size and shape of print is particularly engaging in this book and add to the overall meaning of the text. Some of his words are gigantic, almost filling up a whole page, while others slant as if they are being pulled by the wind of the story.

Noteworthy Features

It may be necessary to discuss some of the vocabulary words that are specific to sailing, such as *dinghy, motor, mooring*, and *lighthouse.*

Teaching Ideas

This book is also particularly appropriate to use as a model in writing workshop once children have heard or read it, perhaps as a read aloud. One possible way of introducing it in the writing workshop is to say, "Let's notice the kinds of things Donald Crews did as a writer so we can try some of those things in our own writing." Children will notice things such as: how the story begins and ends in the same place; the use of sound words (*Whoosh*!); the use of ellipses; different kinds of punctuation ("!"); repetition ("Sailing, sailing")' ;arger print (SEAS SWELL); dialogue ("Shorten sails").

As a mini-lesson in a writer's workshop, one teacher discussed Donald Crews' writing technique saying to her students, "For the last couple of days, I've been sharing stories by Donald Crews. We've been listening to him as readers. Today I want us to think about him as a writer and what he does as a writer. One of the reasons why I love his writing is because he only uses a few words, but he is able to say so much. He uses strong, detailed, powerful words and repeats them. For example in this book he writes, 'Putt...Putt...Putt...Past the lighthouse.' He brings you right in, so you feel like you're there on the boat. He slows down the moment, stretching it out with the sound of the engine, 'Putt...Putt...Putt.' Now let's imagine you're looking at a child on a swing in the playground. Close your eyes. Take a moment to picture it and think about a few words or details you would use

Illustrator
Donald Crews

Publisher
Greenwillow Books, 1995

ISBN
0688110533

TC Level
5

to stretch out that moment. How would you describe what you see, the sounds you'd hear? What words would you use? Turn to your partner. The partner on the left should keep their eyes closed, the partner on the right, share those few words they imagined to describe the scene. Partner on the left, can you see a picture in your mind from the words? If not, think about what word might have made it more powerful. Today everyone is going to try to write like Donald Crews. Take one moment, like the girl on the swing, but chose your own moment, and stretch it out. Think of a few powerful words and details that'll bring your reader into the moment and make them feel like they're right there, too."

The next day, as a follow up to this mini-lesson, the teacher discussed how she noticed that students often write about a lot of different things without focusing on detail. She pointed out again that Donald Crews focused on one thing, a boat, in this case, and wrote around it.

Book Connections

Donald Crews is the author of numerous children's books including *Shortcut* and *Big Mama's*.

Genre
Nonfiction; Picture Book

Teaching Uses
Teaching Writing; Content Area Study

A Field Guide to the Classroom Library, Lucy Calkins and the Teachers College Reading and Writing Project, Heinemann, ©2002 Teachers College, Columbia University; http://www.heinemann.com/fieldguides

Sally's red bucket

Beverley Randell

Book Summary

Sally is at the beach with her mom and her red bucket. Sally's mom reads a book while Sally plays with Chris. The waves take the red bucket away. Mom and Sally run into the waves to get the bucket. Mom retrieves Sally's red bucket, but the waves have reached Mom's book on the beach. "**Oh, no!**" Sally and Mom have to rescue it as well.

Basic Book Information

The PM Readers is a series published by Rigby. The PM Readers tend to come in kits in which every book looks exactly like every other book. Some teachers think this is less than ideal because at every level, a library should be full of books where each has its own individuality. On the other hand, the PM Readers are an important resource for teachers because first, there are many of these at the early reading levels and second, the publishers recognize the supports that readers need and they offer these. The PM Readers are especially good at providing a lot of easy text, full of high frequency words. Instead of saying, "I see the cow/ the pig/ the horse," a PM Reader is likely to say, "I see the cow./ I see the pig./ I see the horse." to reinforce the repetition of high frequency words. Finally the PM readers are special because a great many, of even the earliest books, are stories with characters, a problem and a solution. Often the early books are label-books, organized as a list, and so it is nice to have stories in the collection as well.

Noteworthy Features

This is a book about Sally, who is the character across a whole series of PM Readers. Teachers and children value the fact that the Sally books allow even inexperienced readers to be reading in a series, accumulating knowledge of characters across books. The Sally series represents more than one level of difficulty.

Like all PM readers, this book contains the basic elements of a story. There is a problem (Sally's bucket of beach toys floats away) and a solution (her mom fishes it out). In this book and others in the series, much of the text is carried by dialogue. Early in the story, a friend joins Sally and says, "Hello, Sally! Come and play with me. We can play with my ball."

This book fits solidly with other Level 4 books. There are five or six lines of text on some pages. On some pages, a character is talking and on other pages, the text switches to narration. On some of the pages, a lot of different actions happen (see page 13), but just one is represented in the picture. A child won't be able to rely on the picture alone to discern what challenging words say.

A Field Guide to the Classroom Library, Lucy Calkins and the Teachers College Reading and Writing Project, Heinemann, ©2002 Teachers College, Columbia University; http://www.heinemann.com/fieldguides

Series
Rigby PM Sally books

Illustrator
Meredith Thomas

Publisher
Rigby, 1996

ISBN
0435067052

TC Level
4

Teaching Ideas

If a teacher were to do a book introduction, it could be a light or a heavy one depending on how much support the readers needed. Probably either way it would be good to nudge the child or children to show some independence and do what good readers do on their own before they read. "Why don't you work in pairs to really study the pictures in this book and try to figure out what this story might be about?" These pictures don't help with difficult words but they certainly help with construction of a general sense of the story. The teacher might stop the partnership work after two or three minutes and say, "I noticed you saw that Sally is playing on the beach and her bucket floats away and Mom helps her to get it; that was good reading work you did." (Notice that the teacher is also calling this thinking-about-text work as reading.)

The challenge will be for the teacher to decide what else to teach in an introduction. Typically, many teachers will summarize many of the pages (while turning them) and will get youngsters to chunk words like *shovel* or *bucket*. This is not necessary; it's an option. There is something to be said for letting a reader or a partnership of readers do more of the work than this, and the teacher instead might wait to see what support is really necessary. This is particularly true because most of the words will be accessible.

When the book is part of an independent reading library, many teachers will keep an eye out for a child who is reading this book, and try to catch a moment for a quick introduction. None of this is necessary, however, if the child has enough resources to work her own way through the text. The words themselves aren't particularly difficult (the vocabulary is so controlled it is a bit stilted in some places). If two children who are both ready for this book work in a partnership, perhaps trading off pages and helping each other, providing stamina for each other, the experience should be a good one.

Once children have read the first couple of pages of the book, it would benefit them to stop and talk. They may need to "turn their brains on and really think about what is happening in the story," because the risk is that they might plow along, decoding the words but not using the pictures and print and their own experiences to build a movie in their minds of this summer day.

Book Connections

There are many books in the Rigby PM series that feature Sally, and they span a variety of levels. Books for older children often contain a recurring character, one who becomes more fully developed across books. It's a great experience for children to read about the recurring characters in the *Frog and Toad*, *Little Bear* or *Box Car Children* series. Likewise, titles in the *Sally* series include: *Sally's new shoes*, *Sally's beans* and *Sally's friends*.

Genre
Emergent Literacy Book

A Field Guide to the Classroom Library, Lucy Calkins and the Teachers College Reading and Writing Project, Heinemann, ©2002 Teachers College, Columbia University; http://www.heinemann.com/fieldguides

Teaching Uses
Independent Reading; Character Study; Small Group Strategy Instruction;
Partnerships; Whole Group Instruction

Splishy-Sploshy

Joy Cowley

Book Summary

Mrs. Wishy-Washy is scrubbing her floor when five gnome-like creatures, the meanies, come into her garden shed and splash paint all over the walls and themselves. When Mrs. Wishy-Washy discovers what the meanies have done, she scrubs down the walls and the floor, then puts the meanies into the tub, scrubs them down and hangs them out to dry, warning them not to play "splishy-sploshy" again.

Basic Book Information

This is a *Story Basket* book from the series of easy reading books by the Wright Group. It follows the easier books *Mrs. Wishy-Washy's Tub* and *Mrs. Wishy-Washy*. The story is told in fifteen pages. Although all the sentences do not follow the same pattern, Cowley does use repetitive patterns in several places. The sentences are short, with a simple syntax. Two sentences do contain adverbial clauses as well as reversing the usual sentence order to predicate/subject. Elizabeth Fuller's cartoon-like illustrations are delightful. They connect with the story, facilitating word recognition.

Noteworthy Features

Familiar figures of the cow, dog, duck and pig appear with Mrs. Wishy-Washy on the cover, reminding readers of the earlier books. The layout of the text puts this book on a higher difficulty level than the introductory books in the Wright Group series. The frame on each page includes the print as well as the illustration. Sometimes the print is located at the bottom of the page, at other times it appears at the top. On two pages, some text is at the top, some at the bottom. In most cases the print is on a white background but on several pages, the background, part of the illustration, is a beige color.

The storyline is that of problem/resolution. Mrs. Wishy-Washy discovers that the mischievous meanies have spread paint all over. She cleans it up along with the meanies. Young readers will find this story humorous. The illustrations of the meanies are cleverly done and look too much like little children not to remind the reader of times when they, themselves, may have played that role. The humor of the story, so well depicted in the illustrations, should motivate readers.

This third-person narration is told with simple sentence structure. The action is continuous, so time in the story is clear. There are more than fifty different words used in this story. Although repeated sentence patterns and rhyming pairs of words make word recognition easier, this is still a book for a reader who has acquired more than a beginning sight vocabulary. The story also includes dialogue, another feature that puts this book at a more

Illustrator
Elizabeth Fuller

Publisher
Wright Group, 1997

ISBN
0780283309

TC Level
3

A Field Guide to the Classroom Library, Lucy Calkins and the Teachers College Reading and Writing Project, Heinemann, ©2002 Teachers College, Columbia University; http://www.heinemann.com/fieldguides

advanced level.

Teaching Ideas

Teachers might want to activate prior knowledge by inviting students to discuss some of the "rules" their mothers or fathers have about walking on newly washed floors. They might introduce the characters, the meanies, at this time, using the title page illustration. They might invite students to predict what these meanies might be up to. The full-page illustrations on the next three pages leave no doubt about the mischief done. At this point, teachers might ask what students think Mrs. Wishy-Washy will do. The illustrations that follow answer that question.

Depending on the skill of the students, teachers may begin with a shared reading of the text. In a shared reading, the teacher reads the text aloud, pointing to each word as she reads. The students follow, reading along with her. Once students have read this book with the teacher and are comfortable with the words, they can keep it in a place where they might return to it and reread it independently.

Teachers may want to use this book as a follow-up to *Mrs. Wishy-Washy*. In that case students will recognize the character of Mrs. Wishy-Washy in the cover illustration. Teachers might use the *ish* phonogram in her name as a prompt in decoding the *splishy* part of the title. They should be able to move from *wishy-washy* to *splishy-sploshy* by using the rhyming sounds.

Should an alert reader notice the *a/o* difference, teachers can point out that sometimes words "sound" alike but don't "look" alike in print. That same contrast appears in the rhyming words *shed/said* on the first two pages of the book.

Teachers might have students identify the pairs of rhyming words that appear in the text: *shed/said, floor/door, splishy-sploshy/ wishy-washy, scrub-a-dub, tubbed/scrubbed, by/dry.* They can examine the pairs to see which sound and look alike at the end, and which do not. Teachers might invite students to think of another word that rhymes with the pair. Writing it next to the pair, students might also decide which examples *do* and which *do not* fit the written pattern.

Text features used in the story provide an opportunity for teachers to give a lesson on signals that punctuation marks give the reader. The dash, the comma separating words within a sentence, the end period and the period after Mrs., the exclamation mark, together with the large size of the word *look,* all provide directions for reading aloud.

Book Connections

Students might also enjoy reading Joy Cowley's *Mrs. Wishy-Washy* as well as other books in the *Story* Box group.

Genre
Emergent Literacy Book

A Field Guide to the Classroom Library, Lucy Calkins and the Teachers College Reading and Writing Project, Heinemann, ©2002 Teachers College, Columbia University; http://www.heinemann.com/fieldguides

Teaching Uses
Independent Reading; Whole Group Instruction; Small Group Strategy Instruction; Partnerships; Interpretation; Read Aloud; Character Study; Language Conventions

Sunshine, Moonshine

Jennifer Armstrong

Book Summary

This lyrical story lists things that the sun shines on and brings to a little boy's attention. First the sun shines on a mountain, then the sea, then on the little boy's pillow in the morning. The book then goes on to list things the boy notices throughout one seaside day, with each item linked together by the repeated refrain, "Sun shines on a _____." Meanwhile the pictures tell the story of a boy who joins with other children to notice the seaside objects. Then the boy and his dad row to a sailboat, sail as the sun sets, and return by moonlight.

Basic Book Information

The book contains 32 pages, with an average of either five or ten words and one or two lines of print on each page.

The book is somewhat oversized with sweet pictures showing an idyllic rural life. It is a rhyming text, which helps the reader use some words to read other words, for example, *sea* and *me*. It is also a text that reads, in a way, like a song or a chant.

This book is part of Random House's *Early Step into Reading* series. The books in this series come with a note to parents suggesting they first read these books to their child and "before long the child will say words along with you."

Noteworthy Features

The text has large print, generously spaced. Each page begins consistently, with either the phrase "Sun shines" or "Moon shines," helping the child gain momentum and confidence. Illustrations support some key words on each page, e.g., names of objects such as *mountains*. Text is inconsistently placed throughout the book and embedded in the illustrations, which often contain dark colors. There is some difficult vocabulary, requiring readers to look across words. There is an increasing amount of text per page as the book proceeds. Children inexperienced with reading fluently and listening for rhymes may have difficulty.

Teaching Ideas

This book is appropriate for readers learning to match one spoken word to one written one. If a teacher wants to help readers to self-correct when the matching doesn't work, the teacher can cue the reader to find a known sight word, which will then serve as an anchor for a one-to-one match. References can be made to the word wall in the classroom if the sight word is on it.

A Field Guide to the Classroom Library, Lucy Calkins and the Teachers College Reading and Writing Project, Heinemann, ©2002 Teachers College, Columbia University; http://www.heinemann.com/fieldguides

Illustrator
Lucia Washburn

Publisher
Random House, 1997

ISBN
0679864423

TC Level
4

Opportunities to crosscheck will be presented in this book. That is, there are places in the text where readers will need to use information from the picture and the print in order to read the story. For example, there is a picture of a seashell on page 8 and a crab on page10. A teacher should be able to observe children using the picture as a source of information and then checking against the letters. A teacher has the opportunity to praise the children for doing this.

There are other places, too, where the picture support alone won't be enough to help children produce the needed work. This is just as well because children will need to look at the print and think, "What sound does that letter make?" Mostly children will be relying on the first sounds in words, in combination with the pictures. Teachers will want to support students as they crosscheck one source of information with another, and as they monitor their reading for meaning.

Genre
Picture Book

Teaching Uses
Independent Reading; Small Group Strategy Instruction

Swimmy
Leo Lionni

Book Summary

In this Caldecott Honor book, a small black fish named Swimmy loses all his little red brothers and sisters to a hungry tuna. He encounters many wondrous things as he swims alone scared and very sad. When he comes across another school of little red fish, he encourages them to stop hiding, and "SEE things!" and he thinks of a way to keep them all safe. The school swims in the shape of "the biggest fish in the sea," and Swimmy makes the eye. While swimming together in this formation, they chase the big fish away.

Basic Book Information

This is a very popular, classic work by well respected children's author Leo Lionni.

Noteworthy Features

Text averages from one to five lines per page, though one sentence continues across six double-page spreads. The lines of print seem to "swim" in the ocean-like page spreads and the small typeface may be somewhat obscured in the lush artwork, presenting a possible challenge for beginning readers.

Teaching Ideas

Before reading this book teachers may want to preview a few of the challenging vocabulary words related to the sea: *mussel, medusa, lobster, sea anemone,* and *school* (as it refers to a large group of fish). Students may also have difficulty with some other words like: *swift, fierce,* and *hungry.*

There are many similes and metaphors in the story, but if children miss them, they probably will not miss the main storyline, though they may get sidetracked in their thinking.

A few children have been known to focus in on the similes and metaphors in the text to the extent that it confuses them. Swimmy describes a lobster, "Who walked about like a water-moving machine." They wondered how could Swimmy be saying that the lobster reminds him of a machine? He doesn't know any machines, does he? And a child might ask why do the sea anemones look like "pink palm trees swaying in the wind"?

In a class discussion about the big idea or meaning of *Swimmy*, a teacher may want to start with questions that nudge children toward interpretation, such as: What is really important about this story? What does this story say about the world? What does this story say about my life? What is the point of this story for me?

A Field Guide to the Classroom Library, Lucy Calkins and the Teachers College Reading and Writing Project, Heinemann, ©2002 Teachers College, Columbia University; http://www.heinemann.com/fieldguides

Illustrator
Leo Lionni

Publisher
Scholastic, 1992

ISBN
0590430491

TC Level
7

Most readers decide that there is a message here: that people who are powerless can work together to vanquish the common enemy-if they have a good leader. Readers find other messages too. Some children think the book's message is that if you lose your family, you have to think of a better way to protect your next family. Some children decide the message is that if you are bullied yourself, you will end up trying to bully other people, too. As in any text, the learning comes not in just taking in another person's interpretation, but instead in deciding if that interpretation fits, or in building a different one, always with supporting evidence from the text. If the class has been studying this theme of community, a teacher might want to challenge the class by asking, "If the little fish, Swimmy, helped *people*, what problems would he see, and how would he help them? How would you?"

Book Connections

Many of Leo Lionni's books including *Frederick*, *The Alphabet Tree*, *Tillie and the Wall* and *Mathew's Dream,* are also parable-like animal fables with powerful messages for study either through the read aloud, in a reading center or as part of an author study.

Genre
Picture Book; Emergent Literacy Book

Teaching Uses
Read Aloud; Interpretation; Content Area Study; Critique; Author Study; Language Conventions

A Field Guide to the Classroom Library, Lucy Calkins and the Teachers College Reading and Writing Project, Heinemann, ©2002 Teachers College, Columbia University; http://www.heinemann.com/fieldguides

Sylvester and the Magic Pebble
William Steig

Book Summary

Sylvester Duncan, the donkey, collects interesting pebbles. One day he finds a red pebble that makes wishes come true! As he is walking home to share his exciting discovery with his parents and the neighborhood, he meets a lion. In his panic, a wish turns him into a rock. He is safe from the lion, but now seems doomed to be a rock forever since he can't reach the pebble. When he doesn't come home, his parents are heartbroken and miserable. A year passes and Mr. and Mrs. Duncan have a picnic in the spring, despite their sadness. They sit atop the rock, their son! They find the magic red pebble and lay it on the rock, thinking that Sylvester would like it. Because he is touching the magic red pebble again, Sylvester's wish to turn back into himself comes true! Everyone is overjoyed and they lock the pebble in an iron safe, since they already have everything they could want.

Basic Book Information

This Caldecott Medal winner is a classic favorite of young and old alike. Steig's charming, wiggly-line drawings of the donkey family and their farm-animal neighbors seem to appeal to everyone from the book's first moment.

Noteworthy Features

The story's chronological structure is easy to follow. Time, however does speed up and slow down. In the beginning, the story is told moment by moment; but once Sylvester has turned into a rock, whole seasons pass on one page. By the end of the story, about a year has passed. The bulk of the writing is about the beginning of that year and the end, when Sylvester turns back into a donkey.

The perspective of the story also changes, though not sharply. Once Sylvester has changed into a rock, the story shifts to his worrying parents back at home. As more time passes, it shifts back to Sylvester, and then to the whole family at the end of the story. Most children are not confused by this, though some who aren't used to the abrupt changes in pace don't gather how much time has passed.

Teaching Ideas

Some children use this story to generate conversation about what they would wish for if they had a magic pebble like Sylvester's. They also tend to consider solutions to Sylvester's problem. This kind of talk is valuable, not only because it can make the story exciting, but also because children can see how literature provokes us to think about our own lives.

Illustrator
William Steig

Publisher
Scholastic, 1987

ISBN
0671662694

TC Level
10

Some children make personal connections with *Sylvester and the Magic Pebble*, empathizing with the emotionally intense points of the story. They feel their way into the point where Sylvester finds the magic pebble, where he panics and makes the bad decision that turns him into the rock. The parents grieve the loss of their son, Sylvester makes a simple wish, and the family is reunited again. There is always discussion about whether the family is right to have locked the pebble away, and predictions about what they will decide to do with it later.

Because interpretation is a bit challenging with this book, it should generate rich discussions. What is the book really about? Many children assume it is that getting your wishes granted is dangerous business. Other children think that the family was just distracted for the moment with their son back and that they will use the pebble to its full advantage later. Others will say the book tells us how great children are, or how great a family is-and that they are all you could possibly ever want. There is plenty of room for readers to gather evidence and build interpretations in this text.

Book Connections

William Steig has written many wonderful books for children that could be read in a cluster with this one, including: *Abel's Island*, *The Amazing Bone*, *Doctor De Soto* and *Shrek!*

Genre
Picture Book

Teaching Uses
Read Aloud; Author Study; Interpretation

A Field Guide to the Classroom Library, Lucy Calkins and the Teachers College Reading and Writing Project, Heinemann, ©2002 Teachers College, Columbia University; http://www.heinemann.com/fieldguides

The "Gotcha" Box

Joy Cowley

Book Summary

This book pictures a different colored box on each page. The text of the book begins, "This is the green box." The color of the box changes on each page, except on the next-to-last page, where the box is the "gotcha" box. The last page shows a clown jumping out of the box and yelling "Gotcha!"

Basic Book Information

This is one of the *Story Box* books, and is written by the beloved author Joy Cowley who wrote *Mrs. Wishy-Washy* and countless books for early readers. As a *Story Box* book, this book looks like it belongs in a kit of identical little books. In this library it is interspersed with a lovely variety of shapes and sizes of books. The Wright Company provides professional development as well as books for teachers, and has been a major force in supporting the move towards more literature-based classrooms. The company publishes texts that support early readers.

Noteworthy Features

Every page begins with the same high frequency words, "This is the..." This text is a list of different colored boxes, and like many other similar books, it proves to be "a list with a twist" ending. This change in the repetitive pattern and the location of the print on the last page offers chances to observe, and possibly teach that the print carries the message.

The text alone is not engaging, but the illustrations of the interesting boxes may lead to a lively discussion of what the boxes could be used for. The brightly spotted "gotcha" box needs to be named by some method other than identifying it by its color. The reader is sure to think "huh?" when she reads that this is the "gotcha box," but within the turn of the page, we understand its title.

Teaching Ideas

This is a simple book, designed to support children's first efforts to read print. At this early stage, a child's reading involves either simply looking at the pictures and retelling a familiar story, or if the text is very brief and simple, perhaps matching the print with spoken words. It's very tricky for a child to do this even if he knows exactly what the words say. A child who wants to read the first page of this book and knows what the words say might still read it like this: "This is the green bo-oo-ox." Such a child benefits from a teacher saying, "Did it match? It didn't, did it? Try it again."

A child who is just beginning to read the print *won't* always know what the words say and will need to rely on the pictures for support. The use of the high frequency words *this, is* and *the* serve as anchors for the reader to monitor the reading.

Usually children who are reading this very earliest of book levels don't know many sight words, nor will they be knowledgeable enough yet of letter-sound correspondences to "sound words out." Such a child will probably read, "The green box" instead of "This is the green box." If the child makes this miscue, the teacher is wise to see that the child has done a lot that is right, even though the child's translation is wrong. "Good try," we'll want to say. "That's almost it. It *is* a green box so that would make sense. But let's point to each word to see if that could be it." By focusing the attention on one-to-one correspondence, the child will be more prone to doing this on her own through the pages that follow.

In a book introduction, the teacher may need to familiarize the reader with the slang term *gotcha*. It may also be helpful for the reader to predict the first letter in the word *gotcha* and to locate it in the story.

Genre
Emergent Literacy Book

Teaching Uses
Partnerships; Independent Reading

A Field Guide to the Classroom Library, Lucy Calkins and the Teachers College Reading and Writing Project, Heinemann, ©2002 Teachers College, Columbia University; http://www.heinemann.com/fieldguides

the alphabet tree

Leo Lionni

Book Summary

This parable-like tale told by an ant cleverly describes the relationship between letters, words and sentences while at the same time, reminding us of the importance of community. A wind scatters letters that have been clinging to the leaves of the alphabet tree. They huddle together, in the foliage of the lower branches, fearful this might happen again. A word bug comes along and shows them how they can combine to form words, which will make them stronger, and able to withstand the wind. They do this and see that the bug is right. They make short easy words: *dog, cat*, and more difficult words: *twig, leaf, earth*. But then a strange caterpillar comes by and asks why they don't combine into sentences so they "mean something." The words now combine into sentences to do this. But the caterpillar doesn't stop there. "Mean something important," it advises. When they gather to spell out the words "peace on earth and goodwill toward all men," the caterpillar praises them and tells them to climb on his back. "But where are you taking us?" the letters ask. "To the president," is the caterpillar's reply.

Basic Book Information

There are 30 pages in this book. The green, leafy background sometimes obscures the letters that are the focus of the story, but the text is carefully placed on a white background, making it easy to read. Its placement varies depending on the illustration. On one page, for example, the illustration takes up most of the page, leaving only a small white space at the bottom for the line: "One day the breeze became a strong gust and the gust became a gale." The number of words per page also varies. On some pages, there is a single sentence, whereas on others, we find a paragraph.

The story is told in a logical order: first letters become words then words become sentences.

Lionni's books are favorites among children and adults. Like *the alphabet tree*, most emphasize the importance of a social conscience: working together. Three of Lionni's books have been Caldecott runners-up: *Inch by Inch*, *Swimmy* and *Frederick*. Leo Lionni is an artist and a writer. His stories are told visually as well as verbally.

Noteworthy Features

This simple yet profound story is told in third person (actually we might say it's told in "third bug" since there are no humans, only letters and bugs). The sentence structure is simple and easy to follow. The illustrations-spread across two pages-are close-ups of letters, leaves and bugs with an occasional branch appearing here and there. The vocabulary introduces words that might prove challenging to many children of this age, words like: *foliage,*

Illustrator
Leo Lionni

Publisher
Random House, 1968

ISBN
0679808353

TC Level
6

confusion and *huddle*. But Lionni's illustrations leave no doubt as to their meaning.

Teaching Ideas

For kindergarteners and first graders, this book makes a great read aloud. The story is filled with chuckles and surprises. Children will enjoy the tiny ants that crawl along a branch of this wonderful tree and through whom Lionni tells the story. They'll appreciate the letters clinging to the leaves, the very wise purple caterpillar, and the black and red word bug with bright yellow wings. The illustrations play an important role in understanding the story. Teachers who read the book aloud may first want to do a "walk-through" or picture walk that will allow the children to enjoy and discuss the pictures before they read the story. Students might also discuss how they, too, are learning to put letters together to make words.

The message is embedded in the last lines of the story: "say something really important" and when the letters do that, and then ask where they are being taken, the caterpillar tells them "to the president." Young children might miss the implication in this line. The book was written at the height of the Vietnam War. Although the message "peace" is always "really important," taken in that context, it may have had greater significance at the book's publication.

On reaching this sentence, teachers might ask students why they think "peace on earth and goodwill toward all men" is really, really important. Students may inquire why the caterpillar wants to take this sentence "to the president." Students may also discuss the word *men* and what it is intended to mean and whether it is the best word to use.

In class or partnership discussions with teacher guidance, even young children can begin to look for themes in literature, and Lionni's books are a good place to begin this interpretive work. "What do you think the author is *really* saying?" we could ask youngsters. The point isn't for them to produce "the right answer" so much as to help children look more deeply into texts, growing ideas and substantiating them with evidence from the text.

Young readers often confuse the difference between letters, words and sentences. This book provides another way to remind children of these differences and possibly to engage in word sorts or word-making during choice time.

After reading this book aloud, teachers may remind children that during writing workshop they may try to write sentences that *they* think are really, really important.

Book Connections

Teachers might want to use Bill Martin Jr. and John Archambault's *Chicka Chicka Boom Boom* as another picture book about the alphabet. They may also want to use some of Lionni's other books-*Swimmy* or *Frederick*, for example-as other picture books that speak of the importance of community.

Genre
Picture Book

A Field Guide to the Classroom Library, Lucy Calkins and the Teachers College Reading and Writing Project, Heinemann, ©2002 Teachers College, Columbia University; http://www.heinemann.com/fieldguides

Teaching Uses

Partnerships; Read Aloud; Critique; Interpretation; Teaching Writing; Language Conventions

A Field Guide to the Classroom Library, Lucy Calkins and the Teachers College Reading and Writing Project, Heinemann, ©2002 Teachers College, Columbia University; http://www.heinemann.com/fieldguides

The Baby Owls

Beverley Randell

Book Summary

Down on the farm the cows, pigs, and dogs are asleep, but the owl family is awake up in the tree. The baby owls are hungry and Mother Owl goes out hunting for moths. She brings back a moth for her babies. The book ends with the farm animals still sleeping and the baby owls now contented and asleep.

Basic Book Information

The PM Storybooks, developed in New Zealand and published by Rigby, are written as stories, which are structured around traditional story elements. Even texts that at first appear to be lists are usually stories with characters, a problem, and a resolution. The only exceptions are their very earliest books. The PM Readers are known for including a large number of high frequency words, and for controlling vocabulary so that in books of a comparable level of difficulty, the same high frequency words reoccur. Instead of relying upon an intensive use of sentence repetition, hoping children will be given a book introduction and remember what the teacher has told them, the PM Readers are apt to support very beginning readers by using many high frequency words in longer, more complete sentences: I see a bird./ I see a frog./.

Noteworthy Features

The emergent reader who has recently moved on from Level 1 books will find, on the first page of this book, a repetitive pattern that will get him off to a strong start: "The cows are asleep, the pigs are asleep. . . ." The print is large and well-spaced. The engaging illustrations are supportive, but cannot be totally relied upon for figuring out the text. The illustrations use a dark background to indicate a nighttime setting. Black print appears on white pages and white print appears on pages that have a dark background. The word "not" on page 5 is the only word in the text that is written in bold print. This word is vital to an understanding of the text. Children need to understand that all the other animals are asleep, but the owls are awake in the night. The young reader will probably delight in the speech bubble coming out of the owl's mouth, on page 5, saying, "Hoot, Hoot."

Teaching Ideas

Readers who are new to books in this group will likely need some support in their effort to point as they match their spoken words with written words. A teacher might want to gather a group of readers at this level and teach a strategy lesson on the use of sight words as anchors when reading new text.

A Field Guide to the Classroom Library, Lucy Calkins and the Teachers College Reading and Writing Project, Heinemann, ©2002 Teachers College, Columbia University; http://www.heinemann.com/fieldguides

For example, in the sentence, "Mother owl sees a big moth," there are several high frequency anchor words. These will probably already be on the word wall. "You know 'see,'" the teacher can say. "Here it says 'sees.' Whenever you see this, it says 'sees.' Look at 'sees.' What do you notice?"

Some readers who encounter this book may have been relying upon using repetition and memorization to figure out words and make meaning. For these children, this book will pose new challenges. For example, a teacher might want to teach such a child that, although the illustration can help with the overall meaning when new words are encountered, it is also important to look at the first letter for help with reading the word.

If this book is a bit of a stretch for a child teachers may want to give a brief book introduction. With the student looking at the cover page, the teacher might ask, "What is mother owl doing?" Then the teacher could confirm, "Yes, she is feeding her babies, and it is nighttime." The teacher will probably let readers figure out on their own that while all the other farm animals are asleep the owls stay up at night, and they are hungry. During the introduction, the teacher may want to help children anticipate that the owl is looking for food for the baby. "Let's see what mother owl got for her baby," the teacher could say.

As children begin reading the whole text to themselves with soft voices, the teacher listens in, moving between them and pulling beside readers, one at a time. She may want to coach one child by prompting him to reread when he encounters difficulty and encourage another to look at the picture and get his mouth ready for the first sound. After a child reads a page, the teacher will ask, "Does that make sense?" encouraging children to get in the habit of monitoring for meaning.

When the child finishes reading, the teacher might draw him back to particular pages to make a point. For example the teacher may return to the words: *pigs, dogs, cows, owls,* and *moths* and call attention to the "s" endings asking, "What's the same about all these words?" Children should be able to see that all these words end with an "s." If the child seems able to do this, she could generate other plural words to show how to use this information to solve other words. The same opportunity is possible for the *-ing* ending on the word "looking" on page 7.

This book can also be a fine addition to a reading center on baby animals and their parents. If the book is set alongside *Baby Lamb's First Drink,* another PM reader, young readers may discuss the different ways that parents take care of their babies or the different ways that babies are fed.

In a writing workshop, young children might benefit from trying to write like the authors of books they read. This book, for example, might be used to inspire young writers to use speech bubbles. In a mini-lesson, the teacher can point out how the author uses speech bubbles to show the sound the animal is making, and invite children to try it out in their own writing. The teacher will want to extend this point so children learn that anytime you want to make a character in your writing talk, one possible way of doing this is through a speech bubble.

Genre
Emergent Literacy Book

A Field Guide to the Classroom Library, Lucy Calkins and the Teachers College Reading and Writing Project, Heinemann, ©2002 Teachers College, Columbia University; http://www.heinemann.com/fieldguides

Teaching Uses
Independent Reading; Small Group Strategy Instruction; Partnerships; Whole Group Instruction; Teaching Writing

The Carrot Seed

Ruth Krauss

Book Summary

This beloved classic has been around for years because it is simply written and holds the important theme of keeping hope alive. It is the story of a little boy who plants a carrot seed. Everyone in his family tells him that it won't grow. The little boy continues to believe that the seed will grow, despite the discouraging behavior of his family and the seed's lack of progress. He tends to the plant, and eventually the carrot seed sprouts and grows, "just as the little boy had known it would."

Basic Book Information

Many people credit Ruth Krauss, the author of this book, and Margaret Wise Brown with being the two people to break open the field of picture book writing. Ruth Krauss has also written *The Happy Day*, which is a Caldecott Honor Award winner, and *A Hole is to Dig*. *The Carrot Seed*, like these other books, is considered a classic.

Noteworthy Features

The book is illustrated in single lined drawings with shades of brown and white. When the carrot comes up, green is introduced. Then on the final page, there is an orange carrot. The old fashioned feeling of the book doesn't take away from the brilliance of Crockett Johnson's art. The expressions on characters' faces are especially worth noticing.

Some teachers think this book is easier than it is. There aren't a lot of words on the page but the illustrations won't do a lot to help the readers figure out words. Readers also need to be alert to changing patterns. The book is filled with literary language, which can pose some challenges for readers who are more used to the syntax of oral language. For example, the phrase, "Everyone kept saying it wouldn't come up," isn't the sort of phrase people would normally say.

Teaching Ideas

In the A library, the primary instructional purpose of this book is as an emergent literacy read aloud. Through the teacher's multiple readings of this text, children become familiar with the story. After the teacher has read the story at least four times, copies of the book could join a basket of "favorite story books." When they are given the book to read during independent reading time, readers can then use the pictures and their memory of the teacher's readings to recreate the story. When they have had the opportunity to do this, their reading progresses from simply "labeling" pictures on the page, to telling the story off the pictures using progressively

Illustrator
Crockett Johnson

Publisher
HarperCollins, 1945

ISBN
0064432106

TC Level
4

more dialogue and storybook language, to more "conventional" reading using the print. It is important for children to hear the stories read aloud many times, and to have a lot of opportunities to reread it with a partner while a teacher is near by to thoughtfully coach the reading.

The Carrot Seed is a classic story written around the familiar motif of the youngest child who prevails in the end. This is not unlike the story of Cinderella, the youngest of the daughters who in the end marries the prince or of Titch who has only the littlest things, but whose seed grows into the mighty plant.

The characters' facial expressions provide an opportunity to demonstrate the importance of reading the pictures and how they can be used to help in making inferences. When the mother and father say, "I'm afraid it won't come up," there is a picture of the mother and father leaning into the picture with wide eyes and concern on their faces. When the big brother leans into the picture, he has a smile on his face and he pronounces, "It won't come up." Teachers can point out the facial expressions of the characters and demonstrate, using their own voice inflection, how they imagine the characters might sound when they speak.

One teacher, during a guided reading book introduction, discussed how the illustrated facial expressions help us to understand the story. She said, "The mother looks worried here in the picture. How do you think she would say the words, 'I'm afraid it won't come up.'" One young reader replied, "Oh, she doesn't want to disappoint the boy, so she says it softly, carefully. She doesn't want him to be hurt."

When young readers are working in partnerships, they may alternate the pages, taking on the parts of different characters while reading this book to each other. Readers can practice the different ways the lines could be said. This can develop a reader's sense of fluency and phrasing.

Although this is a Level 4 book, it can be used with more advanced readers in upper grades who are ready to understand that stories often have themes. Some teachers talk about the theme as the "under story," or as the story beneath the surface. In *The Carrot Seed*, the boy's undying belief in his seed illustrates the value of keeping faith in each other and in ourselves.

This is one theme in *The Carrot Seed*, but of course each reader needs to construct her own sense of a book's theme. One first grader noticed that this book is about the way some people and things grow-slowly at first, and then in bursts. This child pointed out that the carrot was rather like Leo from *Leo, the Late Bloomer*. Other readers will think that this book carries the message that if someone believes enough, their belief will come true. This interpretation doesn't always match our life experiences, and readers who know that things don't always turn out well may question *The Carrot Seed*.

All this can make for some great book talk. Teachers may remind children that if they suggest a theme is present in a book, they must demonstrate accountability by returning to the text for supporting evidence.

Book Connections

This book might be added to a reading basket of "Books about people who believe in themselves or others," along with *Leo the Late Bloomer* (Windmill, 1971) and other more recent books by Robert Krauss.

A Field Guide to the Classroom Library, Lucy Calkins and the Teachers College Reading and Writing Project, Heinemann, ©2002 Teachers College, Columbia University; http://www.heinemann.com/fieldguides

Genre
Picture Book

Teaching Uses
Language Conventions; Independent Reading; Partnerships; Critique; Interpretation; Read Aloud

A Field Guide to the Classroom Library, Lucy Calkins and the Teachers College Reading and Writing Project, Heinemann, ©2002 Teachers College, Columbia University; http://www.heinemann.com/fieldguides

The Doorbell Rang

Pat Hutchins

Book Summary

Ma has made a dozen cookies for tea for Victoria and Sam. She makes wonderful cookies, just like Grandma. As Victoria and Sam start to divide the cookies, the doorbell rings and Tom and Hannah from next door come in. Now the four children start to divide the cookies but the doorbell rings again. The story continues until there are twelve children around the table. Each child can now have one cookie, but the doorbell rings again. Luckily, it is Grandma with an enormous tray of cookies.

Basic Book Information

This book has 283 words. The pages are unnumbered. Repetition, sentence structure, and phrasing are written to support early reading behaviors and will help beginning readers find meaning in the book. This book uses many high-frequency words.

Full-page color illustrations are on each page with the text at the top. The illustrations provide moderate support.

Noteworthy Features

The author uses varied, simple sentence patterns. Sentences are short. The pages have one to four lines of text. The print is well-spaced. One sentence continues onto the next page; this may need to be explained to a reader. In this text, children will have the opportunity to implement strategies such as self-correcting, self-monitoring, and searching for visual information.

Teaching Ideas

Because of the complexity of many of the words in this book, independent readers of *The Doorbell Rang* will probably not rely solely on the strategy of sounding it out.

Students should be encouraged to discuss and analyze the book. Young readers of this book will probably be interested in the quandary the characters are faced with every time the doorbell rings. Sharing chocolate chip cookies with an increasingly large amount of people is not always an easy thing to do! Students may want to discuss the plot or characters in book discussions. Young readers might want to put Post-It notes on a favorite page and talk about it, posing alternate solutions to the cookie problem, discussing how the characters might be feeling, and so on.

Children, with keen observation, may notice that the mother is mopping the floor only to have more muddy shoes trample through the kitchen. In addition to the increasing number of muddy footprints, more and more steam comes out of the kettle and pot, more plates go on the table, and the

Illustrator
Pat Hutchins

Publisher
William Morrow, 1986

ISBN
0590411098

TC Level
6

collection of children's toys grows. The illustrations help to create a sense of chaos.

An engaging aspect of the book is that the problem grows in intensity each time the doorbell rings. Young writers in grades 2 and up might want to emulate this "snowball" effect in their writing by setting up a problem in their stories and then adding layers to it. Building suspense could be the topic of a writing mini-lesson.

The Doorbell Rang also provides a strong example of the use of dialogue. The story is primarily told through what the characters say to one another. Teachers may want to coach children on what the quotation marks mean, and then concentrate on how to read dialogue with fluency. At first, children may want to use different voices for each of the characters in order to distinguish them.

Book Connections

There are several other books about these same characters that young readers may want to try.

Genre
Picture Book

Teaching Uses
Author Study; Read Aloud; Language Conventions; Teaching Writing

The Important Book
Margaret Wise Brown

Book Summary

In this classic picture book, Margaret Wise Brown looks closely at the small and everyday things of life: a cricket, a spoon, grass, the snow, wind and sky. She finds what is important about the ordinary things in life. But the most important message of Brown's book for the reader is that "the important thing about you is that you are you."

Basic Book Information

Margaret Wise Brown is the author of other timeless picture books that continue to be cherished by children. She has written *Goodnight Moon*, *The Runaway Bunny*, and *Wait Till the Moon is Full*. *Another Important Book* is a companion book to *The Important Book*.

Noteworthy Features

This book is a cherished read aloud for young children who enjoy the rhythmic, predictable repetition. Each page begins with "the important thing about..." and ends with "but the important thing about...." Each page looks closely at a different everyday, ordinary object in the world. A variety of font styles and sizes support the poetic tone or mood of the text and each object.

Teaching Ideas

This is a very versatile book that can be used in the classroom in many different ways. For young children, it is a cherished, predictable read aloud to be read again and again.

This book also can foster a discussion about identity. The students may talk or write about what they think is important about themselves. This could lead to a deeper discussion about respecting who we are and what makes each of us, as human beings, both unique and similar.

In writing workshop, there are different ways teachers may use this book. After reading it students may be given the opportunity to find the smaller things in the world around them and examine them more closely. Often we rush through the world and do not take an opportunity to truly see what is around us. In turn, the students might sketch or write about what they observe, paying particular attention to detail, and really thinking about what is most important about these things to them.

This book is filled with descriptive language. This is a wonderful time to discuss writing with greater detail and description to tell about an object, using Brown's book as a mentor text.

Students may also study the structure of Margaret Wise Brown's well

Illustrator
Leonard Weisgard

Publisher
HarperCollins, 1994

ISBN
0064432270

TC Level
4

A Field Guide to the Classroom Library, Lucy Calkins and the Teachers College Reading and Writing Project, Heinemann, ©2002 Teachers College, Columbia University; http://www.heinemann.com/fieldguides

crafted book. How did the author construct this book? How is repetition used and how did it lend a structure to this book?

Teachers may use the text as a jumping off point for a discussion about the creative process. Many authors keep a writer's notebook as a tool to help them think about the world and gather ideas for their writing. Artists use sketchbooks. How can we generate ideas or "seeds" for our own writing or artwork? A student sketch might be the seed for a piece of writing or poetry.

Book Connections

Another Important Book, also by Margaret Wise Brown, is the companion to *The Important Book*. Students who enjoy these books might want to engage in a Margaret Wise Brown author study.

Genre
Picture Book

Teaching Uses
Whole Group Instruction; Read Aloud; Interpretation; Teaching Writing; Small Group Strategy Instruction

A Field Guide to the Classroom Library, Lucy Calkins and the Teachers College Reading and Writing Project, Heinemann, ©2002 Teachers College, Columbia University; http://www.heinemann.com/fieldguides

The Lighthouse Children
Syd Hoff

Book Summary

An old couple, Sam and Rose, live in a lighthouse. They are never lonely because a hundred sea gulls fly in every day. Sam and Rose feed the birds, call them by name, paint and photograph them. When a storm damages the lighthouse, the couple moves inland where they have lots of neighbors, parties and cookouts. But they miss their seagulls. So they assemble a searchlight so the seagulls, their "lighthouse children" can once again find their way to the couple.

Basic Book Information

This is a level one book from the *I Can Read* series published by Harper Publishers, designed for what Harper regards as "early readers." In fact, the text often has five or six lines of print on a page, including dialogue in which the speakers are not identified, and a combination of four word- or fourteen word-long sentences. The book doesn't contain chapters. On the back cover, there is a blurb that could serve as a book introduction.

Noteworthy Features

The story fits into the classic story structure. At first, it seems as if the story revolves around the fact that the birds move on each day after they are fed, but in fact, the real problem comes when the storm damages the lighthouse. Sam and Rose abruptly move, and the true problem is revealed: they miss their feathered friends.

Teaching Ideas

This is an endearing story. It's easy to appreciate Sam and Rose, who don't have any children and instead adopt the local seagulls, feeding them bits of bread and cautioning them as one might caution a group of young people. "Be careful on those rocks, Hank, Frank, Molly and Dolly!" Sam calls.

The couple names the gulls with rhyming names such as *Hank /Frank, Dolly/ Molly*. Teachers might use such names to teach students how one can learn to pronounce and/or spell one word by using another one that is familiar to them.

Although the book doesn't have separate chapters, a teacher may ask students to point out the three distinct parts of the story using Post-its, and if possible, to give each a heading or a title. This will help them summarize the story and aid their comprehension.

The lighthouse plays a central role in this story, and it may be interesting for a teacher to see whether a child can read this book and learn about lighthouses from it. The text seems to contain enough of the basic

Illustrator
Syd Hoff

Publisher
HarperCollins, 1994

ISBN
0064441784

TC Level
5

information, so that it might be self-exploratory, but some teachers may want to support a child's understanding of lighthouses with an introductory discussion.

Once children begin reading challenging books such as this, it's helpful to teach them that readers often pause after they've read a story to remember it. One way to do this is by turning the pages of the story and glancing over the text and pictures. This becomes a different sort of a picture walk.

Children might meet with partners after independent reading and, rather than talking over Post-its, they may now revisit the text, leafing through the pages and retelling it. If we want to lift the level of children's retellings, we can mention that a good retelling sounds like a story. We mention the characters by name and say a bit about their traits, and we tell the setting of the story. This book has a clean, clear plot line and lends itself to such a retelling.

Book Connections

Syd Hoff has written many beloved books for beginning readers including *Danny and the Dinosaur, Mrs. Brice's Mice, Barney's Horse, Chester,* and *Sammy the Seal.*

Genre
Emergent Literacy Book; Picture Book

Teaching Uses
Partnerships; Independent Reading; Whole Group Instruction; Small Group Strategy Instruction; Interpretation

The Lion and the Mouse
Beverley Randell

Book Summary

Adapted from an Aesop fable, *The Lion and the Mouse* is a story about how a mouse teaches a lion a valuable lesson. In the beginning of the story, the lion catches a mouse asleep on his chest. The mouse begs for his freedom. The lion thinks this is quite funny, but lets the little mouse go free. Then the lion is caught in a net. He roars all day, but no one comes to help. That night the mouse hears the lion roaring, and helps to set the lion free.

Basic Book Information

The PM Series was developed by Beverley Randell who continues to be a major author of these books today. The PM Storybooks place a priority on always including the traditional story elements. Even texts that at first appear to be lists are, in fact, stories with characters, a problem, and a resolution. Randell claims, "you will find no traces of mad fantasy, certainly no hint of the supernatural, and the very minimum of surprise twists in plots." She values meaning and wants to teach youngsters to monitor for sense.

Noteworthy Features

Sentence structure varies in this sixteen-page book, with some sentences having as many as fifteen words. The text is full of punctuation marks used for emphasis and characterization. Words are bold for extra emphasis. Some sentences include quotation marks that indicate when one of the two characters is speaking. The illustrations are clear enough for early readers to tell the story in dialogue.

Teaching Ideas

This book could be used to teach characterization and "story voice," since there are only two characters, and they have distinct personalities. Children could learn how and when to speak in character by following the prompts provided by the text.

As children read the text, teachers will want to notice their miscues, realizing that these convey the sources of information a child draws upon in order to read. For example, if on page 9 the child reads, "He didn't see the big *neet* by the tree," and acts as if he is planning to continue on undeterred, the teacher will surmise that the child is attending to phonics but is less attentive to meaning. "You said *neet*, does that make sense?" the teacher might say. On the other hand, other children will be apt to read on page 13, "the mouse came out of her *hose*." The teacher will notice that this could make sense but doesn't match the letters. "You said *hose*. I'm glad that you

Series
PM Storybooks

Illustrator
Pat Reynolds

Publisher
Rigby (New PM Story Books)

ISBN
0435067435

TC Level
4

are making sense, but does that look right?"

To teach a strategy for effective reading, a teacher might say that reading is really thinking about a story, and that one way good readers read is they pay attention to things that surprise them in a story. For example, if you were reading *The Gingerbread Boy* and the Fox said, "Get on my back little gingerbread boy and I'll carry you safely across the river," the smart reader should be thinking, "Huh! I thought foxes ate gingerbread boys. Why is he being so nice?" A teacher could say, "To read this book, first look through the pictures and see if anything surprises you. Let's look at the cover together." The cover will generate lots of "huhs!" because it shows a lion looking down at a mouse that he holds gingerly between his paws.

"Sometimes I get the idea, when I'm just starting a book, that this will be kind of like other books I know," the teacher may want to tell children. "You know what I'm thinking? I'm thinking that this might be one of those, 'The little guy turns out to be tougher' stories.'"

Alternately, a teacher could tell children that sometimes authors write stories hoping they'll convey his messages, "Read this and think about, 'What is the author *really* saying?'" Some will conclude this is a story meant to say, "Good deeds will be rewarded." Others will suggest this is about the little guy winning. Others will conclude that this book suggests the importance of all of us, as individuals, working together in a spirit of generosity.

Genre
Picture Book

Teaching Uses
Independent Reading; Small Group Strategy Instruction

A Field Guide to the Classroom Library, Lucy Calkins and the Teachers College Reading and Writing Project, Heinemann, ©2002 Teachers College, Columbia University; http://www.heinemann.com/fieldguides

The Napping House
Audrey Wood

Book Summary

In this cumulative, rhythmic verse, the inhabitants of the napping house each begin to sleep piled up atop a napping granny. One by one they climb on top of one another until the wakeful flea at the top of the pile bites the mouse who scares the cat, who claws the dog and so on, until no one in the house is left napping.

Basic Book Information

This cumulative tale is rich in literary language. It tells of a cozy bed with a snoring granny, a dreaming child, and a dozing dog. Donald Wood's full-page illustrations are lush and intriguing. The author/illustrator team also created *King Bidgood's in the Bathtub*, a Caldecott Honor Book that is similar to this book.

Noteworthy Features

The cumulative pattern and repetition makes this a delightful book to use as a read aloud where excited listeners will join in as the refrain "in a napping house,/ where everyone is sleeping" repeats itself.

Teaching Ideas

The enticing pictures, engaging rhyme, simple cumulative structure, and lush language make this a favorite in early elementary classrooms everywhere. After it has been read to children a time or two, once they get the hang of the pattern and the repetition in the book, it usually becomes easy for children to read along, despite the challenging literary language.

Teachers who work with young readers become accustomed to looking at a book in order to ascertain the supports and challenges it will provide for them. The simple cumulative structure of this book and the repetition that's built into the structure will support young readers and give them the security and confidence necessary to solve the unusual words like *slumbering, dozing,* and *wakeful.* Meanwhile, children's work with this book is sure to pay off because the end result is a story-like reading, and because the illustrations are endlessly fascinating.

This is a great book to use to help children feel rewarded and satisfied by close reading and close observation of the pictures because there is much to find in them. After several readings, children tend to notice that each of the

Illustrator
Don Wood

Publisher
Harcourt Brace, 1984

ISBN
0152567089

TC Level
5

creatures-the granny, the child, the dog, the cat, the mouse, and the flea, can be found in every single picture, even the illustrations in which the character hasn't yet been mentioned. Finding these characters can be fun for groups poring over the pictures.

Next, children tend to notice the color changes in the book as the story progresses. "Why does everything turn yellow?" With a little detective work, children can usually discover on their own that the rain at the beginning of the naptime makes the day dark, and that as the sun comes out, the day gets brighter and cheerier, just as the folks are waking up from their naps.

Very observant or very persistent readers will probably notice the change in perspective that is evident over the course of the book. As each creature joins the pile, the perspective of the viewer changes, until the point where the flea bites the mouse. Thus we move from a perfect side view to a nearly perfect top or overhead view. Then, as everyone wakes up, the perspective slowly, picture-by-picture, moves back down to a side view. These readers may well notice that the book opens and closes with a front view of the napping house, one in rain and one in sunshine, one with everyone asleep and one with everyone awake.

Readers who notice this may also notice that the house in the author photo on the back cover of the book looks suspiciously like the napping house itself. This usually provokes great excitement for young readers.

Sometimes discussion centers around odd questions like, "Why is everyone piling on the granny?" or "Why do they let the flea be in the house?" but even these seemingly irrelevant questions can lead to central issues in the book, like the tone of love and comfort and coziness and snuggling.

Some readers will already know the Woods from their popular book *Quick as a Cricket*. That book has similar illustrations and children might be interested to compare the appearance of the two characters in the books.

Book Connections

Of course, there are many, many books that have this building, repetitious pattern. *Drummer Hoff* by Ed and Barbara Emberly is one well known one, as is *King Bidgood's in the Bath Tub*, also by the Woods. Readers will enjoy comparing *The Napping House* to *Just Like Daddy*, *Who Took the Farmer's Hat*, and *Hattie and the Fox*. This is an "all fall down" story and can be compared to Brian Wildsmith's much simpler book of that title. Books that feature the poem *The House that Jack Built* or the song, *I Know an Old Lady Who Swallowed a Fly* also largely follow this pattern and are great choices for a read aloud and choral reading.

The Woods have also collaborated on *Heckedy Peg*, *Elbert's Bad Word*, and *Piggies*. Teachers may want to collect these books for children to study either in a reading center or as part of an author study/illustrator study.

Genre
Emergent Literacy Book; Picture Book

A Field Guide to the Classroom Library, Lucy Calkins and the Teachers College Reading and Writing Project, Heinemann, ©2002 Teachers College, Columbia University; http://www.heinemann.com/fieldguides

Teaching Uses
Interpretation; Author Study; Read Aloud; Whole Group Instruction

A Field Guide to the Classroom Library, Lucy Calkins and the Teachers College Reading and Writing Project, Heinemann, ©2002 Teachers
College, Columbia University; http://www.heinemann.com/fieldguides

The Photo Book

Beverley Randell

Book Summary

The book is about a family photo album that includes pictures of Mom, Dad, James, Nick, and Kate. But Teddy Bear is missing from the album. Mom takes a photo of Teddy Bear so his picture can be in the book too.

Basic Book Information

The book has five to eight words on each of its 16 pages. The print is consistently placed on the left side of the book while the pictures are on the right. There are a number of high frequency words repeated on every page, including *is, the, here, in,* and *I.*

PM Readers is a series published by Rigby. The PM Readers tend to come in kits in which every book looks exactly like every other book. PM Readers feature Ben, Sally, or other characters across a series of books.

Noteworthy Features

There are several patterns that repeat and change in the book: Here is the photo book. / Mom is in the book. / Dad is in the book. / James is in the book. / Here is James. / Kate is in the book. / Here is Kate. / Nick is in the book. Here is Nick. / Here is Teddy Bear. / Teddy Bear is in the book, too.

The photos are clearly labeled with each character's name providing more support for emergent readers.

Teaching Ideas

The Photo Book provides opportunities to practice early strategies such as one-to-one matching and return sweep. A teacher might introduce this book by saying, "This book is about a family-Mom, Dad, Nick, James, and Kate. Their pictures are in the photo book [show family member's picture in the photo album and pointing out the label-Mom, Dad, etc.]. One family member is missing. Can you read and figure out who is missing?" The teacher may wish to point out and possibly have the children frame the word "here." This word frequently provides difficulty for emergent readers and is the initial word in several sentences (Here is James. / Here is Kate. / Here is Nick.). You may also wish to point out the word "photo" with a quick explanation that this might be a tricky word because you might expect to see an *f* at the beginning but in "photo," the letters *ph* make the */f/* sound.

Book Connections

If children have read any of the other books about Mom, Dad, Nick, Kate, and James they may wish to compare the family's adventures. In *The Flower*

A Field Guide to the Classroom Library, Lucy Calkins and the Teachers College Reading and Writing Project, Heinemann, ©2002 Teachers College, Columbia University; http://www.heinemann.com/fieldguides

Series
PM Readers

Illustrator
Elspeth Lacey

Publisher
Rigby, 1994

ISBN
0435067265

TC Level
2

Girl, Kate is a flower girl and Nick (really Nicola) decides that she wants to be a flower girl, too, and picks flowers from the garden. Beginning readers love following the adventures of this family and knowing the characters provides a natural introduction to the book.

Genre
Picture Book

Teaching Uses
Partnerships; Independent Reading

The Snowy Day
Ezra Jacks Keats

Book Summary

One morning when Peter wakes up he sees that snow has fallen during the night; the snow covered everything "as far as he could see." Peter puts on his snowsuit and goes outside to play. He makes all kinds of tracks, finds a stick and smacks a snow-covered tree. He makes a snowman and snow angels. Before he goes into his warm house, he puts a snowball in his pocket to save for the next day. When he checks his pocket for the snowball, he discovers that it's no longer there. That night Peter dreams that the sun had melted all the snow away. But when he woke, he saw that snow was still everywhere and new snow was falling. The story ends as Peter calls to his friend across the hall and "they went out into the deep, deep snow."

Basic Book Information

The Snowy Day is the recipient of a Caldecott Medal. It is widely regarded as a classic. The book has clear and colorful illustrations made from collage.

Noteworthy Features

This book can be a great example of making a wonderful story out of everyday events. The simple acts of playing in the snow, written carefully and truthfully, make a great story. Children can feel the fun in whacking a snowy tree with a stick, or in makng funny footprints in the snow. Reading aloud stories like this one can help young writers learn to make a story out of their everyday lives.

Teaching Ideas

The Snowy Day is an appealing children's classic. It is a perfect choice for emergent reading. After children have heard the story read over and over, they can construct the story by "reading" the pictures. From hearing the story over and over, children will begin to learn how stories work and understand the structure of language. They will learn to anticipate and connect events. Children will begin to "talk like a book" , as Marie Clay says, and will be rehearsing fluent and expressive reading. Some children will point to the pictures and use them to recreate the story. Others will begin to sweep at the print while "reading." Eventually, some children will begin to notice some words in the text. All of these behaviors are important stages in emergent reading.

The Snowy Day is an engaging read aloud. Children can easily "say something" and make personal connections, sharing these thoughts with a read aloud partner.

The Snowy Day provides an excellent opportunity to teach the strategy of

Illustrator
Ezra Jacks Keats

Publisher
Penguin Books, 1962

ISBN
0140501827

TC Level
6

prediction. An ideal stopping point might be page 24 when Peter puts the snowball in his pocket and goes into his warm house. Readers can use prior knowledge of their own experiences to predict what will happen to the snowball. This provides a clear and simple way for children to begin making inferences.

Book Connections

After children have heard and reread many emergent literacy books, teachers might want to segue into a reading center cycle. Since Ezra Jack Keats has written a series of "Peter" books, such as *Peter's Chair* and *Whistle for Willie*, children might enjoy reading a basket of these books. This provides them with a rich opportunity to discuss the character Peter and how he changes through time.

Genre
Emergent Literacy Book; Picture Book

Teaching Uses
Author Study; Teaching Writing; Read Aloud; Partnerships; Whole Group Instruction; Interpretation

A Field Guide to the Classroom Library, Lucy Calkins and the Teachers College Reading and Writing Project, Heinemann, ©2002 Teachers College, Columbia University; http://www.heinemann.com/fieldguides

The Three Bears
Paul Galdone

Book Summary

This book retells the traditional story of the three bears. Three bears live in the woods: a big one, a middle-sized one and a baby one. Their porridge is too hot to eat, so they go for a walk while it cools. While they are gone, a little girl named Goldilocks goes into their house. She samples all of their porridge and tests all of their chairs, finishing the baby's food and breaking the baby's chair. Then she goes to their beds, and falls asleep in the baby's. The bears come home and discover their bowls of porridge, chairs and beds have been tampered with. They find Goldilocks and wake her up. She flees in terror of the bears, never to be seen by them again.

Basic Book Information

This picture book has about two or three lines of text on every page. The text is positioned beneath the humorous, sketch-style illustrations.

Noteworthy Features

One interesting aspect of this rendition of the classic story is the use of different size type fonts to represent the different bear's voices. The different sizes beg to be read aloud in varying voices. Groups often enjoy, and benefit from, reading the story aloud with different parts played by different group members, including a narrator.

Teaching Ideas

Like Paul Galdone's other well-known folk tales, this one is great to use with struggling readers. The readers know a bit of the story already, so they know what to expect from the text, and may even know some of the repeated phrases by heart. Galdone's folk tales are also perfect for strugglers in that they are fairly simply written, without a lot of adjectives, figurative language and clauses to wade through. They often have repeated activities or repeated phrases, so the text is predictable in that sense, too.

While the stories tend to be easy to read, the topics for discussion can be quite complicated and interesting. This allows children who cannot read on the same level as the rest of the class to participate in the discussion of the story at the same level because they can grasp and refer to the text at the same level as their peers.

One unusual thing about this version of the fairy tale is that in the illustrations of this one, Goldilocks has missing teeth. Kids can read all sorts of things into this. Is she missing teeth because she has lost her baby teeth, or because they are rotten? Is the author trying to tell us that she is not a nice person by making her not look nice? Is that a fair way to judge

Illustrator
Paul Galdone

Publisher
Little, Brown and Company, 1999

ISBN
0395288118

TC Level
6

character?

Once children are trying to figure those questions out, they tend to start to look at Goldilocks' behavior in a new light. How can she enter the house of strangers, eat their food, break their furniture and go to sleep? Why doesn't she try to fix what she has broken, and why doesn't she apologize?

Book Connections

Paul Galdone has also rendered *The Three Billy Goats Gruff*, *The Three Little Pigs* and many other folk tales into simple and fun picture books for kids. Comparing other versions of these stories, especially revisionist versions such as John Scieszka's, like *The True Story of the Three Little Pigs*, can make for great discussions.

Genre
Picture Book; Fairy and Folk Tale

Teaching Uses
Independent Reading; Character Study; Interpretation; Critique

A Field Guide to the Classroom Library, Lucy Calkins and the Teachers College Reading and Writing Project, Heinemann, ©2002 Teachers College, Columbia University; http://www.heinemann.com/fieldguides

The Three Little Pigs
Paul Galdone

Book Summary

This book retells the classic tale of *The Three Little Pigs*. However, this version has a twist. After destroying their homes, the wolf eats Pig #1 and Pig #2. He then proceeds to the house of Pig #3. When he is unable to "huff and puff and blow the house in," the wolf tries to outsmart Pig #3 by inviting him on a series of outings. Pig #3 is too smart for such tricks and goes on the outings alone, always an hour before the wolf has come to pick him up. Finally, the wolf gets very frustrated with Pig #3 and tries to catch him by climbing down the chimney. Pig #3 outsmarts him again by putting a pot in the fireplace, thus catching the wolf in boiling water. Pig #3 feasts on boiled wolf that evening and "lived happily ever afterward."

Basic Book Information

This 37-page book contains sketch-style pictures, which vary in their scope. Some pictures appear to be contained in a bubble, while others spill onto two pages. The pictures are detailed and encourage close examination by the reader (e.g., take a look at the portraits on the walls and the vegetable labels in the garden). Many pages have seven or eight lines of text, but the line breaks are not always traditional. In addition, some of the text is placed at the bottom of the page, some at the top, and some are embedded within the illustrations. Many sentences start on one page and are completed on the next. This version of *The Three Little Pigs* will take longer to read than the more simplistic versions of the same story.

Noteworthy Features

The pictures easily tell the story and children can tell not only what is happening, but also can take guesses about what the characters are saying by studying the pictures. This book contains the usual repeated rhyming dialogue that is used when telling this classic story, "Little pig, little pig, let me come in./Not by the hair of my chinny chin chin." The story also contains some interesting punctuation, such as the use of line breaks and dashes, and sentences that extend from one page to the next.

Teaching Ideas

This is an excellent book to use as a repeated text with emergent readers. The strong storyline allows emergent readers to hold on to the story and to start making sense of the natural rhythms of storybooks. The book has a sense of good and evil, as do many fairy/folk tales. The children may quickly start rooting for the pig and love the demise of the wolf. As this book is read to the children repeatedly, the children will come to be able to "read" the

Illustrator
Paul Galdone

Publisher
Clarion Books, Houghton Mifflin, 1970

ISBN
0395288134

book through the pictures. In other words, they will use the pictures and their recollection of the book to retell the story.

Because of the strong correlation between pictures and words and the fact that most children are already familiar with some version of this tale, children can pick up this book and use the pictures to help them read or retell the story. Over time they will become more and more adept at "reading" the book with the same language and expression with which it has been read to them. This kind of "reading" helps the children to internalize how expression and language helps us to make sense of reading.

The dialogue and repeated lines allow children to read or retell the story with expression and gives them the beginning foundation for how stories sound as they are read. By reading this book many times to a group of emergent readers, we help them to hear and imitate the story voice. As they become fluent readers, this sense of how stories sound will help them in understanding story structure as well as the texts itself.

There is so much in this book to discuss. Students who are studying story elements will find this book a good one for getting started. The children are sometimes so familiar with the book even before starting school that they have a great deal of information about the book stored and ready to use. The characters and setting are easy to identify. The passage of time is noted with phrases like "the next day" and "at two o'clock," but also by the more subtle words like "later."

Book talks that encourage children to compare and contrast texts can deepen their understandings of texts. A study of many versions of this tale allow children to notice the nuances of each version and start to notice the different spin that different authors bring to the tale. More sophisticated discussions might ask children to think about what morals the authors might be suggesting. For example, the storyteller Odds Bodkin seems to ask the audience to value the third pig's work ethic, while Paul Galdone's version seems more interested in the third pig's smarts.

Especially for young readers and writers, we stress the importance of the pictures as much as the words. When we can find a book like this one, where the author also does the illustrations, we can have deep conversations with our students about the decisions the author/illustrator, Paul Galdone, makes about what will be said in words and what will be said in pictures. The simple idea that the words and the picture should match, or go together, can be a big concept for our youngest authors. In addition, this author/illustrator is particularly skilled at showing action in his pictures. When children begin to write, they need their pictures to help them read back their words (just as they use pictures to help them read words in books.) If they can learn from Paul Galdone how to show action in their pictures, their pictures will better serve them when they reread their writing.

Though young writers will scarcely be able to read this text, and therefore be unable to use it as a writing mentor, the story language can be a tool for writing. This story starts with the classic "Once upon a time...." and ends with "lived happily ever afterward." Language like this may show up in the children's writing and can be used in a writer's study of beginnings and endings.

A Field Guide to the Classroom Library, Lucy Calkins and the Teachers College Reading and Writing Project, Heinemann, ©2002 Teachers College, Columbia University; http://www.heinemann.com/fieldguides

Book Connections

Paul Galdone has also retold the classic stories: *The Three Bears* and *The Three Billy Goats Gruff* as well as other folk tales. Adding other versions of *The Three Little Pigs* to a classroom library offers opportunities for great discussions.

Genre

Fairy and Folk Tale; Picture Book

Teaching Uses

Read Aloud; Independent Reading; Interpretation; Language Conventions; Author Study; Teaching Writing; Critique

Tiger, Tiger

Beverley Randell

FIELD GUIDE

Book Summary

This story is set in a jungle. All of the animals are asleep-tiger, mother monkey, and baby monkey. When the baby monkey gets hungry, he strays from his tree branch to feast on some berries below. Unfortunately, the tiger wakes up hungry, too. He goes after baby monkey. Luckily, mother monkey wakes up just in the nick of time and yells below, "Baby monkey! Come up here! Come up here!" Baby monkey scampers up the tree to safety, barely escaping the tiger.

Basic Book Information

This book contains 43 words across 16 numbered pages. The large and generously spaced text does not appear in a uniform location on each page, but is always set against a white background. John Boucher provides colorful illustrations that emphasize the ferociousness of the tiger and the vulnerability of the cute baby monkey. The expressions on the animals' faces throughout the book effectively convey the emotions of the story.

The PM Readers is a series published by Rigby. The PM Readers tend to come in kits where every book looks exactly like every other book. Some teachers think this is less than ideal because at every level, a library should be full of books where each has its own individuality. On the other hand, the PM Readers are an important resource for teachers for two reasons. First, there are many of these at the early reading levels and second, the PM Readers recognize the supports that early readers need and offer these. Also, the PM Readers use complete sentences: I see the cow./ I see the pig./ to reinforce the repetition of high frequency words and simple sentence syntax.

Finally, the PM Readers are special because a great many of even the earliest books are stories with characters, a problem, and a resolution. Just as more sophisticated books may feature characters like the Boxcar Children across a series of books, the PM Readers contain many books about Ben and Sally, or other characters, also across a series of books.

Noteworthy Features

Tiger, Tiger contains a lot of repetition as evidenced even by its title. Though the sentences do not always begin in the same way, they do almost always begin with high frequency words. On several pages, there are multiple sentences, some of which "wrap around" to a second or third line.

The text is fairly straightforward, but there is one instance where the author uses boldface type for emphasis. The last line of the book reads, "Baby Monkey is **safe**." Young readers may not be familiar with an author's use of boldface type for emphasis. Others may have only seen boldface type in dialogue, indicating someone speaking in a raised voice, shouting, or

Illustrator
John Boucher

Publisher
Rigby PM Collection, 1994

ISBN
0435049003

TC Level
2

A Field Guide to the Classroom Library, Lucy Calkins and the Teachers College Reading and Writing Project, Heinemann, ©2002 Teachers College, Columbia University; http://www.heinemann.com/fieldguides

yelling.

The story may be somewhat intense for some young readers. And not all children will infer that when the tiger is hungry, he may want to feed on the baby monkey. Teachers should be mindful of the fact that some children might be upset by the storyline.

The pictures convey a strong sense of the story. John Boucher truly captures the peacefulness of sleep, as well as the panic of the moment Mother Monkey discovers her baby is in danger; however, the pictures are not always directly supportive of the corresponding text.

Teaching Ideas

Tiger, Tiger contains illustrations that are not directly supportive of the text. Children who rely heavily on the pictures to gain meaning may need to be reminded to cross-check the picture with the initial consonant sound of the word. It is important that children who are reading on this level are able to use multiple cueing systems to process text.

The text provides students with an opportunity to predict how they think the story might go. In the beginning of *Tiger, Tiger,* the story reads, "Tiger is asleep. Mother Monkey is asleep. Baby Monkey is asleep." The story is set-up with the vicious tiger and a baby monkey asleep in close proximity. Some children may already predict trouble to come. Making predictions is an early reading behavior that should be fostered in young readers because it provides a framework for understanding the story, and helps keep the reader engaged with the text.

Tiger, Tiger is a wonderful book for helping students develop fluency and phrasing. In coaching and read aloud sessions, it's important for teachers to model the way books should sound when read. This book, for example, provides opportunities to model how different punctuation should be read. On page 15, the text reads, "Here comes tiger!" This page could be used in a reading mini-lesson for children who need to work on how sentences with exclamation marks should sound. Another reading mini-lesson might focus on how to read bold print. On page 16, the text reads, "Baby Monkey is **safe**." Teachers can put extra emphasis on the word "safe" while reading aloud and point out that bold print indicates that this word should stand out from the regular reading of the text. Learning how to read a variety of punctuation enhances children's fluency and improves their comprehension. Emphasizing certain sentences and words can also provide additional emotional layers to the reading of a story.

Tiger, Tiger will surely fascinate children who are interested in animals. This book might be grouped with other animal books in a classroom library. Book discussions may revolve around questions like "Why would a tiger want to eat a monkey?" or, "Why would monkeys sleep so close to a dangerous tiger?" The book also deals with issues of feeling safe and being in danger. These are emotions with which young children will surely identify. By discussing such themes with children as they come up, teachers can help students begin to see that books can be related to their own experiences.

Genre
Emergent Literacy Book

A Field Guide to the Classroom Library, Lucy Calkins and the Teachers College Reading and Writing Project, Heinemann, ©2002 Teachers College, Columbia University; http://www.heinemann.com/fieldguides

Teaching Uses

Independent Reading; Read Aloud; Small Group Strategy Instruction; Whole Group Instruction; Interpretation; Partnerships; Language Conventions

Tracks

Rebel Williams

Book Summary

On a snowy day in the forest, the narrator notices tracks in the snow, wonders who made them, then sees the animal and answers the question. The last set of tracks is from the tires of the truck he is riding away in.

Basic Book Information

This is a Wright Group Book.

This little book has sixteen numbered pages. The pattern is that the narrator asks "Who made these tracks?" and then the next page presents the picture of the animal and the words "A (name of the animal)." This pattern repeats eight times, but the last time the answer is "We did!" because the tracks are tire tracks. This means that readers need to work with three kinds of punctuation, a slight twist in the pattern at the end, and the question/answer format of this book. Usually the text is at the bottom of the page, and most of the time it is only one line.

Noteworthy Features

An element of the story happens in the pictures alone. The next-to-last kind of tracks the narrator sees belongs to a bear, and these tracks are right on top of some tire tracks. The next page shows three people in a truck driving away from a bear, at what appears to be high speed; there is snow flying out around the wheels and they are making a sharp turn! They could be having a narrow escape from a bear! Certainly, they are not pausing to linger, as they are headed in the opposite direction. Some children discuss the page with the tire tracks and the bear tracks and figure out the bear was chasing the truck because its footprints are on top of the other tracks.

Since there are no quotation marks, it isn't clear from the beginning of the story that a character in the book is talking. It could be just an invisible narrator. The *we* at the end of the story that reveals someone in the truck was talking is a surprise that takes some thinking for some readers. Then they often wonder, which of the characters in the truck was talking? Of course, this leads to other questions about those characters, such as whether the narrator is a boy or a girl .

Some children feel confused about the changing scale of the animals in the pictures and wonder why the mouse is the same size as the bear. In partner discussions students might ask why the author has broken the story pattern at the end of the story. Young readers will certainly want to share their ideas about these questions.

Illustrator
Jean Emmons

Publisher
Wright Group, 1998

ISBN
0780290909

TC Level
3

Teaching Ideas

One teacher introduced this text by saying "*Tracks* teaches the reader about the different kinds of tracks, or footprints, that different animals make in the snow. On every other page, the narrator wants to know who made the tracks, and then the answer comes next. Read and look at the pictures to learn more about the different kinds of tracks that animals make." Of course, other teachers will introduce the book differently, possibly putting more emphasis on the meaning of the story in the pictures-the escape of the characters from the bear.

Near the end of the book, the question and the answer appear on the same page, with no picture of the animal to help the reader guess at what the word might be. (The picture is on the next page.) They will have to read *bear* with only the tracks as clues. By watching the reader at this point, the teacher can learn a lot about what the reader has figured out about the book so far. If the reader can't read the word *bear* what does she do? Does she scan the page, looking for the picture of the animal to help her? Does she turn to the next page, thinking the answer might be there? Does she study the footprints and make a guess based on the tracks in the picture? Does she at least guess some kind of animal as she guesses at the word? Depending on what the reader does at this point, the teacher can see what parts of the text the reader has really understood. This can be a good opportunity to teach readers new ways of figuring out words they don't know (i.e. by looking at the structure or pattern of the book and the meaning of the pictures).

Teachers can watch to see if readers are crosschecking the starting sounds of the words with the pictures of the animals. Clearly, if children are familiar with some wild animals common to the northeast, the pictures of these animals will offer a lot of support for the animal words.

There are many things to wonder about in this little book. Why do the characters start out on foot in the beginning of the book, leaving their own tracks, and then end up in a truck at the end of the book? And what were they doing-observing nature, or hunting, or what?

Genre
Emergent Literacy Book

Teaching Uses
Independent Reading; Small Group Strategy Instruction; Interpretation; Critique; Content Area Study

A Field Guide to the Classroom Library, Lucy Calkins and the Teachers College Reading and Writing Project, Heinemann, ©2002 Teachers College, Columbia University; http://www.heinemann.com/fieldguides

Uncle Jed's Barbershop

Margaree King Mitchell

Book Summary

Sarah Jean narrates how Uncle Jed used to travel the county on horseback giving other people haircuts. Uncle Jed would always give her a pretend cut and some lotion on her neck. All the while, Uncle Jed saves and dreams about the barbershop he will have one day. Then, Sarah Jean gets sick, and needs a three-hundred-dollar operation. Uncle Jed uses his savings. It sets back his dream, but Sarah Jean gets well. Several years later, Uncle Jed is again close to realizing his dream, but the Great Depression hits, and he loses his savings. Years pass, and finally, when he is 79, he buys his barbershop. Everyone comes, including the grown Sarah Jean. He dies several years later, but he has taught her that dreams can come true, even when no one else thinks they can.

Basic Book Information

This detailed, colorful book contains gentle pictures that pull the reader into both settings, that of years ago, and that of today.

Noteworthy Features

There is a lot of context and history needed to truly understand this story. Without it, the story can still make perfect sense, but it loses some of its poignancy and weight. The narrator mentions in passing some of the privations and oppressions that Southern African Americans had to live with under the times of "separate but equal" facilities. How these forced inequalities existed is hard to understand even for adults who remember the civil rights tensions of that period. So for children to understand it, in the midst of another story, is often nearly impossible.

However, if readers are only trying to understand the situation enough to read and understand the basics of the story, they may well be able to do so without additional explanations. Children who already know something about these topics will certainly understand these aspects of the book more fully than other readers. Young children, clearly, will need to have this story read aloud to them.

The book follows a very straightforward chronology and narrative style. Most children find the structure simple and easy to follow. However, sometimes children don't realize at first that the modern-looking, grown-up woman in the last picture of the book is the same person as the little Sarah Jean they have seen on the other pages. Some readers aren't used to books spanning this many years without making more of the fact that time is passing. When kids read in a group however, someone usually points this out to the rest of the readers.

Illustrator
James Ransome

Publisher
Scholastic, 1993

ISBN
0590223135

TC Level
10

Teaching Ideas

The values in the book come through strongly and make it a great book for interpretation and discussion. The book ends with the words that most children decide tells the meaning of the story-that dreams can come true if you work hard enough. Other values also come through strongly in the story. Jed puts friends, family and his community above his desire for the money to make his dream come true. He gives his money when it is needed, and performs his services for free when his customers have nothing to give. Even young readers usually notice this, and they notice that this makes Jed's dream even more special. When the barbershop finally opens, it is full of loving customers. Children often find messages about being kind in Uncle Jed's behavior. Because of the strong messages about community, some teachers like to read this book aloud at the beginning of the year, to help form their own communities.

Children sometimes check to see if the author's name is the same as the character's name. Is it written by Sarah Jean? When they find it isn't, they sometimes feel disappointed and decide the whole thing isn't nearly as good a story if it is made up. Sometimes discussions get going about whether the story is real or not or if it could be true in its own way, and how this may affect the reader.

Children may decide to do research to discover if the Jerry Pinkney in the dedication is the same illustrator that they are familiar with from so many other books, such as *The Talking Eggs*, *Roll of Thunder Hear My Cry*, or *Albidaro and the Mischievous Dream*. They gather these books together and search for clues. They look to find the name of Jerry Pinkney's wife, who is also listed in the dedication.

Book Connections

It would be fruitful for children to set this text alongside *Amazing Grace* by Mary Hoffman, to talk about how these two books are similar and different. It's also provocative to set this book alongside *The Giving Tree* by Shel Silverstein.

Genre
Historical Fiction; Picture Book; Memoir

Teaching Uses
Read Aloud; Interpretation; Critique; Small Group Strategy Instruction

We Make Music

Robyn Connery

Book Summary

The book begins with the title page showing a dinosaur peering into what appears to be a toy box full of musical instruments. The text repeats the same pattern, "We make music when we_____" and substitutes different actions that can make sounds and music, into this pattern. Meanwhile, the illustrations support the text as colorful dinosaurs sing and ring bells, tap and clap, bang on drums and clang cymbals, as they make music in this short book intended for beginning readers.

Basic Book Information

There are 7 pages in this book, with only twelve different words in the text, making this an easy-to-read book for beginning readers. The print is in large, bold type. Each page, with the exception of the last one, has a two-line sentence with the repeating phrase, "We make music when we...." The illustrations are of dinosaurs-green, red, yellow, blue-carrying out the actions described in the sentences. The new word introduced in the sentence on each page appears in the illustration as well as in a balloon, but a reader wouldn't be able to deduce the new word from the picture alone.

Noteworthy Features

It's easy to overlook the title page in this book, yet this single page makes a big difference in the text, turning it into a sequential story rather than just a list. First, the dinosaur finds musical instruments in a box. Then the four dinosaurs use the instruments to make music, and finally, they exchange their first instruments for new ones and continue to make music.

This book introduces early readers to simple sight vocabulary words in context. The repeating phrase aids the reader, as do the words that appear in the illustrations (*clap, tap*, etc.). The first and second sentences, third and fourth, and fifth and sixth sentences end in words that rhyme: *sing/ ring, tap/clap, bang/clang.*

Teaching Ideas

This is a Level 1 book which should signal to the teacher that an important challenge will be for readers to point under the words, matching a spoken word to the written word and getting feedback from the print which will lead them to reread when their matching doesn't "come out even."

Children who are reading these very supportive books can also learn to get information from the *meaning* of the story (which for these youngsters usually translates to "reading" the pictures) and from the print (which translates to the first letter of a word, but once in a while refers to the

A Field Guide to the Classroom Library, Lucy Calkins and the Teachers College Reading and Writing Project, Heinemann, ©2002 Teachers College, Columbia University; http://www.heinemann.com/fieldguides

Illustrator
Marjory Gardner

Publisher
Rigby, 1998

ISBN
0947328351

TC Level
1

recognized spelling of a sight word).

When a child who generally reads Level 1 books reads this book, it's asking a lot to expect the child to be able to decode a word like *clang*. The good news is that even if a teacher *really* helps a reader with that word (e.g., "Let's first look at the picture. Oh, look at him clang on the triangle!"), the child is still left to do the important work. Saying the words while pointing at those same words isn't an easy feat even for a child who has been given lots of help knowing what the text says.

Children will feel the rhyme in this book, especially if we read it to them or invite them to reread the book until it's smooth. They can use the rhyme to generate unknown words. They should probably not, however, be expected to do a lot with word families at this point.

There are several topics in this book to ponder and discuss with a partner. What relationship do these dinosaurs have to each other? Are some parents and some children? Why does one dinosaur jump on the drum? Children will love the speech bubbles and may laugh to see that in this book, it's the drum and the cymbals that are "talking."

Genre
Emergent Literacy Book

Teaching Uses
Independent Reading; Small Group Strategy Instruction; Language Conventions; Interpretation

What Floats
Rebel Williams

Book Summary

This book presents a cross-section of land and ocean on each page, showing and naming what floats on the water and what doesn't. For example, whales float while rocks don't.

Basic Book Information

This book has 7 numbered pages. The pattern is that one thing floats, other things don't. Each object is illustrated. The last page breaks the pattern with "Look! I can float!" across the bottom.

Noteworthy Features

The pictures are not exclusively of the objects named in the text. There are birds flying above the water, and boats off in the distance. Under water there are always a variety of starfish, pebbles and sea grass in addition to the named object. This means that the pictures may support readers who have some idea of what the word is, but they won't support others who have no idea of the word and a wide range of objects in the picture to choose from.

Some children notice and wonder why the whales in the picture are unusually small in comparison to the birds and other objects in other pictures.

Teaching Ideas

The child who reads this book will profit from a teacher supporting one-to-one pointing, and also using the picture and the print to try to figure out what words say.

A teacher may want to give a sparse introduction as well. One teacher did so by saying, "In *What Floats?* you will read about some things that float on the water, stay on top of it, and some things that don't and go right to the bottom of the ocean. Read it to find out some things that float and some things that don't. You can use the pictures and the first letters to try to help you figure out what the words say."

A child might look at the illustrations on pages 6 and 7 and read, "Balls float" instead of "Boats float." Although a more sophisticated reader will recognize *all* in *balls*, the very beginning reader will be doing quite a lot of good work to check the picture and see a boat, to check the print and see the word *balls* starts with a *b*, and to read this as *boats*. "You're partly right!" the teacher will want to say. Good checking the picture! And it does start with a /b/. The only problem is...."

The *wh-* words are harder for kids than many other words, and *what* is not a word a child could figure out from the picture or the phonics of the word. A teacher or a friend, then, will probably need to read the title to a child.

Children who really understand the pattern may be interested to look at the cover and back cover of the book where they will find more juxtaposed examples of what floats and what doesn't. The cover features a buoy and an anchor, while the back features a large ship and a treasure chest.

The book is liable to raise questions from readers. Each of the objects that floats: *whales, boats* and *beach balls,* are also known to sink under certain conditions, and children often note this and discuss it. Do the things that sink also float sometimes? And what about the fish in the pictures, what are they doing- sinking, floating or a little of both? The last picture is the one that usually raises the most questions. Is the boy floating? Or is it the inner tube? Do people float or not? Because of the scientific questions the book raises, it can easily be used in science units. Some teachers also use the text to study opposites.

Genre

Nonfiction; Emergent Literacy Book

Teaching Uses

Independent Reading; Content Area Study; Small Group Strategy Instruction; Interpretation; Language Conventions

Where The Wild Things Are

Maurice Sendak

Book Summary

"The night Max wore his wolf suit and made mischief, his mother called him, 'Wild Thing' and Max was sent to bed without his supper." That very night in Max's room a forest grew and Max sails off to the land of the Wild Things where he is named King of the Wild Things. He dances and romps with them and rules them. But, in the end, he misses the world of his mother who loves him, and sails back to his bedroom where his supper awaits him "and it was still hot."

Basic Book Information

This book by author-artist Maurice Sendak is one of the most well known books in all of children's literature. A Caldecott Award winner, the book is a classic. Sendak was also awarded the Hans Christian Andersen Illustrator Award (1970) in recognition of the entire body of his work.

Noteworthy Features

The book has almost 37 pages. The type is an easy-to-read black font on a white background. The detailed, and wildly imaginative illustrations increase in size until the "wild rumpus" begins and in three wild, double-page spreads, the illustrations alone carry the story.

Teaching Ideas

Some children will recognize the "Wild Things" characters and wild beasts from television, magazines and commercial products. If children know the characters only from these sources and not from the book itself, they might come to the reading with incorrect assumptions about the characters and the story. It is easy enough to talk readers through initial (false) assumptions if that problem arises and adds confusion.

Where the Wild Things Are is an appealing children's classic and is a perfect choice for an emergent literacy read aloud. We are basing this instruction on the research of Elizabeth Sulzby, whose work with kindergarten children informed her of the importance of recreating parent-child interactions around the reading of books in the kindergarten classroom. At home, children often ask parents to "read it again" when they hear a favorite story. In school, the teacher's multiple readings of emergent literacy books helps children become familiar with rich narrative and to hear the inflection and pacing of storybook language. They also learn to use the detailed illustrations of picture books to assist them in their rereading of the story.

After *Wild Things* has been read to the class at least four times, multiple

Illustrator
Maurice Sendak

Publisher
HarperCollins, 1963

ISBN
0064431789

TC Level
7

copies of the book could be added to a basket of "Stories We Love." At independent reading time, children in partnerships are invited to read the book to each other "the best way you can." They can be given a time to read quietly to themselves and then time to read to their partner. Children will refer to the illustrations, to their memory of the teacher's reading and to their growing internalization of the story's plot and emotional content as they recreate the story in their rereading.

Given this opportunity to hear and read many books that have a strong storyline, characters that they can personally relate to, and supportive, detailed illustrations, Sulzby has shown how children pass through different reading stages. They go from labeling the pictures on the page, telling the story off the pictures using progressively more dialogue and storybook language, and finally moving towards a more conventional, print-based reading. To go on this journey, it is important for children to hear the story read aloud many times, have many opportunities to reread it to a partner and to have a supportive teacher nearby to thoughtfully coach them in the reading.

Later in the year, *Wild Things* can be used as an engaging read aloud. Children can be assigned "read aloud" partners who they sit next to on the rug during read aloud time. At significant moments in the reading, they can be asked to turn to their partners and "say something." This encourages them to remain anchored to the text and to make important personal connections.

In class or partner discussions, we can try to help children gain a new entrance to the story in many ways. One way to help them begin to think differently about the story is to offer some bit of our interpretation of the story, some bit of thinking that is deeper than they have yet gone, and then ask their opinion of that thinking. We can also help children to ask questions of the story: What is this story really about? Can you account for what is going on in each of the pictures? Are you ever confused or surprised by what the character(s) does? Do you hear echoes within the story, or echoes from other stories?

There are many echoes readers may be able to find in the story. Among others, the words "wild thing" and the phrase "I'll eat you up" come up in different spots in the story, as does the "wolf suit" and the picture that Max drew that hangs on the wall on the second page. When readers try to put together why these echoes might be there, they will probably begin creating a window for themselves into Max's thinking and feeling. These clues more than any other, will be able to lead them into the idea that Max is creating this world of wild things, and that his needs or understandings, lead him to make everyone behave the way they do in that world.

The author of the *New York Times* best-selling *Raising Cain: Protecting the Emotional Life of Boys* has claimed that this story is one of the best and most realistic depictions of a boy's anger available to readers anywhere. Whether or not children come to this conclusion or agree with it, the question "What is this story really about?" is bound to involve the issue of anger.

Book Connections

Maurice Sendak has written and/or illustrated many other books for children that could be read alongside this one, including the *Seven Little*

Monsters and the *Little Bear* series, written by Else Holmelund Minarik.

Genre
Picture Book; Emergent Literacy Book

Teaching Uses
Independent Reading; Partnerships; Interpretation; Read Aloud

A Field Guide to the Classroom Library, Lucy Calkins and the Teachers College Reading and Writing Project, Heinemann, ©2002 Teachers College, Columbia University; http://www.heinemann.com/fieldguides

Writing Places

Pamela Chanko

Book Summary

The book poses the question "What's a good place for writing?" and then answers with eleven different possibilities, from birthday cakes or fridges to the sand or the sidewalk.

Basic Book Information

This book has about fifteen pages. The first thirteen are for young readers, and the last two are for teachers. In the children's section of the book, each page is illustrated with a large photograph of a youngster writing on something. The first page asks, "What are some good places for writing?" Each subsequent page shows a writing place, and below the photograph the name of the place is labeled. One example is "A calendar." A few of the places to write are preceded by *the* instead of *a* and the last page reads "Even the sand!"

Noteworthy Features

Each two-word answer is punctuated with a capital letter at the beginning and a period at the end, although they really aren't sentences.

Because the photographs are very clear-cut, the reader should find lots of support for her guesses as to what the word below the photograph reads. Although there are various possibilities suggested by each picture, such as *blackboard, board,* or *chalkboard,* the range of possibilities is small enough that readers can use the photographs and the initial first letter of the word to help them.

Some readers enjoy trying to read the writing produced by children that is in the photographs, although sometimes it is at odd angles, and sometimes it is not words at all but letters or numbers.

The last pages of the book are apparently words for teachers to use as they read the book to children aloud. Next to each miniature of the photograph is a paragraph elaborating on why children could write in the medium suggested. These words are phrased for children, (except for the entry on "floor"), but most children who pick up this book will not be able to read them.

Teaching Ideas

In addition to the uses for this book common to other books at this level, this book may serve as a strong motivator to children to find some new or suggested writing places of their own to try. Children may often read the book and then go off and write in a new medium, in a new spot. This book may also trigger awareness in children of the environmental print in the

Publisher
Scholastic, 1999

ISBN
0439046092

TC Level
2

A Field Guide to the Classroom Library, Lucy Calkins and the Teachers College Reading and Writing Project, Heinemann, ©2002 Teachers College, Columbia University; http://www.heinemann.com/fieldguides

classroom and in their world. They may find many new places where writing is found.

Some teachers use this book to help them explain to young children about different types of writing, or different types of genres for children who aren't yet able to write very much at a time. The examples in the book offer not only possibilities for places to write, but for different kinds of things to write about as well. Also, a message on a cake will be different, in many cases, from a message written on a chalkboard.

Some teachers also like to have this book on hand when teaching children about book choice. Because of its short summary of itself on the back cover, children can get a good idea of what the book is about easily, in a way different from glancing through the pages. This example can add another strategy for choosing books to a reader's repertoire.

Genre
Emergent Literacy Book

Teaching Uses
Independent Reading; Teaching Writing; Read Aloud

A Field Guide to the Classroom Library, Lucy Calkins and the Teachers College Reading and Writing Project, Heinemann, ©2002 Teachers College, Columbia University; http://www.heinemann.com/fieldguides

Young Cam Jansen and the Missing Cookie

David A. Adler

Book Summary

In this mystery, Cam and her friends Eric and Jason search for who took Eric's cookie from his lunchbox. Jason, Eric, Annie and Cam Jansen are the main characters. Chapter 1 explains Cam's nickname and Cam is tested to prove the power of her amazing memory. Chapter 2 sets up the problem of what happened to Eric's chocolate chip cookie. Cam and her friends confront possible suspects and finally, using Cam's memory and reasoning, they discover the real culprit.

Young Cam Jansen books offer many readers who want to be reading the harder *Cam Jansen* books, a step into the structure of these mysteries without overwhelming them with too much meaning to hold on to. They also help readers develop the stamina needed to read the other *Cam Jansen* books by supporting them with many text supports. The book is divided into four chapters, but the chapters do not stand-alone; they are directly connected to one another because they offer clues to solving the mystery at the end.

Basic Book Information

Young Cam Jansen and the Missing Cookie is 32 pages long with 9 chapters. The sentence structure is simple and the pictures are supportive of the text. This is one book in the *Puffin Easy-to-Read Young Cam Jansen* series. All of the characteristics of the slightly more difficult *Cam Jansen* series books are represented in this series, just at an easier reading level. What makes this text more accessible to beginning chapter book readers is the spacing and layout of the print, familiar vocabulary, additional picture support on each page, and referenced dialogue so that the readers can keep track of which of the characters is speaking. The author even gives the reader a more explicit explanation of Cam's amazing memory and why her name is "Cam"-to support the more literal nature of the readers at this level.

Noteworthy Features

The chapter titles such as "The Missing Cookie" and "The Thief" are supportive and don't play tricks with the reader. The text has underlined words that show emphasis to support meaning.

Teaching Ideas

This is a good book for partner and independent reading for the reader who

Series
Young Cam Jansen

Illustrator
Susanna Natti

Publisher
Puffin, 1998

ISBN
0140380507

TC Level
6

A Field Guide to the Classroom Library, Lucy Calkins and the Teachers College Reading and Writing Project, Heinemann, ©2002 Teachers College, Columbia University; http://www.heinemann.com/fieldguides

is beginning to read longer, more detailed and more complexly structured books. This book can be used to teach readers how to look for clues in the text, gather lists of evidence, notice how the author tries to trick the reader and throw him/her off track, ask and answer questions about the case, and figure out what is important to the story. Readers may use Post-its to mark those places in their reading that are examples of these things. Readers may make little notes to themselves on the Post-its as to what they are thinking, noticing, wondering about the case. They can discuss their observations with other readers, make predictions, reread to find out places where they may have missed a clue, and write lists of clues and predictions to share with other readers.

The teacher might say, "Let's *all* read a mystery and we can think together about how mysteries tend to go, and about the special work a reader of mysteries needs to do." Then the teacher might read this book (or another in this series) aloud while children each select a book at his or her level from the "Mystery" collection the teacher might put out. Some might read *Nate the Great*, some *The Boxcar Children*. In the whole-class read aloud, the teacher might highlight the fact that the reader's job is to figure out what the mystery is, how to solve it, and what clues are important. Often there are red herrings-a sound in the alley that we think may launch the mystery, may turn out to just be a dog knocking over the neighbor's garbage. Whatever the whole class notices, the teacher can ask readers to notice in their independent books. "So do *your* crime solvers have special talents like Cam does? Do yours have a sidekick? Talk about these questions after independent reading, when you meet with your partners today," the teacher will say.

In this fashion, readers can look for, discuss and write about things that seem "universal" in all mystery/detective stories, how the detectives are alike in their methods, what literary devices the authors use consistently and how they differ.

Some meaning challenges may include misunderstanding the "red herring" of the thief picture on page 17 beneath the chapter title. Many students will use the pictures as clues and will expect that the "thief" depicted on the page is really the one who stole the cookie, even though the text will say differently in the next chapter.

Book Connections

Other books in the *Young Cam Jensen* series include: *Young Cam Jansen and the Dinosaur Game, Young Cam Jansen and the Lost Tooth, Young Cam Jansen and the Ice Skate Mystery,* and *Young Cam Jansen and the Baseball Mystery.*

Similar books to *The Missing Cookie* are *Amanda Pig* and *Frog and Toad* by Arnold Lobel. Books that should be read before this are the *Henry and Mudge* series and *Nate the Great. The Young Cam Jansen* books are great transitional books to the regular *Cam Jansen* series.

Genre
Short Chapter Book

A Field Guide to the Classroom Library, Lucy Calkins and the Teachers College Reading and Writing Project, Heinemann, ©2002 Teachers College, Columbia University; http://www.heinemann.com/fieldguides

Teaching Uses

Independent Reading; Partnerships; Interpretation; Small Group Strategy
Instruction; Whole Group Instruction; Read Aloud

Index